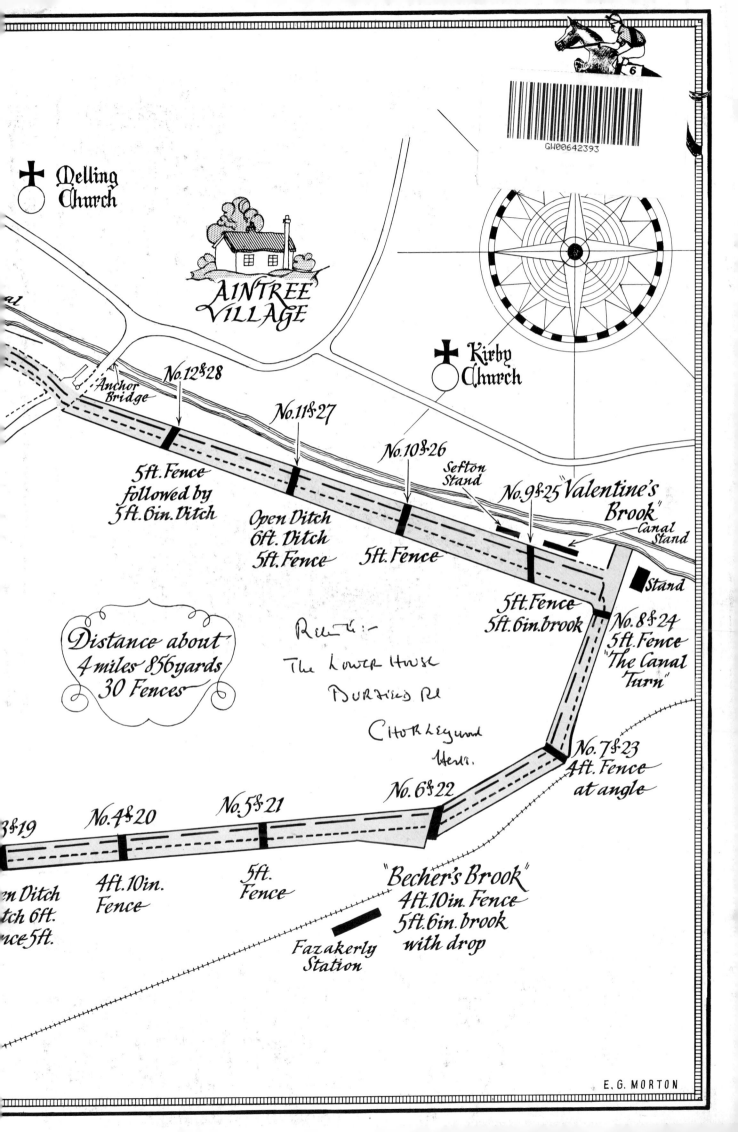

Melling Church

AINTREE VILLAGE

Kirby Church

No.12&28

Anchor Bridge

No.11&27

No.10&26

Sefton Stand

No.9&25 "Valentine's Brook"

Canal Stand

5ft.Fence followed by 5ft.6in.Ditch

Open Ditch 6ft.Ditch 5ft.Fence

5ft.Fence

Stand

5ft.Fence 5ft.6in.brook

No.8&24 5ft.Fence "The Canal Turn"

Distance about 4 miles 856 yards 30 Fences

Route:-
The Lower House
Burfield Rd
Chorleywood
Herts.

No.7&23 4ft.Fence at angle

No.6&22

No.5&21

No.4&20

3&19

4ft.10in. Fence

5ft. Fence

"Becher's Brook" 4ft.10in. Fence 5ft.6in. brook with drop

n Ditch tch 6ft. nce 5ft.

Fazakerly Station

E.G. MORTON

THE
GRAND
NATIONAL

To:- Nigel From Dad   25. 12. 72

"The Hoofs of the Horses, how willing & Sweet"
is the Music Earth Steals of the Iron Shod feet.
No whistle of love, no trilling of bird,
Can stir me as the hoofs of the horses have stirred."

   Wm Ogilvie

Peter Biegel's superb picture of Miss Dorothy Paget's 1934
Grand National Winner, Golden Miller, 'The greatest of them all'.

THE GRAND NATIONAL

An Illustrated History of the Greatest Steeplechase in the World

CLIVE GRAHAM AND BILL CURLING

FOREWORD BY HUGH,
SEVENTH EARL OF SEFTON

Barrie & Jenkins London

© 1972 by Clive Graham and Bill Curling

Published 1972 by Barrie & Jenkins Ltd., 24 Highbury Crescent, N5 1RX

All rights reserved including the right to reproduce this book or portions thereof in any form.

Printed and bound by «Les Presses Saint-Augustin», s.a., Bruges, Belgium

ISBN 0214 65339 0

Designed by Peter Davis

Contents

List of Illustrations

Acknowledgements

FROM CLIVE GRAHAM

This stepping-stone in the rolling, ever-widening stream of the Grand National story, marks another point for those who will one day, perhaps, be entrusted to deliver the funeral oration. Bill Curling and I have tried now to pay our own tribute to a sporting enterprise which for more than 100 years has retained, unwithered and intact, its esoteric appeal.

In the studiously-annotated picture section, fact-seekers will find all they need to know. Pondering over the illustrations, they may well demand of themselves, 'What is the ideal make and shape of a potential Grand National winner?'.

One point will remain inescapable — the degree of courage required by horse and rider. The lay reader, if any such picks up and peruses this work, should also spare a thought for the owners and trainers.

Some will, perhaps, enter their horses in hopes of the attendant rebounding publicity, accompanied by vague dreams of profit and glory. As a general rule, their horses — which have had to show their prowess in qualifying races — are not entered or raced on a mere whim.

Somewhere in these pages you will read about the misgivings expressed overnight by trainer, Reg Hobbs, at the prospect of running the little American entry Battleship, owned by the millionairess Marion du Pont Scott and ridden by Bruce, his 17-year-old son. In our results section, you can confirm the outcome.

With a personal experience of the race spanning close on forty years, and acquaintanceship with many my senior — some alas, no longer with us — it has been the objective to bring a fresh, human element into this presentation, at least from Troytown's year (1920) onwards.

We are in debt to Lord Rosebery, who still retained in his 90th year, such vivid memories of his early days, for his recollections of Manifesto. He was one of the few active racegoers during the 1970s to have seen this supreme Aintree specialist in action.

Mr. J. Marston Spurrier, from Tutbury in Derbyshire, and Mrs. Noel Furlong, widow of Reynoldstown's owner-trainer, are other good friends of the jumping game whose help has proved invaluable.

Particular thanks are due to Mrs. Vera Reynolds, sister of Fred Rimell, and formerly married to the late Gerald Wilson, seven-times champion N. H. jockey. The rough script of Gerry's unpublished memoirs gives a much-needed angle to rounding off the Golden Miller story, and to getting a true perspective on the most-discussed Grand National winner of all time. It gives us much pleasure to recount his version of that unforgettable Gold Cup race against Thomond II at Cheltenham, the happy prelude to the Aintree disaster fifteen days later.

Vincent O'Brien took time off between training his flat-racers and flying to and from the American yearling sales last year, to recall the methods he used to prepare Early Mist, Royal Tan and Quare Times for the O'Brien Grand National hat-trick.

From my good friend 'Mrs. T.' with her memoirs of the long Topham association with Aintree, the writer has received help without stint. This co-operation deserves special mention, for Mirabel Topham's story is also in the publishing pipe-line.

We have an ally here in the old 'reactionary' view that Lottery (1839) was the winner of the first genuine, authenticated, Grand National at Aintree. Readers may note that the co-author of this publication gives credit to The Duke (1837) — influenced (?) by the fact that T. H. 'Dicky' Bird preceded him on the post of 'Hotspur' of the 'Daily Telegraph'. For T. H. Bird originated this theory — or was it pure invention?

1837 or 1839? Does it really matter? 'All history is bunk', said Henry Ford. What we all need to know is what to look for in making our choice for this season's or next season's Grand National.

In giving final thanks to Del Torrione of the Hotel Martinez, Cannes, where most of this book was written in longhand, and to Elizabeth Hearn, who converted it into type, I should like to pay tribute to all members, past and present, of a nameless association which hopes, as I do, that this presentation will be no more than an interim report.

FROM BILL CURLING

This history of The Grand National is different from other books on the National in that it is perhaps first and foremost a pictorial history of the most famous steeple-chase in the world. As a result of help from owners, painters, photographers, riders, trainers, and others interested in steeplechasing I have collected or looked through a thousand Grand National pictures, of which Clive Graham and I have chosen over three hundred for reproduction in this book.

The policy has been to seek out and use action pictures whenever possible. Therefore apart from some nineteenth century National winners, there are few posed paintings of individual horses, rather there are impressions or pictures by such artists as Henry Alken, John Beer, Alfred Bright, Lionel Edwards, D. G. Giles, A. C. Havell, Ben Herring, J. F. Herring, sen., Finch Mason, and F. C. Turner of pre-war Nationals. Up to the outbreak of the First World War the work of artists was far superior to anything produced by photographers.

After the First World War 'action' photography of the National rapidly improved, and began to reach a high standard in the 1920s. Unlike the painter, the racecourse photographer is usually anonymous. The work of photographers who have caught the thrills of the National in fair weather and foul in the last fifty years, has not been praised in print as it should have been. It is deserving of high praise.

Sadly I can mention by name only some of those who have helped with this book. First and foremost I wish to thank Her Majesty Queen Elizabeth, the Queen Mother, for permitting the picture of 'Steeplechase Cracks' by J. F. Herring, senior, in her Majesty's collection at Clarence House, London, to be photographed and reproduced in colour, and also two attractive preliminary sketches by Herring for this particular picture. I should like to mention Mr. Peter Biegel, the artist, who lent me many pictures and cuttings about the race, Miss Georgie Bulteel, granddaughter of the owner of Manifesto, Mr. A. E. J. Church, great grandson of the owner of Abd-el-Kader, Major General Victor Campbell, son of the rider of The Soarer, Mrs. M. N. Carter, great niece of Captain Roddy Owen, the late Mr. Gilbert Cotton, inspector of the course for half a century, Mrs. Noel Furlong, widow of the owner of Reynoldstown, Colonel Sir Martin Gilliat and Lord Adam Gordon of the Queen Mother's staff, Mr. W. H. Harrison, whose dreams of the race came true, Mrs. Home-Robertson, a relation of the rider of Chandler, Mrs. H. C. D. Nicholson, a member of the steeplechasing Holman family, Lord Melchett, son of the owner of May King, Mrs. Mildmay-White, sister of Lord Mildmay, Colonel R. B. Moseley, nephew of the artist Alfred Bright, Lord Penrhyn, son of the owner of Rubio, Captain Geoffrey Poole, a National enthusiast, Mr. E. B. Richardson, only surviving grandson of the rider of Disturbance and Reugny, Lord Sefton, who has given all-important support to the race throughout his life, Colonel J. P. Stanton, whose forbear part-owned the 1837 winner, The Duke, Mrs. Mirabel Topham and her nephew Mr. J. C. Bidwell-Topham of Messrs. Tophams, owners of the course, Mr. Cecil Taylor, nephew of the owner of Grakle, Mrs. J. R. Tomlinson, great niece of the jockey John Page, Captain F. J. Tyrwhitt-Drake, whose family have been connected with the race for over a century, Colonel W. H. Whitbread, a great supporter of steeplechasing, and not least my wife, who has helped me with correspondence over the book.

I have had help too from many trainers and riders including Messrs. G. B. Balding and H. Beasley, Major P. V. F. Cazalet, Major E. G. S. Champneys, Captain N. F. Crump, Messrs. R. Francis, J. H. Hartigan, B. Hobbs, the late H. C. Leader, T. E. Leader, R. Lyall, A. Marsh, B. Marshall, T. Molony, T. Morgan, M. V. O'Brien, J. K. M. Oliver, G. R. Owen, and W. J. Payne, Capt. R. Petre, the late Colonel Peter Payne-Gallwey, Messrs. K. and L. Piggott, Capt. H. R. Price, Messrs. R. Renton, F. Rimell, and W. Stephenson, Capt. P. J. Upton, and Mr. Peter Walwyn, a great Grand National enthusiast before becoming a successful flat racing trainer.

I would also like to thank the editors of *The Daily Telegraph*, *The Sporting Chronicle*, *The Sporting Life*, and *The Yorkshire Post* for publishing my letter saying I was collecting pictures for this book. The publicity given to these letters brought the help I needed in finding pictures. The Tryon Gallery Ltd., London, also gave much help in collecting pictures and putting me in touch with their owners. Finally Clive Graham and I would like to thank all those who have allowed their pictures to be used. They are acknowledged below.

H. M. Queen Elizabeth, the Queen Mother, 14, 16, IV; R. Ackrill Ltd., Harrogate, 304; Associated Newspapers, 248, 250, 274; The Associated Press, 136, 162, 207, 213, 247, 255, 289; Sir Harold Bibby, 65, 66; Mr. Frank Bisgood, XII; Miss G. Bulteel, 55, 298; Mrs. N. M. Carter, 48; Central Press Photos, 106, 108, 115, 116, 120, 126, 127, 135, 138, 139, 143, 144, 147, 157, 161, 163, 165, 167, 169, 170, 175-78, 180, 183, 188, 191, 196, 199, 206, 208, 210, 211, 217, 232, 236, 238, 244, 245, 251, 253, 279, 280-82, 302, 303, 305, 306; Major E. G. S. Champneys, 187; Mr. A. E. J. Church, 33; The late Mr. Gilbert Cotton, 82, 130, 295; Courtauld Institute of Art, London, 4, 28; The Croome Estate, 24; Mr. Geoffrey Dobson, 61, 62; Commander The Hon. D. Edwardes, 46; The Hon. Mrs. R. V. J. Evans, 149; Messrs. Fores, London, 29, 44, VII; Fox Photos, 166, 168, 174, 181, 205, 209, 212, 214, 221, 261, 263; Frost and Reed Ltd., London, XIV, XV; Mrs. Noel Furlong, 152, 153, 156, 158; Gaumont British News Photos, 226-31; Mr. C. T. Gould, IX, XIII; Richard Green Gallery, London, 22, 121, 122; Mrs. A. P. Greenly, 297; Mr. W. H. Harrison, 154, 155; The Hon. Mrs. Aubrey Hastings, 85; Mrs. Peter Hastings, 69, 70; Brigadier W. R. Holman, 18, 19; Illustrated London News, 102, 105, 113, 146; Mrs. W. G. Jameson, 47; Mr. R. B. Kenward, 73-76; Keystone Press, 125, 237, 239, 241, 256, 260, 266-68, 275, 277, 285; The Hon. Mrs. J. B. Kidston, 45; The late Mr. H. C. Leader, 109-12; Mr. T. E. Leader, 114; Mr. R. Leadley-Brown, 34; Mrs. E. Lewthwaite, 25; Liverpool City Libraries, 1; Liverpool Daily Post, 223; Mr. Wallis Loft, 11; Mr. John Longe, 71; Major B. L. Loraine-Smith, 59; The Hon. Mrs. C. P. H. Lucy, Frontispiece; Mr. R. Lyall, 137; Mr. E. F. Manderville, 119, 124; Mansell Collection, London, 5-7, 10, 12, 148; Lord Melchett, 128, 129, 131, 133; Mrs. Ralph Midwood, 134; Colonel R. P. Moseley, 77, 79; Mr. R. McCreery, 15, 17; Mrs. A. G. McGregor, 3; Mrs. H. C. D. Nicholson, 20, 21; Lieutenant General Lord Norrie XI; Mr. M. V. O'Brien, 223-225; The Parker Gallery, London, 63, 81; Mr. W. J. Payne, 118; Pawsey & Payne, London, VIII; Lord Penrhyn, 72; Mr. Lester Piggott, 80, 92; Planet News, 179; Captain G. Poole, 99, 103; Press Association, 95, 96, 98, 100, 197, 198, 200, 201, 219, 246, 252, 259, 272, 293, 299; Mr. K. V. Quinn, 270, 271; Radio Times Hulton Picture Library, London, 9, 60, 94, 101, 107, 159, 172, 192-95; Mr. E. B. Richardson, 26, 30-32, 35-42, I, II; Mrs. Home Robertson, 13; Mrs. P. Rosselli, X; W. W. Rouch, 50-53, 56-58, 83, 84, 86-91, 97, 104; Mrs. John Samuelson, 54; Sport and General Press, 151, 164, 182, 185, 186, 215, 218, 220, 222, 234, 235, 240, 249, 254, 257, 262, 265, 269, 273, 276, 286-288, 290, 291, 294, 300; Colonel J. P. Stanton, 2; Mr. A. F. Studd, 27, V; Syndication Internationale, 93, 264; The Tatler, 307; Mr. Cecil Taylor, 301; Captain Robin Thompson, 64, 67, 68, 78; The Times, 117, 145, 150, 160, 171, 184, 190, 216; Major F. Tyrwhitt-Drake, 8, 23, 43; United Press International, 173, 242, 243, 258, 278, 283, 284, 296; Captain P. J. Upton, VI; Walker Art Gallery, Liverpool, 49, III; Mrs. T. C. Williamson, 140, 142; L.P.A. Sports Services, 292.

Foreword

I am delighted to be asked to write a foreword to this illustrated history of the Grand National. I have been closely associated with Aintree and the National all my life and have known Bill Curling and Clive Graham, authors of this book, since they were young racing journalists before the Second World War.

As Bill Curling points out, the second Earl of Sefton owned Aintree when the steeplechase course was founded in 1836 and for most of the time since then my ancestors have acted either as umpires (not always an easy task in the early years) or as Senior Stewards of the meeting. In the latter capacity I have myself, for several years now, addressed the jockeys in the weighing-room before each Grand National, reminding them that there are four and a half miles to go and suggesting that they approach the first few fences with reasonable caution. By no means all seem to heed this advice but at least we have for some time now avoided the wholesale first fence pile-ups which so disfigured the race in 1951 and 1952!

Enhanced by a magnificent collection of illustrations, many of them hitherto unpublished, the joint authors have produced a book which demonstrates not only how the Grand National has altered down the years but also how much it has stayed the same. The brook into which Captain Becher dived in 1839 may be dry nowadays but it still lies in wait for the unwary and, on the same fateful spot where Devon Loch collapsed in 1956, Lottery had crashed through a stone wall 116 years before. It is this element of continuity which gives the

Grand National its unique character — and which makes such nonsense of any suggestion that it could ever survive away from Aintree. There have, of course been countless changes — notably the modification of the great fences in 1960 since when, as big as ever but more sloped on the take-off side, they have, by common consent, been a much fairer test of man and horse. But although the rise of sponsored races elsewhere has robbed the National of its former absolute preeminence it is still what it has been for at least a hundred years, — far and away the world's most famous steeplechase.

More valuable than ever before in 1972, the National now reaches an audience of many millions by film and television. It attracts enthusiasts from all over the world and remains the one race above all others which most jumping owners, trainers and riders would most dearly love to win.

In an increasingly mechanical and unromantic world I believe with all my heart that it would be a tragedy if we, the British, should ever allow the Grand National to die or even dwindle in value and prestige. And I *cannot* believe that this still sporting nation could be so criminally careless of one of its most precious sporting traditions.

This book, by so graphically illustrating that tradition, must bring home to all who read it just what the great race has meant — and still means — in terms of drama, spectacle and courage. No-one, looking at these pictures and reading the story behind them can fail to be convinced that here is something infinitely worth preserving. So if, as I hope and expect, the Grand National does live on and flourish Bill Curling and Clive Graham will deserve our gratitude.

April 1972

The death, on April 13th, 1972, of Hugh 7th Earl of Sefton, at the age of 73, provides a tragic note to this Foreword, which he so thoughtfully contributed during the last weeks of his long illness.

The family name has been linked with Aintree races since their very beginning, and his presence there during his long years of stewardship always gave the meeting an added air of authority and distinction.

CLIVE GRAHAM

Historical Outline

The Grand National: an Introduction

The setting never varies: the big horses with their riders in the bright jackets parade solemnly as for some religious ceremonial; to their left, on the tiered, spectator-packed stands, the flags of many nations flutter at their mastheads.

It's the sudden hush that hits you: in the quiet you can hear the skylarks singing. The calm, soft-spoken Irishman, Jack Moloney, veteran of so many of these big Aintree occasions would listen for the bird-song as a sign of good omen.

The crowd's tension relaxes when the horses wheel and canter to the starting-point, half-right from the enclosures; renews itself as they line up and then surge forward in a wide, jagged, multi-coloured wave, to break and re-form over the distant first fence...

In all the history of sport the Grand National has achieved an incomparable world-wide interest. This steeplechase is competed for by horses and riders carrying weights assessed on handicap over a double circuit of the pear-shaped course on the outskirts of industrial Liverpool, requiring those taking part to jump thirty fences spread unevenly over the total distance of four-and-a-half miles.

Some turf historians cite 1837 as the correct date of the first running of the steeplechase instituted by the Liverpool hotelier William Lynn. It is debatable whether this race (won by The Duke) can be accepted as the first of the series. A horse called Sir William is credited with winning the 1838 running.

William Lynn must surely be given our affectionate salute for styling a contest of this sort, and attracting the 'bloods' and the betting men to send their horses and jockeys to this then-remote part of our island. At the time of the Grand National proto-type races, the passenger steam-train service had only been instituted on an experimental basis seven years previously in the South-Eastern County of Kent.

And John London Macadam, who died in 1836, had not lived long enough to see his invention of hard road-surfacing become universally popular.

Transport of horses and spectators must have been intolerably slow and dirty compared with later standards. So it says much for the drive and ingenuity of Mr. Lynn that he was able to set spark to a fire which has never since gone cold.

The only credible account of the first 'Great Liverpool Chase' in 1837 reveals that it was won by The Duke, with a margin estimated at '30 yards', ridden by the Cheshire amateur-rider Henry Potts. Police were provided with fire-arms in those days, and a contemporary reporter relates that a member of the force was seen to cock his pistol and wave it around 'alarmingly' whilst apprehending a suspected pickpocket in the crowd.

Sir Henry is shown as the winner of the follow-up race in 1838 in the 'Racing Calendar (Steeplechasers Past)', but T. H. Bird, as Irish as the shamrock, has claimed it for Sir William and his Galway owner-rider Alan McDonough. Both The Duke and Sir William are entitled to honourable mention, even if the clock-holders in 1837 put the winner's time at 15 minutes.

'The course at Maghull where the races were run in 1837 and 1838 is some miles distant from Aintree — and this is why the Tophams, whilst giving full credit to old William Lynn, still insist on a separate date for the authentic running of the first-ever Aintree Grand National'. Mrs. Mirabel Topham makes this statement with a convincing air of hereditary authority which cannot be lightly set aside.

The excitement in the area stirred up by those Maghull steeplechases, spoiled by inadequate management and supervision, was not allowed to die out. A link by rail and a macadam roadway were being set up between industrial Manchester and the sea-port of Liverpool, both passing handily by the flat, open expanses of Aintree.

With the success of two similar races already established, it remained only for an imaginative but realistic touch to transfer the steeplechase to a new and now historic setting — Aintree, a name whose very mention has ever since quickened the pulse-beat of young and old alike, all round our sporting world.

And so it came to be that a different state of affairs prevailed in 1839 on this second and, indeed, final site for *The* Grand National. Three days beforehand, William Lynn let it be known at his Waterloo Hotel that 'due to indisposition' he had resigned from management of the race. We can imagine that the move from Maghull to Aintree, the sudden quickening of nation-wide interest, the meetings, the discussions with members of the Jockey Club almost certainly un-nerved him. He never achieved the same eminence in horse-racing spheres before dying, almost destitute, 31 years later. In his time 'the best fish-cook in the world'.

In this first running at Aintree, two years after Queen Victoria's accession to the throne of Great Britain, the race committee was headed by the local notables — the Earls of Derby and Sefton (whose descendants still act here as race stewards) backed up by Lord George Bentinck and Lord Robert Grosvenor.

I think that the Grand National history book can be justifiably opened on the page setting out the triumph of the horse whose very name has been so closely identified with those instances of drama, luck and high courage which have marked this event as part of England's sporting heritage ever since.

The formidable stone wall has long been replaced by a waterjump, the ploughland has been seeded and changed to turf, the final obstacle is a spruce-fence not a hurdle. In other respects the hazards, although now sloped on the take-off side, and the length of the race, are not significantly different from the February day in 1839 when Lottery and Jem Mason made running nearly all the way, to win easily from Seventy-Four and the remnants of the fifteen other starters.

On his path to victory, Lottery narrowly avoided collision with a bumptious, thrusting amateur rider at the stiffest fence on the course. This was Captain Becher (to be rhymed, please, with 'teacher') on Conrad.

Despite falling into the brook on the landing side, Becher remounted Conrad and nearly caught up with Lottery in the ensuing mile — an indication of how slow the pace must have been — only to part company once more.

Even now, more than 140 years later, the names of Lottery and Becher's Brook are stamped in Grand National lore as firmly as the jealously guarded copyright of the race itself. 'There is only *one* Grand National, and that is here at Aintree,' declares Mrs. Mirabel Topham, who secured rights to the property from the Earl of Sefton in 1949. This claim was upheld by court action in Spain, New Zealand and the USA.

The earlier years of England's unique horse race have been splendidly covered by David Munroe, by my old snuff-loving Irish colleague 'Dicky' T. H. Bird, by Vian Smith, by Con O'Leary — not to mention those talented collaborators Seth-Smith, Willett, Mortimer and Lawrence in their *History of Steeplechasing*.

John Lawrence, so narrowly beaten on Carrickbeg by 'Teazy-Weazy' Raymond's 66–1 chance Ayala and Pat Buckley in 1963, John Hislop, third on Kami to the 100–1 winner Caughoo, in foggy 1947, and Dick Francis, whose version of Devon Loch's slip-up in 1956, with victory assured, still makes the fact sound more unusual than any of his fiction, have all contributed brilliantly written, first-hand accounts of their experiences.

The two Johns, working also for Sunday newspapers, were, obviously, under their contracts, compelled to relay their stories almost before they had wiped the mud off their faces and combed out the sweat from their hair. With the adrenal glands still functioning full-blast, both had stories to tell which competing writers could not equal.

Dick Francis (not then on the working Press) refrained from any immediate post-race comment in the bitter chagrin occasioned by the slip-up of Devon Loch. He returned to the home of his brother Douglas, near Bangor-on-Dee, to puzzle out the mystery of this most inexplicable, unforeseeable and bizarre of all the many sensational Grand National incidents.

His theory, expounded later, was that the enthusiastic roar of the crowd, developing to crescendo at seeing the Queen Mother's horse winning, frightened his mount, causing his collapse. If this was so, why has it never happened to horses before or since, on highly congregated courses such as Epsom, Churchill Downs, Melbourne or elsewhere?

Dick rejected the supposition that his mount took off at an imaginary obstacle, mistaking the shadow cast by the wing of the Water jump.

The conclusion reached independently and unanimously by experts who had scrutinised, frame by frame, the filmed version, was that Devon Loch made a half-hearted attempt to jump, as if at a low hurdle, or a shadow, changed his mind in mid-air, and so ended up splayed out on all fours, before he ignominiously regained his feet. Memory can play odd tricks, and although no one should be qualified to know better than Dick Francis, it seems difficult to subscribe to his opinion that the collapse was caused by the shock-wave of cheering at the prospect of a Royal victory.

Peter Cazalet, Devon Loch's trainer, and a man who has been fated on other occasions than this to receive his full share of misfortune in the Grand National, is still as bewildered as he was at the time. 'There was no suspicion of heart-trouble or physical ailment.' Certainly, he admits to being placed at a loss when asked by the head of a television film-team taking poses of the horse in his stable forty-eight hours afterwards. 'And now, Mr. Cazalet, would you get him to do for our cameras just what he did at Aintree last Saturday?'

Peter half-agreed the Francis version 'for want of a better one'.

When Devon Loch finished lame after running fourth of twenty starters for the Mildmay Memorial 'Chase at Sandown on January 19, 1957, it was decided to retire him from active racing. Top-weighted with 12 st. 1 lb. he looked the probable winner at the second-last fence — he had already assumed mastery over Early Mist and the two Cheltenham Gold Cup winners, Four Ten and Linwell — but Arthur Freeman (taking over in the saddle from Dick Francis), spared the whip, sensing the uncertain movement under him, as the Yorkshire-trained Much Obliged forged ahead.

The Queen Mother made a present of him to Noel Murless, then training the Royal horses leased from the National Stud, as a hack for use whilst supervising his string on Newmarket Heath. Devon Loch carried his new master, day after day, for several years.

Quiet, level-tempered, and without a suspicion of vice, 'but stupid and the clumsiest horse I ever sat on — even in his slow paces, he would stumble walking over a twig'.

Noel, recalling his intimate knowledge of the horse's character, reckons it typical, with Dick Francis waving his whip in salute to the cheering crowds, that Devon Loch — temporarily out of control — should have suddenly vaulted at some self-imagined obstacle, changing his slow-thinking mind in mid-leap to achieve that undignified, sensational sprawl. It must forever, therefore, remain one of the greatest unsolved mysteries of all time associated with the race, which has seldom lacked its moments of drama before, during or afterwards.

How trouble-free, though, it has been from the sort of sinister, crooked happenings which have marked or marred more than one running of the

Epsom Derby, the poisoning of Orme, the substitution of an older horse for Running Rein, the crazy gambling in Hermit's year and the death of suffragette Emily Davison, who flung herself below the hooves of King George V's Anmer in 1913. The 6–4 favourite, Craganour, was afterwards disqualified, in favour of Aboyeur, after a greatly criticised objection.

★ ★ ★

No objection to the result of the National has been registered since Captain Roddy Owen on Cloister (destined to win the race with 12 st. 7 lb. two years later) lodged one to Come Away and Harry Beasley in 1891, only to have it disallowed.

In his record of the 1885 running, David Munroe has seen fit to include an unusual comment on the eight-year-old mare Zoedone, winner two years previously for her owner-rider, the Hungarian Count Charles Kinsky, and the second favourite at 5–1. It was 'poisoned, fell'. The Hon. George Lambton recalled that there were valid reasons for saying the mare was 'got at', but it would not be unusual for an eight-year-old member of her sex to run so far below normal form in the month of March.

There were unsubstantiated rumours in 1961 that a doping gang had endeavoured to knock out a dozen of the thirty five runners, only to give the pill to the wrong grey horse, and not to Nicolaus Silver, when they broke into Fred Rimell's stables at dead of night shortly before the race. Less credence can be given to this story, when one reflects that Merryman II, the strongly supported second favourite at 8–1, disputed the lead most of the way, before eventually filling the place of runner-up.

The robust, sporting character of the Grand National was established from the outset. It reflected an age when the cavalry formed the *Corps d'Élite* in all the European armies, where it was highly important that not only should their officers display skill and courage in the saddle, but that they should be mounted on horses combining speed and stamina, with weight-carrying ability. More so, even than the Derby, this event aroused the keenest interest from the English, Irish and Continental aristocracy.

Lord Craven owned the winner, Charity, in 1841, to be followed two years later by Lord Chesterfield's Vanguard, from a field which included Consul, running for the second year in the name and colours of Baron

Rothschild. Lord Strathmore, ancestor of Queen Elizabeth the Queen Mother (who was to adopt his racing colours, blue, buff stripes, blue sleeves, black cap, gold tassels, a century later) took the mount on his own horse Red Lancer in 1847, failing to complete the course.

The Marquis of Waterford fielded one or more runners most years from 1840 to 1845, and in 1862 the Vicomte de Namur had the thrill of triumphing with Huntsman, after Baron de la Moote, Vicomte Talon, Vicomte F. de Cunchy and other French venturers had fallen short of their objective in previous years.

The Topham family first became connected with the management side of the race in 1856, and in the ensuing ten years until the formation of the National Hunt Committee in 1866, the race slipped into disrepute, for reasons then more readily understandable than now. Criticism against the Topham administration was directed against its policy of cutting down the size of the obstacles into 'little trappy fences', instead of the formidable jumps which Lottery and the first winners were required to face. The majority of the runners during this period were set to carry between nine and ten stone. The critics, therefore, had every reason for accusing the management of transforming the race as suitable only 'for lightweight thoroughbred weeds'.

The whole story of the Grand National and steeplechasing during the nineteenth century needs to be judged against the military background of that era. Only the name and repute of Lord Coventry (who lived another seventy years to found the 'halfbred' Verdict breed, but not long enough to see its inclusion in the General Stud Book) sustained the virtues of the full-sisters Emblem and Emblematic, winners in 1863 and 1864, but rejects from flat-racing.

Both were in the safe and sure hands of George Stevens, who had enjoyed the first taste of his five Grand National celebrations when riding Freetrader at 9 st. 6 lb. to a 25–1 win in 1856. Stevens was later to partner The Colonel (1869-1870) before meeting a stranger-than-fiction death, when thrown by his hack on Cleeve Hill which overlooked his Cheltenham home, in June 1871.

He set a winning style which Bryan Marshall and Pat Taaffe were able to imitate profitably many years later. No dare-devil thruster, but a paid and honoured servant, he preferred to keep his mounts in hand and free from interference until such time as the racecourse strip turned away from running parallel with the Canal, left-handed towards the distant grandstand and the judge's box.

With the passing of its fiftieth year, a pattern began to emerge. The weights, jumps and prize money had all been increased and the then-impoverished Irish farmer was quick to seize on the notion of marrying sport to business. On their limestone-rich land, the Irish reared and trained over earthen banks and formidable bull-finches a breed of horse with three markets in view: (1) Liverpool, (2) the hunting field, (3) the cavalry.

The invention of the internal combustion engine, the machine-gun and other modern weapons of war, sealed off the third channel, but anyone earnestly seeking the other two commodities will still, without prompting, head for Dublin and thereafter for points West and South of the bustling city straddling the Liffey River.

The French and German interests, incidentally, waned due to the Franco-Prussian War; but before the Irish first began their continuing series of assaults the race was largely dominated by Captain James Octavius Machell, an officer in the old 59th Regiment, who resigned his commission in 1863 to manage and train horses for Lord Lonsdale, Mr. Henry Chaplin and others at Beaufort House, Newmarket, where he conducted the skilful preparation of 1867's never-to-be-forgotten Derby winner, Hermit.

It was Machell's theory that the correct running distance of any racehorse could be ascertained to the length of a walking stick, and unusual genius enabled him to become one of the rare individuals in turf history to effect the Epsom Derby-Grand National double.

The late George Lambton thought him an even greater judge and trainer of steeplechasers than he was on the flat, an opinion borne out when he both owned and trained three Grand National winners in the space of four years Disturbance (1873), Reugny (1874) and Regal (1876). Machell continued to be closely identified with the great steeplechase until 1891, when Emperor failed to complete the course. Ill-health then compelled him to retire from the racing scene, although his death was not recorded until 1902.

This period in which Captain Machell exercised such a telling influence overlapped that of another memorable name in the Grand National story Henry Eyre Linde, a farmer in County Kildare. Mr. Linde had his stables at Eyrefield Lodge near the Curragh, a property which was subsequently acquired by Lieut-Col. Giles Loder. Here the immortal Pretty Polly and Spion Kop, the 1920 Epsom Derby winner, were bred and all the other good flat-racers who carried the blue-and-yellow jacket.

During the 1880s the Linde-trained steeplechasers became the most famous in Europe. The decade began with a win for the five-year-old Empress — what a marvellous feat of horse-mastership in itself to produce a horse of this age (and a mare at that) to outjump and outstay two previous winners, Regal and The Liberator. These triumphs were to be followed in 1881 by that of Woodbrook. Once again Tom Beasley, one of the four jockey brothers, rendered his powerful expert assistance to the Eyrefield Lodge favourite, and only an almost-incredible short-head defeat foiled trainer and jockey from making it three in a row with Cyrus the next year.

This 1882 triumph of Seaman, discarded from Linde's stable the previous October, was what largely inspired Lord Mildmay years later in his many gallant attempts. For this bay son of Xenophon was ridden by his owner, Lord Manners, having his second race under rules.

Linde never came so close again, but in addition to two Grand Nationals he has the distinction of sending Whisper Low and Too Good to beat the French in the Grand Steeplechase at Auteuil. Few members of his profession before or since have 'schooled' their horses so vigorously or so successfully and no doubt he had learned the value of discipline and routine during earlier years when he was a sergeant in the Royal Irish Constabulary.

By a slow process the Aintree course, the prize money, the training, the riding and the type of horse required for the Grand National were all alike improving. One may well wonder how far, if at all, the best of our steeple-chasers now racing can be considered as peers of the 1893 winner, Cloister. Second the two previous seasons, and unlucky to have been beaten in 1891, Cloister, now carrying 12 st. 7 lb., vindicated the solid faith of his admirers by setting off in front, steadily increasing his lead until he jogged past the winning-post, alone and with only a light sweat breaking over his neck, forty lengths clear of the next-nearest, Aesop. On the firm, powdery going, he set a new time-record of 9 minutes $32\frac{2}{5}$ seconds, a figure never to be equalled nor surpassed until Kellsboro' Jack, Golden Miller and Reynolds-town each won those keenly competed races forty and more years afterwards.

No horse can ever enjoy an easy race in the Grand National, and Cloister proved incapable of standing up to the preparation to fit him for a fourth attempt, although winning the Grand Sefton' Chase in November of '94 under no less than 13 st. 3 lb. In thirty-five starts, this exceptional horse won nineteen and was unplaced five times only. Had he remained sound or, indeed, not been smitten by sudden lameness in the 1891 finish, he would have had his name inscribed as the fifth dual winner following:

Peter Simple	1849, 1853
Abd el Kader	1850 & 1851
The Lamb	1868, 1871
The Colonel	1869 & 1870

This big, long-backed straight-rumped bay, whole-coloured except for a light smear down his forehead, was first of three Grand National winners for Sir Charles Assheton-Smith — he changed his name from the plainer Charles Garden Duff after unexpected inheritance of properties on the Welsh border.

The increasing prestige of the great Aintree event brought the race to the attention of the Prince of Wales, who visited the 1878 running as the guest of Lord Sefton. The Duke of Hamilton (whose first jockey, Richard Marsh, was many years later to become the trainer of the three royal Derby winners Persimmon, Diamond Jubilee and Minoru) joined forces with Lord Marcus Beresford to advise him, and the Prince bought and registered The Scot to carry his name and colours in 1884.

A loyal public made the royal jumper favourite at 6–1, only to learn that 'somewhere out in the fog on the second circuit' their fancy had straddled the fence (it was Becher's) and thrown his jockey, Jack Jones. Ironically the winner, Voluptuary, destined in the twilight of his days to appear on Drury Lane's revolving stage in a melodrama entiled *The Prodigal's Daughter*, had been bred and reared in the paddocks of the old Royal Stud-Farm at Hampton Court and auctioned as a yearling on Queen Victoria's behalf for less than £700.

From 1884 until 1908, the purple, gold and scarlet colours figured regularly in the Grand National parade for their owner, who succeeded to the throne as King Edward VII in 1901. What excitement, therefore, greeted the finish in 1900, when Ambush II, trained for the Prince of Wales at Linde's old stables, Eyrefield Lodge in Ireland, by Joe Hunter and ridden by Algie Anthony, was seen to be drawing away from his two closely challenging pursuers.

The cheers for Ben Battle's son, soon to be re-echoed at Newmarket, Epsom and Doncaster, when Diamond Jubilee became one of the select band of fifteen colts to capture the Triple Crown, were equalled by those for the third horse, staggeringly weighted with 12 st. 13 lb., and at twelve years old passing his best yet, set to give 24 lb. to the winner, and no less than 43 lb. to the runner-up.

This was the one-and-only Manifesto, already winner twice and destined to be placed third again in 1902 and 1903 before completing the course to finish sixth behind Moifaa in his Grand National farewell at the ripe old age of sixteen.

In the chequered and glorious story of the world's most famous steeplechase, who can be judged the equal, let alone the superior of this lion-hearted gelding, with his amazing constitution and courage and that perfectly formed shoulder which enabled him to jump with such facility at full, extended length over the broad span of Aintree's most formidable fences?

Perhaps more than any other horse, Manifesto, in his heyday and in his declining years, typified all that is and was best about the Grand National. Only once during the seventy-odd years which have passed has the Aintree roll of fame been marked by another dual winner. For sheer brilliance he may have been out-pointed by some of those who came after. For determination, skill and soundness never!

★ ★ ★

From its very beginnings, and more so as the race developed in prestige, the big Aintree triangle came to represent a challenge to horse and rider which could not be parallelled by any other racecourse in the world. As the emphasis turned to a demand for testing the quality of speed rather than bottomless stamina, so the ploughland reverted to grass, and the turf which resulted remains the object for admiration of all who tread and gallop over it.

In retrospect, the conception of the Canal Turn obstacle would not possibly have passed any safety measures laid down by a modern inspector of courses. Modified and protected by railings designed to prevent competitors from careering into the old Leeds-Liverpool waterway (which once carried so much Yorkshire cloth and coal to the Lancashire seaport), its circumvention still requires the handy skill of a polo-pony or a show-jumper.

Some other of our major steeplechasing circuits, such as Haydock and Cheltenham, contain fences where the ground on take-off stands higher than that on the landing-side, but none have to be crossed with the same urgency and expertise called for by Becher's and Valentine's in the Grand National.

The records of the race pay their own tribute to the multiple winners from John Elmore, owner of Lottery (1839) and Gaylad (1842), the immortal George Stevens, astride those five Aintree firsts in the fifteen-year period between 1856 and 1870, the great amateurs, Tom Pickernell, J. Maunsell Richardson and the Irish Tommy Beasley, so dominant towards the latter half of the nineteenth century, down over the years to such latter-day heroes as Vincent O'Brien and Fred Winter.

Some passing thoughts, too, should be spared for the array of horses and men who tried so hard and failed. Horses such as Old Tay Bridge, The Bore and owner-rider Harry Brown (remounting after breaking his collar-bone to finish second in 1921), Easter Hero, Bright's Boy, Delaneige, Thomond II, Mac Moffat from the Border country, Wyndburgh and Freddie from Scotland, not forgetting Lord Sefton's Irish Lizard, or little Lough Conn, who helped to gather the hay-harvest at his owner's Irish farm as a relaxation from his visits to Aintree; all deserve honourable mention in this group.

Her Majesty Queen Elizabeth the Queen Mother, Lord Bicester, Mr. James Voase Rank, Mr. John Hay Whitney, Mr. Edward Courage and Lady Lindsay, all notable past or present supporters of National Hunt racing, are readily recalled amongst the many who could claim no better than minor honours.

During the past fifty years there have been nineteen individual champion jockeys under National Hunt Rules. Of this number only F. B. ('Dick') Rees, Jack Anthony, Ted Leader, Gerry Wilson, Bryan Marshall, Fred Winter and now Graham Thorner, have realised every cross-country rider's supreme objective. Terry Biddlecombe, Josh Gifford, Stan Mellor and Tim Molony have all had to bear the disappointments suffered earlier by predecessors such as Jack Dowdeswell, Fred Rimell, Billy Stott and Eric Foster.

One can recount also the reverses endured by so many highly skilled trainers, with George Beeby, Peter Cazalet, Tom Dreaper, Bob Turnell and Arthur Stephenson springing to mind. Between them these men have had through their hands a high proportion of the top steeplechasers to have carried colours in England and Eire before and since World War II. Their combined efforts have yielded ten place-money prizes, without one solitary victory.

What a tantalising challenge is presented by this race, for horse, owner, trainer and jockey, to win even just the once, a challenge which will last so long as the race continues and which can never be equalled by any other sporting enterprise.

During the twentieth century only Major Noel Furlong's Reynoldstown (1935 and 1936) has prevailed twice in the Liverpool Grand National. Opinions differ whether Poethlyn should not deservedly figure in the select band of double laureates, gaining, as he did, the prize under 12 st. 7 lb. in the authentic 1919 running at Aintree the year after Ernie Piggott (Lester's grandfather) and he had also been greeted by a host of supporters in the wartime substitute at Gatwick. This race, held on the site of the modern airport, bore little relation except in title to its Lancashire synonym. Right-handed, with a short run-in from the last fence, it had no hazards to compare with the Canal Turn, or the drops down to the landing side of Becher's and Valentine's. Mrs. Hugh Peel's bay gelding started 3–1 favourite, ridden once more by Ernie Piggott, in 1920, only to fall at the first fence. At the risk of seeming to damn with the faintest of praise a steeplechaser who must certainly be rated the best of those available at that particular period, I incline to Mrs. Mirabel Topham's decree: 'There is only *one* Grand National, and that is at Aintree'.

Poethlyn, who had been sold by his owner-breeders as a weakly foal for seven guineas, and bought back by them as a two-year-old for fifty guineas, might even have had luck on his side when winning in 1919.

It was this year that Lord Wavertree's All White (remounted and third to Shaun Spadah in 1921) made the first of his seven attempts. An injury to the booked jockey, Bob Chadwick, caused a replacement to be sought at short notice to take the mount at 9 st. 10 lb. Tommy Williams, little known of then, or for that matter thereafter, and many years later a potman in a public house off Jermyn Street in London's West End, was given the assignment.

'Going to the Canal second time round, we had Poethlyn stone-cold' he would tell anyone who cared to listen. 'And then, what with the pills and the wasting and no food and the desperate, cold, wind, I got the stomach-cramp. I had to pull up and be sick.'

These hard-luck tales are so interwoven into the Grand National fabric that it may not be surprising that there have been so few triumphs duplicated, by comparison, for instance, with the Cheltenham Gold Cup (which is, of course, run on level, weight-for-age terms). If we disallow the right of Poethlyn's entry and concede without demur the qualifications of Manifesto and Reynoldstown, the record books show only four horses to have won more than once and none more than twice. These dual successes were gained in the twenty-two year period between 1849 and 1870 inclusive. And now, all these years afterwards, some serious doubt is being expressed as to whether one of this quartet might not be accused of being an impostor.

For purposes of the narrative, let us look at the four in alphabetical and not chronological order beginning therefore with

Abd el Kader (1850, 1851). There can be certainly no reason to quibble at the pedigree (by Ishmael out of English Lass) or the identity of this little, square-cut bay gelding, owned as he was by Joseph Osborne, a nineteenth-century equivalent of turf-writing amateur-riders such as John Hislop and John Lawrence. Joseph contributed to *Bell's Life* (ancestor of *The Sporting Life*) and also edited *The Horsebreeder's Handbook*. In this latter publication he told the story of his father (David Osborne of County Meath), who, whilst on a visit to England took a fancy, riding on the box, to a handsome brown mare, one of the leaders drawing his coach during the final stage from London to Shrewsbury.

Certainly not the last of the Osborne family to be a shrewd judge of horseflesh, Mr. David bought her for forty guineas and shipped her back home, where she not only won flat races for him, but also carried him brilliantly to hounds. He had ascertained that English Lass, although half-bred, had some Herod blood in her and the mating with Ishmael doubled the quota. It came as no surprise to those who knew the blood-lines of this era that a male product of such a mating might be nappy and difficult to handle. Castration made it inevitable that the colt named Abd el Kader should be schooled for jumping, a decision soon justified by his prowess in Irish steeplechases. He crossed to England early in March, where he ran and won at Worcester. Despite this victory, he was not even honoured with a quotation when he lined up in the then-record turnout of thirty-two runners for the 1850 Grand National. (The space of 113 years was to elapse before Ayala, the 66–1 Grand National winner of 1963, was to follow the footsteps of 'Little Ab'.)

His weight was raised only 6 lb., from 9 st. 12 lb. to 10 st. 4 lb. the following year, when he started joint second-favourite at 7–1. It was a desperately close thing between him and the mare, Maria Day, all the way from the last fence

16

Opposite. I The Christening of Becher's Brook by Finch Mason.
II 'What price Mr. Hobson and Austerlitz, Aintree, 1877' by Finch Mason.

to the winning-post, where the judge gave the old-fashioned verdict of 'half-a-neck' in his favour. Two further efforts in 1852 and 1853 both failed, and he passed out of the Aintree scene when falling at the second fence in 1858.

If the country of Shropshire can claim some reflected credit by virtue of David Osborne's percipience in finding within its boundaries the dam of Abd el Kader, it established a reputation as a production-area in which to rear champion racehorses, when

The Colonel (1869, 1870), was foaled at John Weyman's stud-farm near Ludlow in 1863. Although technically a half-bred, he was closely related on his sire's side of the pedigree to Stockwell, winner of the 1852 Two Thousand Guineas and St. Leger, and champion stallion for a decade and more thereafter. Unlike the Marquis of Exeter's blaze-faced compact chestnut with the two white hind stockings, The Colonel is shown in Harry Hall's painting to be a brown-black horse of the accepted Aintree stamp, whole in colour except for a rosebud-shaped white marking in the upper centre of his forehead.

Three horses are recorded as winning the Grand National in successive years. To the tough, painstaking little Cheltenham professional George Stevens goes the unique fame of being the only jockey to partner the same horse in two consecutive victories, and his second win on The Colonel in 1870 brought his triumphant total to five, a record still unequalled and likely to remain so for all time.

Stevens helped John Weyman and Matthew Evans to break and school this handsome, strongly-built entire, and he donned the racing colours first of Weyman and then of his partner (to whom he was related by marriage) on those two halcyon afternoons at Aintree. However, on the eve of his thirty-eighth birthday, came the abrupt termination to the career of this frail, delicate, dedicated race-riding genius.

Could it have been sheer carelessness, or a loss of concentration after having 'one for the road' with his cronies at 'The Rising Sun', which resulted in George being unable to control his hack that June day on Cleeve Hill above Cheltenham in 1871? Instead of jogging on homewards up the hill, the horse took fright after his rider's hat was blown off, wheeled and bolted in the opposite direction, throwing Stevens to his death-fall against a pile of road-mender's stones. Due largely to ill-health, he rode less than a hundred winners during the twenty years which spanned the period between 1852 and 1871;

17

Opposite. III The Steeplechasers Lottery and Valentine, by F. C. Turner.
IV The Steeplechase Cracks 1846, by J. F. Herring, senior.

contemporary reports allude to his winning races in France, which would enhance this meagre total but the details of these victories, if they ever existed, cannot be traced.

His Grand National record of victories — and let us not forget that he could go to scale at nine stone with a man's saddle on his arm — remains supreme:

1856 Freetrader   (9 st. 6 lb.)
1863 Emblem   (10 st. 10 lb.)
1864 Emblematic   (10 st. 6 lb.)
1869 The Colonel   (10 st. 7 lb.)
1870 The Colonel   (11 st. 12 lb.)

The Colonel was sold afterwards to Germany and it is said that the Emperor of Prussia rode him on parade when reviewing his troops on their return from conquering the French in the Franco-Prussian War. The Germans have ever since shown a marked preference for horses of The Colonel's image, big, sturdy-limbed and chocolate in colour.

Compared with their record as flat-racers, unusually few grey horses have achieved distinction over jumps and then mainly over hurdles and not over fences. The successes by greys on the flat during the past fifty years have been gained in major part by horses of The Tetrarch breed. These have inherited with their coat-colour speed in excess of stamina and a predisposition towards bulk which causes the effort of leaping over raised obstacles to become all the more arduous.

Only two greys from the scores competing have ever triumphed in the Grand National. When Charles Vaughan's Nicolaus Silver, ridden by Bobbie Beasley and the second of three winners trained by Fred Rimell (preceded by E.S.B. in 1956 and followed by Gay Trip in 1970), beat thirty-four rivals for the 1961 race he also conquered a jinx which had been attached to horses of his colour for ninety years.

The Lamb (1868, 1871), his predecessor, a little Irish-bred grey reared in County Limerick, was measured at no more than fifteen hands two inches when he won the Grand National for the first time as a six-year-old in 1868, carrying the cerise jacket, blue sleeves and cap of Lord Poulett.

This sixth holder of the title, a godson of King William IV, was renowned as the most famous amateur sportsman of his day, master of the Hambledon Hounds, a keen cricketer and supporter of the Hambledon Cricket Club, an excellent yachtsman, and a better-than-average rider on the flat, over jumps and between flags. He was past forty when he leased The Lamb from the Dublin veterinary surgeon Joseph Doyle, acting on a lucky hunch, for the little horse had been 'spun' by more than one of the lessor's colleagues, and fortune came to his aid again when he decided to hand over the ride at Liverpool to George Ede, a seven-years younger Hampshire neighbour who had been his friend and companion riding to hounds and on the cricket field.

Under the conventions of those far-off days, when a spirit of modesty was held to be the hallmark of a true sportsman, George Ede, Eton-educated and son of a wealthy landowner with estates bordering on the New Forest, preferred to ride under the alias of 'Mr. Edwards', a polite fiction approved by the turf authorities to help smooth out an awkward father-son relationship.

Tutored by the rough-and-ready Ben Land, this tall, elegant but sad-faced young amateur developed his talents until he, the pupil, had exceeded the skill of Ben in his prime. After Poulett's acquisition of The Lamb and his prevailing on George Ede to ride, it was only to be expected the little grey's Grand National preparation should be entrusted to Land.

By all accounts, the race-riding technique shown by George Ede on the little six-year-old in the 1868 Grand National, after a hard-fought duel against the professional Tomlinson on Pearl Diver, deserved the fullest praise. The big race was held on the fourth of the month this year.

Eighteen months later, whilst riding in the Grand Sefton 'Chase at Liverpool', George Ede was thrown from a horse called Chippenham at the Chair fence. Unable to disentangle his foot from the iron, he was dragged a hundred yards, trampled on and never regained consciousness.

Tom Pickernell took his place in 1871, when The Lamb, who, for one reason and another, was forced out of competition in 1869-70, won for the second time with much greater ease than on his first bid, although carrying 11 st. 4 lb. against the earlier 10 st. 7 lb.

Ben Land, a heavy and unpredictable gambler at cards and dice, saddled The Lamb for a third attempt in 1872. Mr. Topham put his weight up to 12 st. 7 lb., which clearly proved too much for him although he struggled gamely to take fourth place behind the lightly-weighted mare, Casse Tete.

The lease from Mr. Joseph Doyle having expired, ownership passed from Lord Poulett to the German Baron Oppenheim. Faced with the news that his old favourite would henceforth be transferred to Germany, followed by a bad run at the gaming tables, Ben Land must have felt that the very core had irrevocably gone from his way of life. He chose a rough mode of exit, slitting his jugular artery with a cut-throat razor on 11 August, 1872. A month later, The Lamb, racing in a steeplechase at Baden Baden, fell, broke a leg and had to be destroyed.

Such a fate has sadly been the portion of many another Grand National winner when called on to race over steeplechase circuits whose smaller fences have possibly created a feeling of dangerous over-confidence, unbalancing the judgment of a horse who knows what it is to go round Liverpool.

The fatality rate ranks high, too, in the list of their riders, even if George Ede must be counted among the few to meet their end on the scene of his supreme triumph. What an occasion that must have been in the 1858 running, when the youthful amateur on Weathercock ran second to Little Charley, mounted by William Archer (whose son, the immortal Fred Archer, had been born in January of the previous year)!

The also-rans included Escape, ridden by 'Black Tom' Olliver, best man at William Archer's wedding, and Lough Bawn, the mount of the one-and-only George Stevens.

If wasting brought no problems for George Stevens, this was one of many to beset his older but contemporary rival, 'Black Tom' Olliver. The old Cheltenham trainer, Ben Roberts, father of young John (who trained Four Ten to win the 1954 Cheltenham Gold cup), related to me what he remembered of this famous, if not notorious, character, companion of the youthful and equally wild Adam Lindsay Gordon, over a dying fire and an ebbing pint at 'The King's Arms' about forty years ago: 'He was a rough 'un — a gipsy, with all the gipsy's ways with horses and women. Gay as a lark, but a real terror in drink. Hopeless with money. If he had any and was in the mood, why, if he saw a beggar in the street, he would turn out his pockets and give him every penny he had.'

It is easy to see why such a man should have built up a legend, for Ben could have been only just out of the cradle when 'Black Tom' died in 1874. He knew about him, though, and his explanation why he preferred to sign his surname with two 'l's' bears the ring of truth. In those days, this cypher signified also a £1 note. Tom rarely out of debt, and at times behind bars for this reason, added the extra to the technically correct 'Oliver' on the joking pretext that he never wanted 'to go short of a pound or two'.

In his later years Tom Olliver set up as a trainer at Wroughton, near Swindon in Wiltshire, proving the worth of the downland gallops which were afterwards to provide the schooling facilities for Ascetic's Silver, Ally Sloper, Master Robert, Kellsboro' Jack and Royal Mail. Tamed, after his vagaries of youth, he carried with him the enviable score of three firsts astride Grand National winners, Gaylad (1842), Vanguard (1843) and Peter Simple (1853).

From time to time it is shown in the sketchy records of those days that he rode as an amateur and he is credited in the 1845 Grand National return as both owner and rider of Vanguard, top weight with 12 st. 10 lb. following this horse's success (also ridden by 'Black Tom' but in the ownership of Lord Chesterfield) under 11 st. 10 lb. in 1843, the first occasion that the race was run on handicap terms.

Peter Simple. The laxity of regard given to registrations is further shown by the fact that the name of Peter Simple crops up almost continuously in the early Grand National annals from 1841 until 1854 inclusive. It has been ascertained beyond doubt that there were two steeplechasers of this name. Might there possibly have been a third? Let the record-book speak:

1841.   Peter Simple, ridden by Walker, owned by the Hon. F. Craven, 3rd to Charity. S.P. 6–1.

1842.   Peter Simple, ridden by Mr. Hunter and owned by him, 3rd to Gaylad. S.P. 6–1.

1843.   Peter Simple, ridden by Frisby, owned by Mr. W. Ekin, 8th to Vanguard. S.P. 3–1, despite the welter-weight of 13 st. 1 lb.

1844.   Peter Simple, again mounted by Frisby for Mr. W. Ekin, a faller against Discount. He carried 12 st. 12 lb. but was not given a betting quotation.

1845.   Peter Simple, ridden by Frisby, owned by Mr. Thornton, 2nd to Cure All. Carried 11 st. 12 lb. and offered at 9–1.

1846.   Peter Simple. Frisby in the saddle once more for Mr. W. Ekin, weighted with 11 st. 2 lb. Unplaced to Pioneer and priced at 100–6 in the betting.

The Peter Simple which ran between 1841 and 1846 was a grey horse by Arbutus. 'The Druid' remarked of him in lyrical terms: 'Peter, for whom John Elmore (Lottery's owner), offered £700 in vain, was a most beautiful horse to look at and when he paced he seemed fit to carry a King. He could go up to his knees in dirt, but his mouth was not first-rate and he was far too impetuous at his fences.'

A print of this horse by Ferneley has long been in possession of the Malton trainer, Bill Elsey.

Then a gap until:

1849. Peter Simple, ridden by Tom Cunningham, owned by Mr. Mason jr. (the first 'Finch' Mason). Carried 11 st., won from The Knight of Gwynne (10 st. 7 lb.). S.P. 20–1.

1850. Peter Simple, ridden and owned by Mr. C. Cunningham. Carried 12 st. 2 lb., unplaced to Abd el Kader (9 st. 12 lb.) and The Knight of Gwynne (11 st. 8 lb.). Started 5–1 favourite.

1851. Peter Simple, ridden by D. Tubb, owned by Mr. Cunningham. Carried 11 st. 7 lb., unplaced to Abd el Kader (10 st. 4 lb.). Not named amongst the first eight in betting, although prices ranged from 6–1 La Gazza Ladra to 100–1 Royal Blue.

1853. Peter Simple, ridden by Tom Olliver for Captain Joseph Little. Carried 10 st. 10 lb. Won from Miss Mowbray (10 st. 12 lb.) and Oscar (10 st. 2 lb.) with Abd el Kader (10 st. 10 lb.) and The Knight of Gwynne (11 st. 2 lb.) unplaced. S.P. 9–1 in strong contrast to the odds presumably available in 1851 and 1852. 5–1 Miss Mowbray, 6–1 Oscar.

1854. Peter Simple, ridden by C. Boyce for a Mr. Bignell. Topweighted with twelve stone, unplaced to Bourton (11 st. 12 lb.). Fifth in the betting at 12–1. Oscar, carrying 11 st. 12 lb., 24 lb. more than in 1853, was knocked over. Bourton 4–1 favourite, 15–1 Oscar.

The story of this second Peter Simple's first win in 1849 has been dramatically related many times. His rider, Tom Cunningham, who also trained him had been staying at the Old Rose and Crown Hotel in Beverley, Yorkshire. He took a lucky chance bet of £3,000 to £30 with Tom Davies, the William Hill of his day, whilst both were waiting on a station platform for the Liverpool train.

He is said to have refused considerable inducement in running to stop his mount, was paid out £3,030 — no betting tax in those days — within a few minutes of passing the scale, got married on the proceeds and accepted an offer to train in France, where he met with considerable success.

The 1849 winner is generally agreed to have been a bay half-bred gelding by Patron. The difference between him and the grey Peter Simple who ran between 1841 and 1846 cannot be disputed. What of the 1853 winner?

Finch Mason, who owned him in his year of triumph in 1849, ran two against him four years later — Miss Mowbray (the '52 heroine) and Oscar, which finished second and third.

If so much is known and authenticated about the 1849 race, why should so few details be left to us when Tom Olliver and the gallant Captain Josey Little confounded Finch Mason's plans four years later?

Captain Van Burton, until recent retirement an official racecourse-judge at many of our principal meetings, and Dick Whitford, a highly respected private handicapper, expressed their individual doubts on this issue last year in the correspondence columns of *The Sporting Life*. Van Burton wonders why Finch Mason makes so little of this second win in his own history of the race. Whitford points to the discrepancy in the weights allotted. To cloud the issue further, there is evidence of another horse called 'Peter Simple' in existence at this time, not a half-bred by Patron, but a thoroughbred of the same colour, 'By Cataract or Pompey'.

Van Burton puts forward the suggestion that Finch Mason may have switched Oscar for Peter Simple. If a conspiracy of silence was necessary, would Tom Olliver have been the right man to engage for such a shady enterprise, unless, maybe, the bailiffs were once again at his heels? And why, in the 1854 handicap, should Oscar have been set to meet Peter Simple on 6 lb. worse terms? Did 'the Wizard', as Mr. Topham was known, suspect something? It strikes the seeker after truth as curious that Mason should even have accepted the challenge to run Oscar from such an unfavourable handicap mark.

On reflection, I give those concerned the benefit of the intriguing doubts which have arisen, and the final word, to my eminent colleague Major John Fairfax-Blakeborough, M.C., of Whitby, Yorkshire: 'For over half a century I have been responsible for the answers to Turf historical queries, and every year the mystery of the Peter Simples crops up. My reply is that after much research, I have come to the conclusion there were only two Peter Simples (I) the grey by Arbutus which ran first in the 1841 Grand National, and lastly in 1846. (II) The Peter Simple which won the Grand National in 1849 and 1853, a half-bred by Patron.'

The eighty-eight year-old major enjoys the reputation of being a ferret in the field of turf lore. The possibility of a scandal being associated with that 1853 Grand National is a rabbit which he would surely never have allowed to escape. So let us stand fast by the official records and allow Peter Simple's right to keep his place in the select group of dual Grand National heroes.

Manifesto's record stands for all time. It has never been equalled, and owners of other great Liverpool jumpers who came later on the scene with horses such as Reynoldstown, Kellsboro' Jack and Freebooter, never sought seriously to challenge it. The raising in prestige and value of the Cheltenham Gold Cup, and the institution of heavily sponsored, long-distance 'chases such as, notably, the Whitbread Gold Cup at Sandown in April, preceded by the Hennessy, the Massey-Ferguson, Kempton's King George VI 'Chase, etc., broadened the whole scheme of operations for owners and trainers. Anne, Duchess of Westminster, for instance, refused even to countenance entering Arkle for the National, and Aintree was also missed from the campaigns of Cottage Rake, Hallowe'en, Mandarin and Mill House. The cancellation of the Sefton meeting in November, as an economy measure by Mrs. Mirabel Topham, from 1966 to 1971, deprived potential Grand National candidates of invaluable schooling experience and the public of much-needed aids to forming an opinion.

Old-timers have always had a special high place in their estimation for the 1920 Grand National winner, Troytown, third in the Grand Steeple, after slogging so indomitably through the Liverpool mud three months earlier. Troytown was never seen again in England, for he was doomed to meet with a fatal accident in his second venture at Auteuil that season.

Seaman won both the Grand National and Grand Steeple in separate years. So, too, did Jerry M.

If Manifesto is to be lowered from his eminent position, the horse with strongest claims to usurp him is one who must be judged on his all-round excellence and on the courage he showed — admittedly only the once in seven tries — over a course which he thoroughly detested. Viewed against the background of five triumphs in the Cheltenham Gold Cup, the victory of Golden Miller, easing up by five lengths under 12 st. 2 lb. in 1934, establishing a time record of 9 minutes 20 $\frac{2}{5}$ seconds, which still stands supreme despite the subsequent sloping and consequent easing of the Aintree fences, tells its own story of the winner's exceptional prowess.

There are some who still maintain that by virtue of winning this Grand National on top of his Cheltenham haul, 'the Miller' must be considered Arkle's superior. Needless to say, on that March day in 1934, against twenty-nine rivals, which included the previous winners Gregalach and Forbra and quick-jumping Liverpool 'stars' such as Thomond II and Delaneige, his performance could not have been bettered.

If only the processes of time could have been halted for all concerned and the winner's unsaddling enclosure draped by a final curtain, then and there on that golden afternoon! Plump, plain-faced Dorothy Paget, that eccentric twenty-eight year-old millionairess, looked as near as she ever came to being radiant as she walked in with her horse's leading-rein in her hand holding the arm of her frail old father, Lord Queenborough, who was overjoyed at the realization of his £1,000 betting win to supplement his monthly allowance. Mick Boston, Golden Miller's Irish-born lad and still to be seen apparently little changed in general physique picking out his fancies and sipping his half-pint in the saloon-bar of Newmarket's 'Golden Lion' of a lunch-time, strode along, proud as a fighting-cock, at his horse's flank. Stan Tidey, Basil Briscoe's head-lad, destined to retrace this same coveted route with Oxo, Michael Scudamore and Willie Stephenson twenty-five years later, led the way. On the horse's back, the tough, square-cut Gerry Wilson, brought up in a hard school by 'Sonny' Hall and still to receive countless more knocks of one sort and another before he retired from riding and training to become the landlord of a Berkshire pub, raised the wan smile of a professional who rarely let his feelings be known, although these moments of acclamation, achieved now so swiftly, represented the summit of his ambition since his rough-riding boyhood days in the hunting field. And, somewhere in the background, delayed by handshakings and back-slappings from numerous friends, pausing for a second to light up his fiftieth or sixtieth du Maurier of the day, the trainer — his path tracked by that hilarious, infectious cackle of a laugh — pushed his way through the milling crowd from the Press enclosure at the top of the stand where he had accompanied me to watch the race.

The romanticized story of how the three — horse, trainer and owner —

were thrown together is as follows. Miller's Pride, the mare, had been bought by a young officer whilst he was on leave from the French battlefields during the '14-'18 war, to ride out hunting in County Meath. When his time expired, he left the mare with a local farmer Mr. Laurence Geraghty, promising to collect her and pay his dues on his next visit. He was never heard of again.

As the years went by, the farmer decided to make his own use of her for breeding. Her first two foals, May Court and May Crescent, both eventually succeeded in making minor names for themselves as point-to-point and National Hunt performers in England, during the 1920's. The claimant to the honour of being the legitimate owner of Miller's Pride at the time of her mating with the local five-guinea stallion, Goldcourt, in 1926, was a Mr. Julius Solomon of Dublin.

Three years later, Golden Miller was bought by Basil Briscoe, inheritor of a comfortable fortune from his parents' sheepfarms in Australia. He had established temporary residence with his brother Dick at Longstowe Hall on the outskirts of Cambridge, after some agreeable years at Eton and his local University followed by a pupil-trainer course with Harvey Leader at Newmarket. He felt unsuited to understudy his brother's role in politics, one of the few decisions which created mutual harmony in this household.

Stabling was built, galloping grounds were marked and laid out in the park. All through the winter, hunting was to be readily available with the Newmarket and Thurlow, the Cottesmore and the Quorn. Election to White's Club in London and the acquisition of a limousine Bentley made the West End an inevitable magnet.

In the chic chemin-de-fer parties of that era, run by 'Skipper' Ward and others, he rubbed shoulders at cocktails and swapped badinage and chips across the green baize with London's elite gamblers, Lord Harewood, Mr. Jimmy de Rothschild, Sir Abe Bailey, Alfred Butt, Sidney Beer, Phil Carr, Tim Birkin and on rarer occasions, Dorothy Paget.

It could not be considered surprising that a man prepared always to stand pat on a draw of five, or to call 'suivi' against a winning bank, should be willing to play his hunches in the racing game. This sharp impulsiveness, after a winning night at the table, prompted him to snap up the telegraphed offer of £500 for the then three-year-old Golden Miller, without even taking time off to inspect him first.

He knew the potentials of Golden Miller. He remembered, too, the favourable remark passed on to him about this very horse some months earlier by Nat Galway Greer, for so long one of Ireland's unexcelled judges of the young, immature racing prospect. The days which elapsed between the posting of the cheque and Golden Miller's arrival at the end of a rough sea-rail journey, were buoyed up by excitement; the disappointment can be imagined when this long, lanky, three-year-old unlimbered himself from his motor horse-van and stumbled puppy-fashion across the yard to his box.

Basil, however, was nothing if not an optimist, and when his friend, Phil Carr, came to visit him, the initial shock was soon forgotten. The Nottinghamshire sportsman (whose son Arthur had the reputation of being the best heavy-weight rider to hounds in the Midlands when able to take time off from his extensive top-class cricket commitments) formed an immediate and instinctive fancy for the son of Goldcourt. And, furthermore, when offered him at original cost-price, he refused point-blank to pay less than £1,000 for him, although knowing full well that he had finished unplaced on his only English start in a minor hurdle-race at Southwell some six weeks previously.

Golden Miller's career, and Basil Briscoe's whole future, would have differed unpredictably but beneficially if this owner-trainer relationship could have remained intact. The confidence instilled by the purchaser seems somehow to have passed itself on to the horse. On his next outing in a Newbury hurdle, ridden by Bob Lyall (due to win that season's Grand National on Grakle) he ran second and earned high praise from his partner. Lyall again had the mount when Golden Miller gained the first of his twenty-nine victories, at Leicester, to be quickly followed by another in a hurdle-race at Nottingham, with Ted Leader in the saddle. Briscoe made an unusual choice for the four-year-old's final appearance of the season, promoting him to fences and racing him for the Spring Chase at Newbury's February fixture.

Gerry Wilson, who was to be more closely identified with the horse than any of the other jockeys who rode him, had the mount in this, first-ever, race by the Miller over fences. He had been to ride his mount in a school at Longstowe some days previously. Here is his own account of this experience.

'I motored to Longstowe the night before, and during our conversation that night Basil Briscoe said he thought that he had, not only the best horse in England, but also that he would make the best chaser ever seen. I agreed that he might be the best young horse out that season, but if he could beat the old ones at the weights, I was very doubtful. As for making the best horse we had ever seen… well, I had heard that tale before, especially at night!

Next morning I threw my leg across The Miller for the first time, thinking as we walked and trotted round what a great strong sort of devil he was, and what a good ride he would be if only he would wake up. As it was, he slouched along as if tomorrow would do. In the preliminary canter he was just the same, and it was not until we had jumped three or four baby fences that he began to take an interest in the proceedings. Mr. Briscoe then put a very light lad on a good plater, with orders to lead me a striding gallop over six nice fences, which would be about a mile. Away went the plater, and for the first two fences The Miller could not get within two lengths of him. Over the next two he was upsides, and over the last The Miller was pulling and out-jumping the old horse.

At breakfast, talking over the morning's work, Basil surprised me by saying:

'Ride Golden Miller at Newbury next week, and keep yourself for the Four-Year-Old 'Chase at Cheltenham'.

I was delighted to do so, but added 'Don't you think you are asking rather a lot of the horse to jump Newbury with so little schooling?'

'Unfortunately that is his only engagement over fences before Cheltenham', came the reply.

I was not worried about myself. I would ride anything on four legs in those days. Newbury is a grand racecourse with ample room for a horse to see his fences, and Golden Miller ran a great race, and after making a couple of mistakes was only beaten a short-head by Rolie, a first-class handicap hurdler with years of racing experience behind him. Golden Miller had only been broken for nine months. It was a great performance for a four-year-old.

Unfortunately the Cheltenham National Hunt Meeting was off owing to the weather, and it was decided not to run The Miller again that season.'

The trainer's lucky hunch had survived early misgivings, greatly helped by Carr's backing and ownership of others in the stable, such as the young Achtoi gelding, Insurance, and the slow-but-sure jumper Solanum. Now tragedy struck. Carr summoned Basil to his bedside, 'The doctors have given me bad news,' he said: 'I have only a few months to put my affairs in order. Sell all my horses and take a lower price if you can continue to keep those you want to train.'

At Sir Melville Ward's next chemin-de-fer party, Briscoe called Dorothy Paget's bank three times on the turn, killing each coup. For a few moments between play, he was able to take her to a quiet corner and outline the offer: '£10,000 for Golden Miller and Insurance as a pair, on condition they stay with me. Otherwise no deal. £3,500 for Solanum under the same terms or £5,000 if he leaves the stable.'

Within forty-eight hours, the veterinary certificates were posted to Leeds Castle near Maidstone in Kent, and a reciprocating cheque in prompt settlement encouraged the move of the Briscoe horses to new premises at Beechwood House Stables, Exning, on Newmarket Heath's western fringe, giving access to the vast range of gallops and schooling facilities.

Here Golden Miller grew to maturity, stretching his muscles on the long expanses from Southfields to Choke Jade and sharpening up his precision over fences on the old steeplechase course which still made the circuit of the golf links, hard by the raised Ditch. He had his home in the biggest box of the open square, bounded on one side by a clock-tower and on the other by the house where Basil Briscoe, his assistant Jim Pilkington, the flat-race jockey Harry Beasley, Grouse the huge Great Dane, and a pack of dachshunds and Cairn terriers shared a bachelor establishment.

As 'the Miller' thickened and thrived, increasingly contented with his way of life, the relationship between owner and trainer bucketed over a series of flash-points. An occasion when Miss Paget arrived more than two hours late for evening stables, requiring the urgent summons to Stan Tidey and the task of arousing the horses who had been untethered for their night's rest, remained as a remembered source of grievance. It was aggravated when she refused to enter the house, sending instead her chauffeur to the kitchen to put boiling-water in the teapot whose contents she shared at the back of her Rolls-Royce with her two secretaries.

Briscoe's optimism about all three jumpers was vindicated in full. Insurance became the first horse to take the Champion Hurdle twice (1932-3); Solanum's wins included the then still-important Lancashire Chase at Manchester; and Golden Miller, in his first ten starts for Dorothy Paget, registered six victories (one disallowed on a technical objection for carrying the wrong weight). The most important by far was that in the 1932 Cheltenham Gold Cup, when his way became easier due to the two favourites, Grakle and Kingsford, both falling — but nonetheless a noteworthy archievement by a horse only five years old.

Ted Leader, a member of the famous Newmarket family, had the riding of him in most of his races, but the following season his place was taken by the champion National Hunt rider, Billy Stott. (During his career 'the Miller' was handled in one or more of his races by fifteen different jockeys). Powerful, short-legged Billy could do no more than win all five, beginning at Kempton in December, visiting Lingfield twice and Hurst Park once before landing the Gold Cup at Cheltenham again and this time, to uproarious acclaim, by ten lengths.

Twenty-two days elapsed between the Gold Cup and the Grand National date that year, and Miss Paget, spurred on by the rivalry of her American cousin 'Jock' Whitney, decided to run at Aintree, where her champion had 12 st. 2 lb. against the 12 st. 7 lb. to be carried by Gregalach and the 12 st. 1 lb. on the back of another previous winner, Shaun Goilin.

It is none too easy after this lapse of time to sort out why Stott was now deposed and Ted Leader reinstated. Stott had let it be known, although not to owner or trainer, that he doubted whether the horse would get round the Aintree circuit. This story was repeated, as such stories are, and came to the ears of Miss Paget. That was enough. (Stott recanted, too late, and then changed to Pelorus Jack, who fell at the last fence when in the lead.)

'I had vowed never to ride for her again — she was *very* difficult in those days — but Basil pleaded with me to come to his rescue and so I consented,' explained Ted.

The first Liverpool experience proved as unhappy as several in later years. 'He was too heavy in the shoulder for this course,' went on Ted. 'He shuddered when he saw the drop-down on the landing side of Becher's and I couldn't keep with him at Valentine's. For a parting present, he gave me a nasty kick in the back. That was the last time I rode him.'

Whatever Ted's feelings, his mount had the good sense to avoid injury to himself. The thought of having him accompany Insurance to Auteuil was discarded in favour of another long summer's rest.

Now came the season of glory for Gerry Wilson, Miss Paget's new jockey, beginning in November of 1933 by the defeat of Kellsboro' Jack and Thomond II at Lingfield. The owner had continued to extend her scope of interest to flat-racing and the Paget string at Exning now amounted to a round dozen, with the acquisition of some high-priced yearlings at the September Sales.

In the heavy Lingfield going, the Miller finally won easily from his two distinguished rivals. Basil Briscoe's last words to the rider as he left the paddock were 'for God's sake keep him straight over the last three or four fences'.

'I kept him fairly straight', recalls Gerry, 'but I had a job, as he began to hang badly to the right down the hill, and going into the last three fences, I had to hit him on the shoulder and check to keep him from running right across his fences. I never had to hit him to win a race, although every now and then for a race or two, he needed a reminder to keep him straight. He would never have won a National, or beaten Thomond II in that momentous race at Cheltenham if he had been allowed to keep jumping to the right, as both those courses are left-handed'.

Golden Miller's next race was a two-mile-and-a-half affair at Kempton Park on Boxing Day with only three or four runners. The going had dried up considerably, and with Thomond II receiving seven pounds on the fast track, it looked like a match between the two. And so it was. Speck jumped Thomond II off, and try as I might The Miller could never quite get on terms with him. Thomond II won a very fast race by a length and a half, the Miller trying hard to jump to the right over the last two fences'.

Again, round the sharp turns of Hurst Park, Southern Hero, receiving 28 lbs. and later to win two Scottish Grand Nationals under big weights, proved much too nippy for him, and these two defeats naturally set tongues wagging, but they were promptly silenced when — on the soft ground which he loved — he succeeded in easily winning his third successive Gold Cup. Always up with the leaders, he took over at the third last fence, as Wilson later said in explaining his tactics to Basil Briscoe.

'I sent him clear so early, because I feared he might try to run across to the right, and probably be involved in an objection for crossing, if he did so at the last fence'.

Not all the critics were convinced, though, by his style of jumping. The late James Hylton Park of the 'Evening Standard', remarked:

'I noticed that Golden Miller reached for the fence on two occasions. He will not have to do this in the National.'

Wilson's own account of this historic race cannot be bettered:

'I was quietly confident that we would win. The only worry I had was, could I escape trouble all the way to Becher's first time round? The Miller hated being hurried early in a race, and everyone knows what a gallop they go down to the first fence. We were bound to be in a bad position when we arrived. Luckily the four or five which did fall did not interfere with us. The Miller was jumping deliberately and well over the first three or four fences, gradually making up his ground in his own time. We were about tenth or twelfth approaching Becher's with the field spread all over the course. The runners were a little thicker on the inside and with Forbra (a wonderful jumper) going for the middle of the fence, I went on his right and had a perfectly clear run into the fence. A good job I did, as The Miller was not prepared for the drop, and landed all sprawling and ran along on his knees with his nose touching the ground for a couple of yards before recovering himself, losing quite a lot of ground in doing so.

'Well done Gerry', shouted one jockey as he passed us.

We were soon striding along again with the Canal Turn just in front, where he had parted company with Ted Leader the year before. Safely round that with the leaders still a dozen lengths in front. The Miller now well warmed up, was going great guns, and I took closer order with the leaders coming on to the racecourse first time round, being fifth or sixth going into the Chair Ditch in front of the stands, which Basil Briscoe had warned me he had not jumped very well the year before. The Miller did not do it very well this time either, leaving his hind legs on the fence, having to give an extra heave to get going again. He was quickly in his stride again, absolutely eating the ground going into the water, which he jumped magnificently, and on landing I gave him a kick, and shot up to the leader, which was Delaneige. All the way down to Becher's, we were upsides, galloping and jumping to-gether.

'How are you going Gerry?' asked Jack Moloney.

I was too busy to reply.

Going into Becher's the second time, Gerry Hardy, on Forbra, came up on the inside of us. That was the only other horse apart from Delaneige that I saw all the way round. We came round the Canal Turn with the usual bump, catch-as-catch-can, associated with that acute left-handed in-an-out. Taking a deep breath, (The Miller generally did that a couple of times in a race, and I needed a refill now) over Valentine's, then the last big open ditch and on to the racecourse again, with still nothing in it between the two of us. Delaneige still holding a slight lead all the way round that long gallop into

32

Opposite. V Silks and Satins of the Field 1866, by Ben Herring.
VI The Canal Turn in the 1892 National, by G. D. Giles.

The Grand National 1899

Over the Water

the second-last fence, which he jumped slightly quicker. The Miller by now had started to hang to the right with me. Delaneige still led into the last fence, but although Golden Miller jumped out to the right rather, losing about a length, he soon recovered it, and drawing away from the other with every stride, he galloped by the post in the record time of nine minutes, twenty and two-fifth seconds, five lengths in front of Delaneige, with Thomond II, whom I had not seen since jumping the water, third, realising for me my life's ambition of winning the Grand National'.

What a superb performance it had been — and the writer still recalls the gasp when Golden Miller barged through the Chair Fence in front of the stands, leaving a mighty hole in his wake, and the sheer joy at watching him lengthen his stride on the long run home from the final fence.

Only Speck on Thomond II, of the beaten jockeys, was heard to declare that he might have beaten the winner if he had not been the subject of interference when old Gregalach faltered at the Canal Turn, causing him the loss of much valuable ground at a vital stage in the race.

Celebrations for this victory were, as always, during the 30s, held at Liverpool's Adelphi Hotel. The winning owner had a reserved place in the centre of a horseshoe-shaped table on a stage overlooking the band and the ball-room.

Soon after eight o'clock, the waiters began moving among the five hundred £5-a-head customers, packed around the dance-floor, on the balconies and the two restaurants on either side. Up on the stage, Miss Paget's fifty-or-so guests gyrated with increasing uncertainty around the temporary bar, as nine o'clock and nine-thirty passed by.

Joe Orlando, baton poised, waited anxiously for his boys to give out with a special version of 'Here comes the bride' on the appearance of the millionaire hostess.

It was not until past ten o'clock that Miss P. joined us, almost unnoticed, by a side-curtain clutching to the arm of her father. Without ado, her plain, plump, face semi-circled by lank strands of hair, dressed in a heavy-weight, crumpled, maroon-coloured ankle-length gown which fitted where it might, the 28-year-old millionairess wasted no time on ceremony before seating herself.

Sometime after midnight, Lord Queenborough arose to propose his self-appointed toast: 'My daughter, her horse Golden Miller — and the British

33

Opposite. VII Mr. J. G. Bulteel's Manifesto, winner in 1897 and 1899, by A. C. Havell.
VIII At the Water, in the 1899 National, by W. V. Longe.

Empire'. Few present, alive or dead, could have given you next day a verbatim report of that sleep-inducing oration.

It served a purpose which none of us guessed. Close at hand, behind a screen, Miss Paget's secretaries were peeling off £5 notes from a thick pile — one for every member of the Adelphi Hotel staff, page-boys, lift-attendants, chambermaids, commis-waiters, and all. 'Funny thing!' mused Joe Orlando, recounting this incident, 'only me and my boys were left out'.

★ ★ ★

The summer of 1934, relaxed and peaceful for Golden Miller, found a heightening of tension between his owner and trainer. Miss Paget spent most of it in Germany, continuing though to gamble heavily, telephoning Exning several times a week, usually at two or three in the morning, for an hour and more each session. Briscoe did not have the same flair for training two-year-olds that he showed for the jumpers. The two-year-old Racla colt (later called Radamedes) ran the great Bahram to a neck for the Rous Memorial Stakes at Goodwood, before coming up trumps at Manchester and Newmarket to compensate in part for a series of expensive failures.

To all outward appearance, the 1934-35 campaign for Golden Miller began smoothly enough with an odds-on canter for a £117 steeplechase at Wolverhampton on Boxing Day. Typical of the uncertainty brewing between the principals, Briscoe only advised Wilson of the plan two days before Christmas. By this time, Gerry, champion jockey for the second successive season — he topped the list on seven occasions between '33 and '41 — and fully booked with six rides at Kempton Park, expressed his concern that he had not been asked earlier, with regrets that he could not be available.

Jack Baxter, Golden Miller's exercise-rider, and a competent young jockey, who was killed three years later in a fall from a bad horse at Taunton, took over, and did all that was needed of him. The two champions, however, were successfully re-united at Derby and Leicester in similar small-money races. The slip-up by Scottish Wood racing immediately in front into the water-jump at Derby, gave Gerry Wilson a fresh insight into his mount's uncanny cleverness. 'The way he side-stepped him could have been a lesson for any light-weight boxer', he said on unsaddling.

There followed, in mid-February, at Sandown Park, a thorough-going test for any champion — The Grand International Handicap Chase, with Miller carrying top-weight of 12 st. 7 lb. (175 lb.) against six experienced jumpers, which included Delaneige (receiving 12 lbs.). Owen Anthony, seeing him draw clear to win by ten lengths, ever afterwards rated this his greatest performance.

All was set clear for a repeat of the 1934 programme — the Gold Cup at Cheltenham, the Grand National at Aintree, for horse, trainer and rider. And then the wheel of fortune which had been spinning so merrily for all involved, changed its capricious pace.

As rarely before and seldom since, the traditionally 'fill-dyke' month of February, was marked by searing winds and no rain-fall. Cyril Luckman, then 'The Scout' in the London 'Daily Express' described this end-of-February drought as 'phenomenal', and detailed the injuries brought about by the hard going. 'Nearly every day of late, more than one horse has broken down, leading riders have been involved in serious falls, and fatal mishaps have been above average'.

Briscoe was forced to soft-pedal the Miller's training schedule, and at Gatwick on the second of March (twelve days before the Gold Cup) Wilson was pitched hard onto his left shoulder by D'Eyncourt, when challenging for the lead at the second-last fence in the Grand National Trial 'Chase. On the advice of his friends, the trainer 'Sonny' Hall and Mr. Ronald Holbech, it was arranged for Sir Morton Smart, the royal doctor, to give the injured rider special treatment. 'I suppose it made some difference', said the patient, 'The pain seemed not too bad when I was warmed up in the daytime, but it was hell at nights'.

He felt fit enough to book several rides at the three-day Cheltenham meeting, starting with Lion Courage in the Champion Challenge Hurdle Cup, feature of the first afternoon's programme. Briscoe and he had noticed that, on the Thursday, Thomond II was named amongst the final five acceptors for the Gold Cup, but had an alternative engagement for the two-mile Coventry Cup, which looked at his mercy. Jack Anthony, playing his cards very close to his chest, refused to commit himself. 'We have beaten you once, and we shall do so again!' he remarked, in jesting fashion to Basil when they happened to meet outside the Cheltenham weighing-room before Tuesday's racing started, careful not to specify any exact date for the decisive match between the two champions owned by the Whitney cousins.

Jack's alert beady-brown eyes, helped clinch the Thursday decision when watching Gerry Wilson dismount from Lion Courage after they had won the Champion Hurdle. The rider could not lift his left arm and hand to undo the girths. In his words:

'Lion Courage stood off further from his hurdles than any horse I have ever ridden, and it was this way of standing off and reaching for the jumps which caused this to happen. No pain — but the whole of my left arm just weak and useless'.

As Gerry cancelled all booked rides until the Gold Cup, and left for electrical treatment in London, Jack stumped off to contact 'Jock' Whitney and advise on a fighting policy, advice that resulted in a race which those lucky enough to see will never forget. The Hon. George Lambton — and who could know better the full score of racing on the flat and over jumps — summed it up for all of us when describing this with admirable brevity as 'the finest steeplechase I ever watched in all my life'.

All five acceptors stood their ground — the other three being Mrs. F. Ambrose Clark's Kellsboro' Jack (the 1933 Grand National winner), Mr. J. V. Rank's Southern Hero and Mrs. H. Mundy's six-year-old Avenger.

In a race which had such close bearing on the Grand National, due to be run only fifteen days later, we can do no better than re-live it again, sharing the misgivings of the man in the Dorothy Paget 'blue-and-yellow'. Fearing his own fitness, that of his mount and the state of the ground (so greatly favouring Thomond II), he left the jockeys' dressing-room reflecting in his quiet way that everything was 'not quite what one might have wished'.

'In the Parade Ring before mounting, Basil Briscoe said he did not want a fast run race, as The Miller was short of work. If he had known Thomond II was going to run, he would have given The Miller more fast work. I disagreed, saying that The Miller's natural staying power would carry him through a fast-run race. What I was afraid of was a slow-run race, with Speck on Thomond II sitting in behind, coming to beat me for speed at the finish. Neither of us need have worried.

There were five runners; Golden Miller, Thomond II, Southern Hero, Avenger and Kellsboro' Jack. The only ones I saw after the second fence were Thomond II and Southern Hero. Jack Fawcus on The Hero had jumped off in front at a nice gallop, with myself a length behind on his inside, and Speck on my right, just wide of Southern Hero. Going down the hill to the water first time round, Speck came close into me. I could see what he wanted; to go up to Southern Hero on his inside. I steadied The Miller for a stride to let him do this, thinking 'just what the doctor ordered. I can watch *you* now, Billy!'

Jack Fawcus glanced over his left shoulder and saw Thomond II's nose, and from that second to the end of the race, not one of us could have gone a stride faster. Southern Hero seemed to be flying along, the two of us at his heels. In all my races, I have never experienced anything quite like it. Three crack horses on very fast ground, going absolutely all out all the way. It was a question of which of us cracked up first. Little Thomond II was skipping along, flicking over his fences, loving every second of it. The Miller had his neck stretched the whole of the journey, hitting the ground with his great big feet like sledge hammers. It was not until coming down the hill into the third last that Southern Hero cracked up, Speck and I both going by him in mid-air over the fence, just as if he was not there. Speck and I jumped the second last together, coming round the turn into the last with not an inch between us. Into the last Speck drew his whip. I did not hit The Miller, keeping hold of his head and booting him into it, concentrating on keeping him balanced and straight. We landed together, still not an inch between us until half way to the winning post Thomond II cracked up, leaving The Miller to stay on and win a great race by three-quarters of a length. Kellsboro' Jack with D. Morgan up was third, with Mrs. Mundy's Avenger, trained by T. R. Rimell fourth, while Southern Hero on whom Jack Fawcus had led us such a dance, eased up last.

It was marvellous. The crowd were cheering like mad. Speck and I having a job to get back to the unsaddling enclosure to weigh in. We shared the same valet, Fred Taylor. A really good chap. But his patience was sorely tried by the crowd round us both in the dressing-room.

That great sportsman, Sir John Grey, came in asking both of us to his box after racing to have a drink. There was the usual crowd there. Sir John filled our glasses, everyone congratulated us and so on. When it had died down a little, Billy pulled me into the corner of the room, and clinked my glass with his own.

'Well done mate. Well there's one thing, when we are old and grey, sitting back enjoying a drink, we can tell them how we did ride at least one great horse-race one day in our lives'.

And so 'the Miller', although his unique record had not yet been fully written into the Cheltenham Gold Cup chapters, had now won four in a row. All recriminations on other matters forgotten, a rapturous owner and trainer once again stood patting and admiring their paragon, cheered by the curious and admiring throng around the winner's unsaddling enclosure.

In the euphoria of the moment, bookmakers would lay no more than 6–4 against his Grand National chance, as the champion returned home to Exning to rest and recuperate after this most gruelling battle of his career. More nervous than ever, Basil's equanimity was rattled before the week was out. Wilson sought an urgent, personal talk. 'I think you and Miss Paget ought to know, guv'nor, that I have had an offer of £3,000 to stop the horse at Aintree, and that I've turned it down,' he said, in his stolid matter-of-fact way refusing to name the source of this nefarious enticement. And then on the Monday at Wolverhampton Wilson had a heavy fall in a steeplechase, causing a fresh bruise to his damaged collar-bone. It seemed possible he might not be fit to ride, and Eric Brown was confidentially asked to stand by. However, with his right side tightly strapped up Gerry was back in action at Sandown, landing a gamble for Gil Bennett there in a selling-hurdle on Saturday. He did not take a mount over fences after his fall on March 18 until getting the leg-up on to Golden Miller in the Aintree paddock on March 29. As usual, until after World War II, the Grand National was then held on a Friday.

Special security guards had been keeping twenty-four hour watch over the favourite. The trainer slept fitfully, with a loaded 12-bore at his bedside. On arrival at Liverpool the horse looked splendid; the trainer was wan and distraught.

The number-board showed a line-up of twenty-seven starters, the smallest since Troytown's year. Bookies extended odds against the favourite to 2–1, in view of the heavy betting on Thomond II (second choice at 9–2) now receiving 8 lb. carrying 11 st. 13 lb. against the 12 st. 7 lb. on the topweight. The Cheltenham win by Tapinois made him a popular bet at 8–1. Amongst the longer-priced, opinion seemed split between the Furlong family pair Really True (18–1) and Reynoldstown (22–1).

The parade in front of the stands was watched by the Paget party from their box. Some distraction was caused when a wild hare, roused from its lie, careered into the water jump and drowned itself.

'Dammit! There goes my daughter's last chance of a husband!' said old

Lord Queenborough, in a quiet aside to Basil Briscoe, who recalled later that this unexpected observation afforded him his last laugh for a long, long time.

They set off at a fast clip on the firm going, not easily identifiable as they streamed away over Becher's and then, clearing the Canal Turn jump, made back towards us on the grandstand. Bill Hobbiss (from the Canal) and Bob Lyall (from an extension to Lord Derby's top-floor box) were covering the running for the B.B.C. Bob Lyall was seen suddenly to poke his head out of his sound-proofed kiosk, making excited thumbsdown gestures. Golden Miller was out of the race...

Confirmation came speedily when the riderless bay horse, carrying the No. 1 cloth under his saddle, separated himself from the others and cantered back to the paddock. The ensuing hubbub deflected much of the interest remaining in the race, and the acclaim for Reynoldstown's triumph over Blue Prince and Thomond II. What had happened to the favourite? With not a hair to be seen out of place anywhere, it was up to the horse's rider to furnish the explanation.

Wilson had been undergoing treatment every day for his injured arm and shoulder from an old masseur in Church Stretton, Shropshire, treatment which was continued until the eve of the big race. He claims, though, that on mounting, he found himself fitter and in less pain than for several weeks past. His story continues:

'The preliminaries being over, we were away to a good start, The Miller, as usual, taking his time to warm up. This did not worry me at first, but instead of gradually lengthening his stride and catching hold of the bridle, he was shortening his stride and not going into his bit at all. Landing over the third fence, I shook him up, sending him nearer the leaders, and by the time we reached Becher's first time round, we were in a good position, although The Miller was not jumping in his best style.

Round the Canal Turn, over Valentine's, Mr. Peter Bostwick, the American amateur was making the running on one of his own horses (Castle Irwell). I was lying about third when two fences later, going into the last open ditch first time round (fence 11), the Miller really tried to refuse. In fact he had pulled up to a standstill with his head down in the bottom of the ditch, shooting me up his neck.

Then he did what no other horse I have ever ridden would or could have done. He jumped it from a standstill in that position. In mid-air I knew

I could not keep on him, as I was half-way off when he decided to jump, and the tremendous heave and twist in slow motion did the rest. While he was jumping the fence, the film showed three or four horses jumping by him, one after another. All the critics seemed to have missed that; thinking I had fallen or thrown myself off just because he twisted in mid-air.

How the tongues did wag, and the pockets talk. It was even said I was seen meeting a man in an A. A. uniform on the way home, and receiving bundles of notes from him!

Wilson's version was largely substantiated by an onlooker, a Mr. Edgar Turner, who was standing by this fence, which, for the record, is 5 feet high and 3 feet wide. The ditch on the take-off side is 6 feet wide, 2 feet deep, with a guard rail 1 ft. 6 inches high in front of the ditch.

'Golden Miller came to the fence lying third on the inside position, and then suddenly jibbed and came to a standstill in front of the guard rail. By some amazing effort, he then jumped, screwing to the left, but landing safely on the other side. Wilson had no chance to stay in the saddle, having understandably been taken completely by surprise at this unexpected unprecedented leap'.

All this, in the days before the invention of the film patrol camera, was unknown to owner and trainer, as they agitatedly sought Wilson for his explanation.

Briscoe admitted later that the possibility of the bribe being increased passed through his mind, and he was somewhat sceptical about Wilson's halting explanation. The jockey riled the trainer when he bluntly gave it as his opinion to Miss Paget that exercise given to Golden Miller at Newmarket since the Cheltenham race, had caused the horse to become temporarily unsound, and that, in other words, the fault lay with the trainer rather than with the jockey — an inference which sent Briscoe almost incoherent with fury.

A visit to the racecourse stables in company with two vets, disclosed nothing seriously amiss.

'He will run in tomorrow's Champion Chase', decreed the grim-faced Miss Paget, before returning to the Adelphi Hotel.

Basil followed an hour or so later, repairing, with a few friends, to the suite booked for the occasion by his old friend, George Foster, who had two horses in training at Beechwood, and there to mull over the tragic events of the afternoon.

Word reached the party that downstairs in the cocktail bar, Gerry Wilson's old father had boasted of winning heavily by laying against Golden Miller. (This was found afterwards to be pure invention, sparked off by taunts about his son's incompetence.)

This scurrilous bit of tittle tattle should, of course, have been checked, or at least treated with some scepticism, taking into account the rider's splendid reputation for integrity, and the open-handed way in which he had admitted the offering of a bribe.

Briscoe, still rankling after the interchange in the paddock, impulsively contacted Miss Paget on the internal hotel telephone.

'If your horse runs tomorrow, I am not having Wilson. Eric Brown rides'.

'I am the owner, the horse runs, and Wilson rides'.

There have been few such outbursts of booing on any English racecourse, as that which marked his second venture. Golden Miller, even-money favourite, jinked and threw Gerry Wilson, this time at the very first fence.

The tempestuous sequel erupted almost immediately afterwards. The owner was ordered to take all her horses, including Golden Miller, away from Beechwood within the week, with the threat that 'otherwise they will be turned loose on Newmarket Heath'.

A few days later, in London, the Grand National newsreel film, with the motion slowed down for Valentines and the two following jumps, was shown to Miss Paget and Press representatives.

The detail confirmed Gerry Wilson's story.

Golden Miller now went out of Basil Briscoe's life leaving him a broken man, never again to be the same, gay, carefree individual and to die, widowed, sick and poor, in 1951, pre-deceasing the horse he loved by a full six years. Miss Paget chose as his successor Owen Anthony, a bluff, hearty, rumbustious Welshman, one of the famous brothers, who told her straight out that he would not tolerate being bothered. 'My bed-time is usually ten o'clock, when I take the telephone off the hook.'

He won another Gold Cup for her, Golden Miller's fifth, with Evan Williams replacing Gerry Wilson in the saddle, but he could not restrain her from submitting the horse to three further ordeals at Aintree. Fulke Walwyn contrived to finish second on him in the Becher 'Chase 'the old fellow groaned, though, as he touched down over the drop-fences'. Evan Williams (1936) and Danny Morgan (1937) were picked as his Grand National partners. Neither could get him past the ditch beyond Valentine's. 'He hated the very sight of the place by the time I rode him there,' said Evan, who chose rightly the following year, when switching to the smooth-jumping Royal Mail.

Golden Miller would almost certainly have made the 1937 Gold Cup his sixth if snow and frost had not caused cancellation. The unbroken sequence was finally halted when he ran second to Morse Code in 1938, his last-but-one public appearance, before bowing out, a shadow of his old self, unplaced at Newbury the following year. As his record shows, he deserves bracketing with Manifesto as the best steeplechaser ever to win (and to lose, for that matter) this historic steeplechase.

Miss Dorothy Paget forfeited much of the public esteem, which could have been hers, by insisting on running the horse in the Champion 'Chase or, indeed, at Liverpool thereafter. Although she had ridden horses out hunting with the Tickham Hounds and the Ashford Valley in Kent, and even on one occasion taken part in a point-to-point, her knowledge and interest were confined to her horses' prospects as a means of gambling.

'Well,' remarked Owen Anthony in extenuation some years later, 'wouldn't it be enough to turn any girl's head coming down to breakfast one morning on her twenty-first birthday, and opening a letter containing a cheque for a million pounds from her solicitor, and the promise that there was plenty more to come?' We must suppose so.

★　★　★

The Golden Miller story overlapped that of three superb Grand National winners — Reynoldstown and Royal Mail, who followed him, and Kellsboro' Jack, who preceded him. The two former were both jet-back, and both by My Prince. This stallion had also sired a third winner in Gregalach (1929) and the placed horses Easter Hero (of whom we shall hear more later) and Thomond II.

Brief reference has already been made to Reynoldstown winning in the year of Golden Miller's disgrace, and how the romantic triumph of the Furlong family was overshadowed by the publicity attaching to the favourite's failure. Major Noel Furlong and his wife had come to settle in Leicestershire from County Cork, returning home from time to time with the object of buying a horse to race or hunt. Their elder son, Frank, in his boyhood years had a positive distaste for equestrianism in all its forms, and it was not until nearly twenty that he took to it, learning the art military fashion before being gazetted to the 9th Lancers.

He proved a natural cross-country jockey, coming second on Really True in the 1933 National before this victory with Reynoldstown two years later. A propensity to put weight on his thickset frame cut short his career in the saddle. His close friend and brother-officer, Fulke Walwyn, took his place in 1936, when even the black horse's increased weight of 12 st. 2 lb. was beyond him.

Frank became one of four World War II casualties amongst winning Grand National riders. He survived combat missions in the Fleet Air Arm, and the ordeal of a near-miraculous air-sea rescue after three days and nights in a storm-tossed rubber dinghy 200 miles south of Iceland, the sole survivor of a crashed amphibian bomber, only to crash his damaged aircraft on Salisbury Plain at the end of a reconnaissance flight.

Bob Everett, partner of the 100–1 1929 hero Gregalach in that record-sized field of sixty-six starters, took on a hero's role himself, returning to the Navy as an officer in the Fleet Air Arm, flying cata-fighters to help defend Merchant Navy Atlantic convoys. He accounted for several submarines before the almost-inevitable death by drowning.

Young Mervyn Jones, nephew of the Anthony brothers, winner on Lord Stalbridge's Bogskar in 1940, the last to be run at Aintree until resumption there in 1946, also felt the appeal of the air, joining the R. A. F. A flight-sergeant, he set off one summer's day in 1942 for photo-reconnaissance of the Norway fjords in his high-altitude Spitfire, and was never heard of again. And poor Tommy Cullinan, the cheers greeting his 1930 epic ride on Shaun Goilin long since forgotten, joined up in an English Anti-Aircraft unit as a private, and blew his brains out with his rifle in a fit of depression.

The hardihood and gameness of Reynoldstown, the first dual winner of the Grand National at Aintree since Manifesto and the fifth in all, did much to counteract the long-standing prejudice against black horses, for he amply proved his qualities as a marathon hurdler before having his attentions switched to fencing. His odds of 22–1 in 1935 were due to a careless fall at Gatwick in his final public test, the Grand National Trial. After Golden Miller had quit the scene so dramatically, Reynoldstown and Thomond II drew away from the pack towards the end of the second circuit. They jumped the last fence upsides with the little Whitney horse, obviously dog-tired, unable to retain second place when pursued and passed on the run-in by Blue Prince.

Reynoldstown's second victory also suffered by being diminished in the press-reports on the race, due to the extraordinary mishap which befell the 100–1 outsider Davy Jones between the last two fences. This tubed former selling-plater, ridden by Anthony Mildmay and owned by his father, Lord Mildmay of Flete (to whose title he later succeeded), held a clear lead at the second-last with Reynoldstown and Fulke Walwyn seeming to make no progress. Suddenly, the tall amateur rider was seen to be hopelessly unbalanced in the saddle. He was frantically tapping Davy Jones's head on the left side with his whip. Closer scrutiny revealed the brand-new reins flapping loose on either side. The buckle had become unfastened. There was nothing Mildmay could do. He was as helpless as the driver of a moving motor-car from whose grasp the steering wheel has been abruptly removed. Davy Jones ran off the course to the left (just as another 100–1 shot Zahia was to do, but for a different reason, in the year of Sheila's Cottage), leaving Reynoldstown out clear.

'He was such a redoubtable stayer, would run till he dropped, that he might have won anyway,' reported Fulke Walwyn to the jubilant Furlong family. An hour or more later, Anthony Mildmay and his close friend Peter Cazalet in the grandstand tea-room were indulging in a tug-of-war with Davy Jones's head-set. Pull how they might, the hasp stayed firm in its slot. 'I consciously didn't tie a precautionary knot. Davy has such a tremendously long neck, I needed the full extent of rein for those drop-fences,' explained the dejected amateur.

When, next year, the weight-range became increased to 35 lb. (from 12 st. 7 lb. down to 10 stone) Major Furlong, in protest and out of consideration for his favourite, refused even to enter Reynoldstown. Never a match for Golden Miller on the park-courses, he fully deserves his special place in the Grand National annals.

His successor to the winner's unsaddling enclosure was a leaner, lighter-framed black, son of My Prince. Royal Mail's victory under 11 st. 13 lb., a not-inconsiderable achievement, had an all-Welsh flavour, owned as he was by Mr. Hugh Lloyd Thomas (fated to be killed less than a year later in a race-riding accident at Derby) ridden by Evan Williams and trained by Ivor Anthony.

This registered the sixth victory during the twentieth century for the Wroughton stable, which had first won with Prince Hatzfeldt's Ascetic's Silver, trained and ridden by the Hon. Aubrey Hastings, in 1906. Although the owner was German by birth and married into American wealth, he preferred the spacious, gracious ways of life in England's Edwardian era: he rented for many years a big estate in Wiltshire so as to be near his horses and his close friend, their trainer. Better cast in the role of English country gentleman than many of those born to be, the news of his death from a heart-attack in Claridge's Hotel, London, in 1910, at the age of 57, was received with genuine dismay.

Ascetic's Silver might have brought off the double in 1909, but for breaking down and thus being unable to complete the course against Lutteur III, a French-bred five-year-old — the fourth and final winner of that age — owned by M. James Hennessy, of cognac fame, and ridden by France's ace jockey, George Parfrement.

Ally Sloper, ridden by Jack Anthony, proved Wroughton's next at Aintree in 1915, the first-ever triumph for a woman owner (Lady Nelson). This was swiftly followed by Ballymacad, in Gatwick's 1917 war-substitute event. Master Robert, once considered too slow for racing and relegated to working as a plough-horse in a bid to help the agricultural war effort on the fields which London Airport runways now cover, and where a motel now commemorates his name, was returned to racing in the early 1920s. Lord Airlie, his new owner, sent him to Aubrey Hastings, and profiting from a superb ride by Bob Trudgill, he landed a 25–1 chance in 1924.

With the demise of Mr. Hastings in May 1929, his widow passed the licence on to his assistant, Ivor Anthony, and it was a bitter-sweet occasion for both of them the following month, when the five-year-old gelding Brown Jack (by Jackdaw) registered the first of his six successive triumphs in the Queen Alexandra Stakes at Royal Ascot. Fifteen months previously, Sir Harold Wernher's great stayer had rounded off his hurdling career (he never ran under National Hunt Rules again) by trouncing his seniors for Cheltenham's Champion Hurdle.

Ivor Anthony, even without this ready-made and unsought opportunity, would always have made his mark as a trainer. Less effective in the saddle than brother Jack, who won the National on Glenside, Ally Sloper and Troytown, less flamboyant than Owen, he found his true metier in the stables and at the desk. His calm demeanour hid a power to voice his mind when he felt so inclined. Under the shield of Mrs. Hastings, he ruled the fortunes of Wroughton, owners, jockeys, and staff alike, with a firm, sure hand. Insistent on the domestic virtues of punctuality and neatness, a confirmed bachelor (and maybe something of an old woman), his shrewd appraisal of men and horses was never called into question.

In the autumn of 1930 a big, unfurnished four-year-old gelding by Brown Jack's sire arrived from Ireland in the Wroughton stable-yard. His owner, the American millionaire-sportsman, F. Ambrose Clark, one of the heirs to the considerable Singer Sewing Machine fortune, had struck up friendship with Aubrey Hastings on the international polo-grounds, and in the Leicestershire hunting-field. 'Brose', a chubby, rubicund-faced character who might have stepped straight out of the pages of Mr. Pickwick, with his knee-length covert-coat, his grey curly-brimmed bowler and his gruff staccato style of speech, continued his liaison with Wroughton, choosing Ivor Anthony as tutor to his young relatives the two Bostwick brothers, and Louis B. Stoddard jr.

'The horse was Kellsboro' Jack, and the very moment I set eyes on him, I liked him,' the trainer related to me some years later. Too deliberate to make his mark as a hurdler, it was not until December 1931 when fourth to Golden Miller in a steeplechase at Newbury that Kellsboro' Jack began to justify this favourable estimate. One niggling doubt continued to irk the trainer. 'You're unlucky. Give the horse to your wife,' Ivor remarked in a peremptory tone one day to Mr. Clark. It was Brose's turn to demur, with his own brand of superstition: 'Gift-horses are as unlucky as hell.' Floss Clark, scenting a compromise, pulled a £1 note from her pocket-book. 'It's a deal. The horse is mine,' she declared.

With the jinx lifted, Kellsboro' Jack won three of his next four races: the Spring 'Chase at Newbury, the Stanley 'Chase by twenty lengths at Liverpool's spring meeting and the Stroud 'Chase at Cheltenham under 12 st. 7 lb. Next season, with his sights set on Aintree, no attempt was made to try out his stamina in public. He won a two-mile 'chase at Newbury in December, trailed behind Golden Miller in the Cheltenham Gold Cup after being held up in his work, and then got the better of a bumping finish with Theras over three miles at Wolverhampton.

Thirty-four runners turned out for this 1933 Grand National, run in spring-like weather with even the furthest jumps clearly visible from the grand-stand. All bar eleven survived the first circuit, but Pelorus Jack, Kellsboro' Jack and Delaneige had outpaced the rest by the second-last fence. The two Jacks rose together at the final obstacle, though only Dudley Williams and Kellsboro' Jack came away with the race at their mercy.

Dudley, a product of the same Welsh county as the Anthony brothers, Carmarthenshire, remarked of the 25–1 winner that he had been foot-perfect all the way, gaining a length or more at every jump. For a lightly raced seven-year-old carrying 11 st. 9 lb. this ranked as a performance of considerable merit. There was to be no hope of repetition. Mrs. Clark announced determinedly: 'He will never run in another Grand National, or at Aintree again'.

Ivor Anthony eventually persuaded her that no cruelty was involved in letting this superb jumper show his prowess at Liverpool. Somewhat reluctantly, the owner agreed to start him for the 1936 Champion 'Chase. He won effortlessly, as he did again in the same race the following year. He was retired then to one of the Clark estates at Cooperstown in northern New York State. And there, on the summit of one of the Adirondack foot-hills, his grave is to be found underneath a simple head-stone, alongside that of Sorley Boy, winner in the same colours of the 1936 Welsh Grand National.

Every August after World War II on his visit to Saratoga races, Ivor Anthony would accompany his host to their resting-place and tell his American friends:

'Kellsboro' Jack was the greatest horse round Aintree I have ever known. Those big fences were no more trouble to him than they would be to a bird.'

That would be the signal for Brose to uncork a bottle of Dom Perignon and the two old men would then go down the hill to the big mansion and try to cheat each other like crazy at a game of ten-cent bridge.

★ ★ ★

One of the most unusual transactions in the long and tangled story of Anglo-American horse-dealing concerned the export to the States of Diomed, first winner of our Epsom Derby (1780), for a paltry fifty guineas. He was twenty-one when he first sniffed the invigorating air from those blue-tinted hills and for buyer, Col. John Hoomes and his fellow-enthusiasts in Virginia, he turned out a remarkable bargain, continuing to be active and fertile until past his thirtieth year. Before the close of the eighteenth century, he was joined by five other Epsom Derby winners, the short-lived Saltram (1783), John Bull (1792), Spread Eagle (1795), who was moved from Virginia to Kentucky, Sir Harry (1798) and Archduke (1799). They were followed, to this day, across the Atlantic by nineteen other winners of our Blue Riband. Two (Blue Gown and Kingcraft) died at sea. Three others, Iroquois (1881), Sir Ivor (1968) and Nijinsky (1970), were returning triumphant to the Continent of their birth.

The American attack on the British turf was spear-headed by the Dutch-descended Ten Broeck, Pierre Lorillard (of French extraction, the owner of Iroquois) and that fabulous stock-market gambler James R. Keene, whose colt Foxhall was not entered against his compatriot for the 1881 Derby, but who still revealed his exceptional combination of speed and stamina by winning the Grand Prix de Paris, the Cesarewitch and the Cambridgeshire all in that same year.

James R. Keene had diced for millions on the Wall Street market with the dollar-giants of his era, Rockefeller, J. P. Morgan, Harriman, that canny Scot Andrew Carnegie, Jacob Schiff (the equally shrewd Jewish banker) and last, but not least, William Collins Whitney. 'No-one ever loved his horses so well or knew them better,' was remarked of him in an obituary notice after his death in January 1913.

Keene and Whitney, one-time friends and partners, fell out over the struggle for control of New York's Metropolitan Railway in 1893. Keene sold short. Whitney, with the undisclosed help of his nominee Thomas Fortune Ryan, hooked him for $5 million. He used the proceeds to establish a racing stable, and beat Keene again on the turf. In 1901 Volodyovski, leased by Mr. Whitney from his breeder, Lady Meux, won the Epsom Derby. And Whitney also headed the list of American owners, as he did for the next two years.

Keene and his son, Foxhall, died without further heirs, although their name is commemorated by the racetrack and famous thoroughbred auctions in Kentucky. The Whitneys live on. Golden Miller's owner, Dorothy Paget, derived her fortune from her Whitney-born mother, Pauline. Her first cousins, Cornelius Vanderbilt Whitney, John Hay Whitney and his

48

Opposite. IX The Canal Turn, 1907, by Lionel Edwards.
X Mrs. Hugh Peel with Poethlyn 1919, by Sir Alfred Munnings.

sister, Mrs. Joan Payson, survive as owner-breeders of world-wide repute.

John Whitney, founder-father of the American Whitneys, could trace his yeoman Hertfordshire background to the year 1313. He emigrated with his wife and five sons to Watertown, Massachusetts, in the summer of 1635.

William C. Whitney, after serving with distinction in government posts (he was Secretary of the Navy from 1884 to 1888) turned his talents to commerce at the age of forty-seven. His will was proved at more than $20,000,000 when he died in 1902.

Against this background of acquired, increased and inherited wealth, his grandson, the young John Hay Whitney, seventh in direct male line from his emigrant English ancestor, came to New College, Oxford from Yale in 1924. It was a year after Stephen ('Laddie') Sandford, another young compatriot with similar tastes and interests, an undergraduate at Cambridge, had achieved the first-ever Grand National victory for an American owner, with the thirteen-year-old Sergeant Murphy.

Sandford's prime concern in acquiring this old steeplechaser from the book-maker Martin Benson was to cut a dash out hunting with the Leicestershire packs. Between his none-too-serious pursuit of knowledge as an undergraduate, he rented a 'hunting box' near Melton, where he was joined on occasions by Jock Whitney.

Sergeant Murphy proving too great a handful for his new owner, he was sent back into training at Newmarket with George Blackwell. This 1923 Grand National is the only one to have been won by a thirteen-year-old this century. 'Laddie' Sandford tried again, unsuccessfully, the following year with the old horse, and also bought expensive replacements, Mount Etna, The Drifter and Bright's Boy.

This involvement with steeplechasing by American owners during the 1920s did much to help revive the sport.

Gordon Selfridge, the American founder of the Oxford Street store, was another to become fired with the Grand National 'bug' but the New York stockbroker Charles Schwartz outsmarted him for possession of Jack Horner who was bought for £4,000 within a few weeks of his 1926 victory, the second for the U.S.A. What a fantastic story can be told about that plain-looking gelding, who as a five-year-old had carried Lord Barnby, M. F. H., who owned him at that time, fifteen miles across country in an historic fox-hunt with the Blankney pack. The year previous to his win, as an eight-year-

49

Opposite. XI The Canal Turn, 1920, by Cecil Aldin.
XII Easter Hero leading at Becher's 1929, by T. P. Earl.

old, he was ridden in the Grand National by the American amateur rider, Morgan D. Blair. Nicknamed 'Bam' from his habitual exclamation as he stuck a syringe full of heaven-knows-what into his forearm before any race in which he was competing, to the terror of his fellow-riders in the dressing-room, Blair could boast of a superhuman constitution.

That March day in 1925, he rode Jack Horner with a fourteen-day old appendicitis operation scar still raw having sweated off eighteen pounds in weight over the preceding forty-eight hours. He won his side-bet to get round, finishing seventh of nine who completed. Bill Watkinson and trainer Jack Leader made a better job of things for lucky Mr. Schwartz a year later. Bill did not live long to enjoy his fame, or the £1,000 present from the owner. He was dead within the month from a fall in a £100 steeplechase at Bogside.

Jack Leader and Charlie Schwartz had been introduced to each other by a mutual friend at Claridge's in London. The conversation made up in impact for what it lacked in duration.

'What, in your opinion, Mr. Leader, will win the National?'

'Bright's Boy.'

'Buy it.'

'Can't. Your American pal Laddie Sandford got him last week.'

'What next?'

'Sprig.'

'Buy it.'

'Can't. The old lady who owns him, promised her dead son she would never part with him.'

And so the to-and-fro continued until by a process of elimination rather than choice, the Jack Horner deal was agreed.

'We tried to do the same again three years later,' recalled the Newmarket trainer, 'but it misfired. Charlie returned home, married, and gave up any notion of a third bid.'

That spirit of high-powered rivalry (whether in sport or business) which so animates the Americans and to which reference has already been made, received a further boost when Howard Bruce's Billy Barton, the champion timber-horse in the U. S. A., all but won the 1928 National. This was the year when the brilliant bright-chestnut Easter Hero created havoc by running up and down the open ditch at the Canal Turn jump on the first circuit and putting thirty-five of the other forty-one runners out of the race.

Easter Hero at this time raced for the European financier, Captain Albert Lowenstein. Before the year was out Lowenstein had flung himself out of his private plane to his death over the English Channel, one of the many victims of that universal Depression.

On the advice of trainer Jack Anthony, 'Jock' Whitney succumbed eagerly to the lure of that Grand National will-o'-the-wisp, to find that he had bought the 1929 Cheltenham Gold Cup winner and the 9–2 Aintree favourite. (He launched out on the English flat-racing scene too, paying a worth-while £15,000 for the brilliant Royal Minstrel.)

Easter Hero must rate with Mr. James V. Rank's Prince Regent and Lord Bicester's Silver Fame as one of the greatest steeplechasers to contend for the supreme Liverpool prize without winning. And how ironic that success should have so persistently eluded all three, although in the sixteen-race period between 1929 and 1949 they mustered between them eight places.

Jock Whitney's prime horse-racing interests have been principally concerned with the flat, but his mother campaigned a team of jumpers in the U. S. A. and he shared in the jubilations when his first wife, Liz Whitney, won the 1931 American Grand National at Belmont Park with her four-year-old Green Cheese.

'Easter Hero was a marvellous horse in every respect, and a great pleasure to own and to ride,' recalled Mr. Whitney when discussing his old Grand National ventures one day in London this spring. The former U. S. Ambassador (1957–61) retired him to Virginia after he had dead-heated with Coup de Chapeau for Liverpool's Champion 'Chase in 1931, having been brought down in the previous day's Grand National.

'Although not really up to my weight, he gave me some great hunts in Virginia, and became a really superb post-and-rail jumper but one had to sit very tight when hounds were running.' He was eventually put down at the ripe old age of twenty-eight.

Although not in the same class, Sir Lindsay was probably the unluckiest carrier of the Whitney colours not to win the big Aintree prize. In 1930, he came to the last fence in line with eventual winner Shaun Goilin and Melleray's Belle, only to stumble on landing, and cause Dudley Williams to lose both irons. In sorting himself out Williams forfeited considerably more than the distance of less than two lengths by which he finished third. In doing so, he just beat Glangesia, owned by another American millionaire, Mr. (later General) Richard K. Mellon.

Mellon made two more unsuccessful attempts with his almost-white American-bred jumper, for whom he engaged the crack transatlantic amateur rider Mr. James E. Ryan in 1932. Sparing no expense, he sent Ryan over on the old *Mauretania* in early March of that year, accompanied by an athletic coach, who had orders to see that Ryan's weight was reduced to the necessary 10 st. 9 lb. The science of dieting was then in its infancy, and on Mellon's rigid order the brawny Irish-born rider was forbidden steak, but to subsist instead on a diet of toast and caviar. Not surprisingly, he was still overweight on arrival in London, and it was only when he reached the sanctuary of the Hammam Turkish Baths in Jermyn Street, sneaking out occasionally to Scott's Restaurant for a meal of oysters and filet mignon, that the scales tipped in his favour.

Andy Wilson, on Sea Soldier, a combination well known in U. S. hunt circles, sought in 1932 to copy the bright example set by Billy Barton four seasons previously. The good Irish mare Heartbreak Hill carried the hopes of Mrs. Charles S. Bird from Pennsylvania, and considerable support, which caused her to start equal favourite with the previous year's winner, Grakle. This was the year of the 50–1 outsider, Forbra.

It should be mentioned here that there had already been one American-bred winner. This was Rubio, in 1908, foaled ten years previously at the Rancho del Paso Stud Farm in California. Sent in a draft of yearlings to Newmarket Sales by James Ben Ali Haggin, he was knocked down for fifteen guineas to Major F. Douglas-Pennant. He broke down at five, but the Major got him sound again by loaning him to draw the hotel horse-bus, to the landlord of the 'Prospect Arms' at Towcester.

Thirty years are to go by before we read of the next American-bred on the list (Battleship, 1938), followed after a similar period of time by Jay Trump (1965).

The du Ponts have been a great name in American industrial and social life, ever since the family business in Delaware provided George Washington with arms and ammunition to conduct the War of Independence. Marion du Pont of Montpelier Farm, Virginia, and Camden, South Carolina, along with her brother William, of Foxcatcher Farm, Maryland, became identified with racing, hunting and breeding from the early 1920s and they instigated the purchase and import into the U. S. A. of the Aga Khan's 1930 Derby winner, Blenheim, for $225,000 in 1936. After marriage to the handsome cowboy film-star Randolph Scott, she achieved her ambition, perhaps even closer to her heart's desire, when her horse, Battleship, a seven-year-old entire by Man O'War, won the 1934 American Grand National at Belmont Park.

In the autumn of 1936 Mrs. Scott sent him here to Reg Hobbs at Lambourn, to gain experience over English fences, and qualify for the Grand National. He seemed to go well for the trainer's long-legged son, Bruce, and the pair teamed up eventually for the 1938 National, the 17-year-old boy and the miniature eleven-year-old stallion. 'She's a lovely person, the owner, but she must be mighty tough to even think of running this dear little horse over Aintree,' Reg remarked to a small group of friends and acquaintances late on big-race eve in the Adelphi Hotel lounge. 'He's only 15.2, too small to see over the Chair Fence, let alone Becher's, and I can't bring myself to have a shilling on him.' Bookmaker Percy Thompson broke in almost angrily:

'That's ridiculous! I'll lay you 66–1. You *must* have £1,000 to £15, just in case you have to buy the champagne.'

The trainer accepted the challenge reluctantly and, indeed, had entirely forgotten the transaction until reminded of it twenty-four hours later. How Battleship and Bruce landed the wager pegging back the two-length lead inch by inch up the long straight, from the big Irishman, Royal Danieli, and his hefty rider, Dan Moore, is a matter of history. It is still hard to convince the Irish that they were beat, but the judge, after an unconscionable pause, raised the other number first. Battleship, the smallest winner since The Lamb in 1871, was the last to wear blinkers until the barely credible victory of Foinavon twenty-nine years later.

Bruce Hobbs, now training a fine string of flat-racers at Newmarket, was Mrs. du Pont Scott's guest at her Montpelier Farm on several occasions after World War II. To his pleasant surprise, he found Battleship still hale and hearty and siring winners despite advancing old age. Bruce related that he topped the list of winning jumping stallions for five seasons in America, and also fathered some smart flat-racers. Battleship remained happy and contented despite losing his eyesight over the last five years of his life. It was not until 1958, when he had reached the advanced age of thirty-one that it was found necessary to put him to sleep.

Although the enormous crowds, 100,000 and more, conveyed in special trains and coaches from many parts of the country, continued to flock to Aintree for several years after racing was resumed there in 1946, the break in continuity had caused a slackening of U. S. interest in the race. We over here were still saddled with restrictions and rationing — an owner had virtually to forego a new suit for himself if he wished to buy a set of racing colours for his jockey — and due to lack of horses the sport lost that distinction which had marked it in the 1930s.

In America a prejudice by the betting public, which has certainly not diminished, set in against steeplechasing, and severe taxation limited the number of that Scott Fitzgerald and P. G. Wodehouse class of leisured rich who could afford to spend time and money on polo-playing and foxhunting. The Irish were able to reap the reward of wartime neutrality and of the first thirteen winners following and including Lovely Cottage's year (1946) ten were bred and five were trained in Ireland. By far the best steeplechaser to race in England or Ireland during that war-time period was Mr. James V. Rank's Prince Regent, trained in County Meath by Tom Dreaper.

★   ★   ★

After Bogskar's victory in 1940, World War II, so far as the United Kingdom was concerned, began in earnest and there could be no thought of carrying on with racing in the heavily bombed area of Liverpool. Nor was there any thought of staging a substitute, as in World War I, at Gatwick, as the fences had been razed to make way for an airfield and underground storage for mustard-gas.

The racecourse area at Aintree, when stretched to maximum capacity, housed 16,000 troops (mainly Americans) and served as a depot for trucks and all sorts of armoured fighting vehicles. From their stronghold, Paddock Lodge, near the parade-ring, Arthur Ronald Topham, his wife, Mirabel, their nephew Jack Bidwell and his sister Patricia, safeguarded their family interests, preserving intact the turf on the two-mile Grand National circuit.

Arthur Ronald was the grandchild of Yorkshire-born Edward William Topham (clerk of the course and handicapper from 1843). This younger son of a younger son became unwillingly involved in family-business arguments during the mid-thirties after the death of his elder brother, Edward Anthony Christopher. He chose the easy way out, for with good grace he handed over the reins to his wife, a former musical-comedy actress, who severed connection with the stage whilst still retaining her eye for publicity, on her marriage. In 1949, the racecourse was purchased by Messrs. Tophams Ltd. from the Earl of Sefton, who was advised on financial grounds to sell rather than accept rent. Arthur Ronald Topham died, and his widow Mirabel took over full control — she had assumed this ten years earlier — with a determination that the years have not quenched. Her charm of manner and delightful presence, her flair for newsworthiness and her inventive talents have alike been nullified and bedevilled by a grasshopper-type of mind which has sparked off so much misunderstanding and litigation over the past thirty years.

Newspaper-cuttings are crammed with Mirabel-made rows. The matter of resale created an argument with Lord Sefton which had to be referred to the House of Lords. Construction of a motor-racing track in 1954, even if the European Grand Prix was staged there in 1957, proved little more than a seven-year wonder, and severely affected drainage on the flat-race course. She teamed with Charles Langlands of Epsom in trying to institute an idealistic but unworkable conception of copyright for major international events such as the Grand National and the Epsom Derby. Her intransigence in dealings with the B. B. C. resulted with her being forced to raise her own scratch-team of commentators for the 1952 Grand National broadcast — Mrs. T's greatest-ever disaster.

One key-member's admission to the course was denied due to some betting disputes; her principal gateman Mr. Kilpatrick, found himself at the 'mike' with ten minutes to fill impromptu, due to a delay at the start; the eventual winner, Teal, was wrongly announced as a first-fence faller; the commentator at Becher's, overcome by nerves, could stutter no more than 'Up and over' without mentioning one horse by name.

This was the first Grand National occasion to be denied the B. B. C. control since Meyrick Good of *The Sporting Life*, standing alongside King George V, called Sprig and Ted Leader home for 'cat's whisker' set listeners in 1927. By 1971, the race was being televised live (and by Eurovision to fourteen countries) for the twelfth year with a set-up of nearly two-hundred production staff, seventeen cameras and forty miles of cable.

All such developments lay in the misty future as the crowds flocked back to Aintree in 1946 for the first post-war National after a five-year gap. On

5th April a Friday (the traditional pre-war day), assembled a motley crew of thirty-four starters including the thirteen-year-old Bogskar, the 1940 winner, and the fourteen-year-old Mac Moffat, runner-up on that occasion, and also to Workman the previous year.

Past their best and rusty from war-time idleness, both Bogskar and Mac Moffat figured among the twenty-eight who failed to complete the course, adding to the flock of loose horses who hampered and distracted Mr. Jimmy Rank's 3–1 favourite, the Irish champion Prince Regent, top-weighted with 12 st. 5 lb. Owning to the same sire (My Prince) as Easter Hero, he had much in common with the famous Whitney jumper. They shared the brilliance which enabled both to win the Cheltenham Gold Cup, but also lack of staying power which found them wanting in all their Grand National ventures.

With six riderless companions, some swerving in front, Tim Hyde had a nightmare experience on Prince Regent. All of twenty lengths behind this pack at the second-last fence, an amateur-rider on another Irish-bred horse (bought three months previously for £2,000) scented the faint hope of victory. Bobby Petre, serving captain in the Scots Guards, suddenly saw the loose horses run clear and only the favourite, stone-cold, in front of his 25–1 mount, Lovely Cottage. He rode Lovely Cottage to victory with the skill and vigour of a professional in only his second Grand National ride.

It was estimated that a crowd of 400,000 attended the race and certainly, despite petrol-rationing, there were literally hundreds of motor-coaches sardine-packed on the in-field car park. Another enormous throng turned out in 1947, despite conditions of acute discomfort and limited visibility to hear rather than to see that the 100–1 chance Caughoo had won by twenty lengths from another Irish challenger Lough Conn, nearest of his fifty-six rivals. Caughoo had been bought as a yearling for fifty guineas by the County Dublin 'vet.' Herbert McDowell and his brother John and trained by them on the foreshore of Sutton Strand.

Eddie Dempsey, the victorious jockey who was having his first-ever ride in England, later became involved in a punch-up followed by a law-suit over this little-expected triumph. It was alleged by his assailant that he took Caughoo through the mist across the plough after jumping the fence before Becher's on the first circuit, joining in at the fence after Valentine's on the second round, thereby missing twenty of the thirty fences.

The magistrates rightly upheld Dempsey's integrity. Rightly? Yes, indeed. I acted that year as race-reader to Victor Smythe, of B. B. C. radio, from the Canal Turn sector. Raymond Glendenning, grandstand commentator, handed over to us before the first fence, although they did not come into our ken until fence 6 (Becher's). Of the fifty-seven competing, only three jockeys wore white caps. One of them was Dempsey. All three jumped twice over the fences, Becher's, the Canal and Valentine's, inside our restricted area of vision.

Caughoo's victory ranks with Tipperary Tim (1928) and Foinavon (1967) as the longest-priced this century. Davy Jones, of course, could have brought off another 100–1 shot in 1936, and Zahia, at the same odds, must be considered equally unlucky when running off the course giving way to Sheila's Cottage in that hectic 1948 finish, to the eternal chagrin of her previous owner — trainer James 'Blather' Farrell — deservedly styled 'the greatest talker in Ireland'.

Eddie Reavey, now the successful Berkshire trainer, than a little-known twenty-eight-year-old 'rough-riding' National Hunt jockey, mistakenly steered the Irish mare to the left of the last fence and up the old open galloping-ground which ran parallel to the racecourse. And so victory went to another Cottage-sired mare, first winner of her sex since Shannon Lass in 1902. She was owned by the Grimsby trawlerman John Procter, who directed the Lord Nelson Hotel at Brigg in Lincolnshire as a profitable sideline.

She was trained by Neville Crump, an ex-cavalry major, and her victory was the first of three for him. He moved to Middleham in Yorkshire after being demobilised at the end of World War II. On a points system, he would come out top of post-war Grand National ratings, winning also with Teal (1952) and Merryman II (1960) and gaining four places. He had a special regard for the Scottish-bred Merryman II, the first clear favourite to win since Sprig in 1927 and, indeed, the last at the time of writing this review.

'There's no doubt Merryman was the most successful of my three Grand National winners, although Teal may have been more brilliant. I shall always think that Teal would have won the 1953 Cheltenham Gold Cup if he had not suffered a fatal internal rupture during the race.'

Crump thought Arthur Thompson's jockeyship on Sheila's Cottage played the key part in the 1948 finish. His opinion of her was 'a good, game plodder, but an "ornery old cow"'. Arthur also had cause to criticize her. On going to fondle her in the stable after her Grand National win, she turned on him and bit off the top joint from one of his fingers.

A romantic story lies behind every Grand National winner, and that of the 1960 hero, Merryman II, proves no exception. One morning in the breakfast-room at Hopetoun, on an April day in 1949, the head of this ancestral Midlothian household and estate, the former Viceroy of India, looked out from behind *The Times* and delivered a pronouncement. His wife, his twin sons and his daughter, heard his words with considerable surprise. 'Poor as I am, it is beyond my means to aspire to breeding the Derby winner, but it would give me the greatest satisfaction to breed a Grand National winner here at Hopetoun.'

At home with his family, the Marquis of Linlithgow had uncovered a yearning that he had kept hidden for a long time. 'I was so surprised, I nearly spilled my porridge off the plate — just to imagine my father becoming interested in horse-racing.' — His daughter Lady Joan Hope wondered how this hope could possibly be fulfilled.

Within the week a telephone-call came from (Sir) Harry Floyd, a brilliant staff-officer in Italy and Normandy, a close friend and relative of the family. He was a widower with two young daughters and a young half-bred mare (Maid Marion, of the old Gretton breed), which was too fiery and impetuous for them to handle. 'Take her — she's yours for the cost of the transport.' And so the dam of Merryman II arrived at her Midlothian home.

Lady Joan rode her to hounds for one season, but mated her in the spring of 1950, and retired her to the paddocks. The Marquis saw and approved the offspring but he died in January 1952 and was never to know the realisation of that million-to-one breakfast-time wish.

Four months later Lady Joan married Col. Billy Gore-Langton, following him in his service appointments to Crete and Cyprus. Charlie Hopetoun, elder of the two twin sons succeeded to the title, the estate and Merryman II. He asked the local trainer, Stewart Wight, for his opinion, and whether he would consider taking the horse into his stable. 'Ach no, me lord,' replied the cautious Scot, 'he has no pedigree to speak of on the dam's side. He'd be better in the hunting-field.'

Wight did not take into account the potent influence of the stallion, Carnival Boy, of whom Hughie, Duke of Northumberland, had given a free service. A big, exceptionally good-looking horse, Carnival Boy had been a winner, in moderate company admittedly, on the flat, over hurdles and over fences. He had a near-classic pedigree, being by Lord Glanely's brilliant Colombo, from a mare by the redoubtable stayer, Son In Law, and the next dam by the great Hurry On.

As a youngster, Merryman was sent to George Beveridge, landlord of the Plough Hotel, Yetholm, one of those sporting innkeepers who rode to hounds, and was renowned for his handling of green horses. Asked to find a buyer, he was unable to do so, and the horse was returned to Hopetoun.

Miss Winifred Wallace, a keen all-round sportswoman, who fox-hunted in the winter, rode at point-to-points in the spring and went Alpine climbing for her summer holiday, was a subscriber to the Linlithgow and Stirlingshire pack, of which Lady Joan Hope was M. F. H. She boarded her hunters at the Hopetoun Stables, for it was too far a journey to van them from her home on the outskirts of Edinburgh. She had therefore known Merryman since his earliest days, and had bought his younger half-brother, Robin Hood.

In 1955 Robin Hood met with an accident, and had to be put down, and Miss Wallace, then in her mid-thirties, negotiated the purchase of Maid Marion's oldest offspring.

Charlie Hopetoun, who had succeeded to his father's title, recalls: 'I could probably have got a bigger price for him, but this would have been beyond Winnie Wallace's pocket, and it was of sentimental importance for us all in the family to know that he would be in good, sympathetic hands.'

The first time she rode Merryman to hounds nearly ended his career. Scared by a squealing litter of pigs, he jinked abruptly, throwing his new owner, and disappearing, with the sow chasing after him. It was three months before his injuries were healed.

In time he developed both strength and speed, encouraging the idea of running him in ladies' point-to-point races. After winning three for his exuberant owner-rider, he was started for the first time under National Hunt Rules, at Kelso in April 1958, winning the Buccleuch Hunters' 'Chase by twenty lengths, before a crowd which included Neville Crump, who was greatly impressed by this performance.

After hunting him again in the early part of the next winter, Miss Wallace sent him into training at Middleham, with his objective the Liverpool Fox-hunters' 'Chase at Aintree in March. He never made the semblance of a mistake, going clear at Becher's, in the hands of the noted amateur rider, Charlie Scott.

He showed his class at Bogside in April against top handicap 'chasing horses, by carrying 10 st. 12 lb. and professional Gerry Scott (no relation to the horse's amateur rider) to a tremendously polished twelve-lengths victory in the Scottish Grand National.

Crump needed no convincing now that he had a very possible third Liverpool Grand National winner in his hands, and with this in mind, when he took over training for the full season later, he gave him only four races before the big day. Although failing to win any of them, his strong finish when third at Manchester in February, combined with his superb performance in the Foxhunters' 'Chase and again in the Scottish National, caused him to start favourite at 13–2, when the twenty-six runners lined up at Aintree.

Once again Gerry Scott followed similar tactics to those successful in the Foxhunters', taking the lead at Becher's, and retaining it with fifteen lengths to spare at the winning post.

'No doubt, though, that Merryman II was the best Liverpool horse I have trained — one of the few greats,' recalls Neville Crump. 'He was kicked so severely on the stifle by Jimuru at the start when trying to win the National a second time in 1961 it was a near thing he was not withdrawn.' With Gerry Scott injured, Derek Ancil took over. It was a tremendous effort, half-lame, ridden by an unfamiliar jockey and carrying 11 st. 12 lb. to finish such a close second to Nicolaus Silver, who was getting nearly two stone.

The identification of Neville Crump with Aintree begins from the late 1940s. Another trainer of three Grand National winners, Fred Rimell, has an even longer experience. He was there, as a lad of eighteen, helping his father, Tom, with Forbra, 50–1 winner for Ludlow owner Bill Parsonage in 1932 and ridden by the Cheltonian Tim Hamey. Tom's original plan had been to keep Forbra for '33, but an unexpected win at Taunton made the seven-year-old ineligible for competing in the Stanley 'Chase and a bolder policy was therefore taken up.

Fred, who rode his first winner on the flat at the age of twelve and later headed the National Hunt jockeys' list three times, had another experience of Liverpool's strange breaks of luck four years after Forbra's win. Astride Mrs. Hilda Mundy's Avenger — 'the best jumper I ever trained,' said his father — he lay second over the water jump. Going away for the second circuit, the

60

pair faltered when crossing the Melling Road. The form-book records that at the next fence Avenger 'fell and broke his neck'. According to Fred's version, this tragic accident should have been interpreted differently: 'He must have suffered a heart-attack. I felt him dying as he took off and dead, under me, before we rolled over on the far side.'

This grim and painful memory was stirred up again for Fred, watching the race from the trainers' stand, twenty years later. In the paddock, he had given a hand to long-legged Dave Dick, on the big brown gelding E. S. B., wished him good luck and watched him, in the easily recognizable green-and-white colours of Mrs. Leonard Carver, try unsuccessfully to challenge Devon Loch between the last two fences.

Through his raceglasses, he peered at Dick Francis in the Queen Mother's colours land safely on the flat, followed, equally safely, by E. S. B. 'What a marvellous result!' thought Fred, as he lowered his glasses, reflecting on what seemed about to be the most popular Grand National victory of all time, and on the fact that his own stable's runner had given a first-rate performance, fully entitling the husband-and-wife Carver partnership to second prize money of £1,700.

This idea of the 1956 Grand National result became so implanted in Fred's mind during the few seconds which remained that he found himself groaning with the rest of the crowd 'What a tragedy!' as Devon Loch slipped and fell. 'It was several seconds after E. S. B. had passed the post before I realised that instead of feeling so dejected on your behalf, Ma'am, I should have been shouting and cheering,' Fred was later to recount to the Queen Mother.

If E. S. B. profited by amazing good luck, there was no semblance of a fluke about Fred's other two winners, Nicolaus Silver (1961) and Gay Trip (1970). Bobby Beasley, grandson of the Harry Beasley, who rode Come Away to victory in 1891, was able to hold off Merryman II by a confident five lengths on this grey nine-year-old, the first horse of this colour to be entered on the roll of honour since The Lamb, ninety years previously. Owner Charles Jeremy Vaughan, who gave 2,600 guineas for this Tipperary-bred jumper at Ballsbridge in the previous November, thus went one better than his father who had owned First of the Dandies, runner-up to Sheila's Cottage in 1948.

The Nicolaus Silver race was made memorable by the first and only appearance on an English racecourse of two Russian-trained horses, the big, ungainly Reljef and the handsome little chestnut, Grifel, ridden respectively by the Red Army soldiers, Boris Ponomarenko and Vladimir Prakhov. They showed themselves as unsuited to the Aintree fences as the earlier middle-European challenger Gye Lovam thirty years previously, although Grifel, after being remounted, completed one circuit. The Russian Minister of Agriculture informed me gruffly during my Moscow visit to see them training on the snow-covered local hippodrome that he resented the horses being given top-weight of twelve stone in the handicap and that they should be required to pay entry and transport expenses. There seems little likelihood of the attempt being repeated.

Fourteen of the thirty-five starters completed the full course — a satisfactory percentage which justified the sloping-off of the fences, making them easier to jump, which was carried out under the supervision of Wing-Commander Peter Vaux, a former amateur rider and at the time the chief National Hunt steward.

Nicolaus Silver was to try again the following year. In the rain-sodden ground which he hated, he could finish no nearer than seventh behind the Fred Winter-ridden Kilmore, who was followed home by Wyndburgh and Mr. What. (It was the third time the gallant Wyndburgh — retired afterwards to the hunting-field — had filled this position, having been second also to Mrs. Geoffrey Kohn's Sundew in 1957 ridden by Fred Winter, and to Oxo in 1959, after a famous feat of horsemanship by the stirrup-less Tim Brookshaw.)

Fred Rimell's third Grand National trophy came somewhat unexpectedly back to Kinnersley, brought there in 1970 by little Gay Trip. In his previous races, this bay son of Vulgan, very similar in size, colour and shape to another of the breed, Team Spirit — winner in 1964, had indicated that his best distance was in the region of two and a half miles. Gregalach, in 1929, and Russian Hero in 1949 had both surprised and confounded their critics by showing that the ability to skip over the Aintree fences without strain can be a more valuable asset than sheer stamina.

And so, mindful of these two examples, the trainer, who also saddled the shorter-odds French Excuse (ridden by Ken White), instructed Pat Taaffe to 'hunt the horse around for the first circuit and ride your own race on him after that'. The orders suited horse and rider to perfection.

62

Pat, taking over from the injured Terry Biddlecombe, who followed the race on his bedside television set in hospital, lined Mr. Tony Chambers' eight-year-old on the right wing of the field. An easy-going sixth over the water jump, he went fourth at the Canal Turn fence, and after a brief tussle with Eddie Harty on the American-owned Dozo he sauntered away from Vulture and Miss Hunter for a winning margin estimated officially as twenty lengths. This was even easier for the popular, lanky Pat Taaffe than when he had rounded off another triple success for a trainer on Quare Times in 1955, the third on the books since World War II, and the most remarkable of all.

Willie Stephenson, as a flat-race jockey in the thirties, performed miracles of self-discipline by wasting the flesh of his tall spare frame to go to scale at 7 st. 1 lb. He lost the battle against increasing weight during Army Service in World War II, and on demobilisation set up as a trainer of flat and national hunt horses at Royston in Hertfordshire. Success came quickly. For Mr. Joe McGrath, he sent out Arctic Prince to win the 1951 Epsom Derby by six lengths at 28-1, brought off some hefty betting coups, including three successive Champion Hurdles with Sir Ken (1952, '53 and '54) and further proved the versatility of his talents by training Mr. John Bigg's Oxo, ridden by Michael Scudamore, to win the 1959 Grand National.

Willie thus became the second trainer this century to bring off the Aintree-Epsom double. George Blackwell (with Rock Sand in 1903 and Sergeant Murphy in 1923) had so far enjoyed this unique distinction. They were to be joined and surpassed by a third — Michael Vincent O'Brien, born 9th April 1917 — an Irishman who trained three Grand National winners in a row, and retiring from the National Hunt scene has now won twenty-two flat-racing classics, of which three were in Epsom's Blue Riband — Larkspur (1962), Sir Ivor (1968) and Nijinsky (1970).

Vincent took out a training licence in 1944, winning with his first runner, Good Days, at Limerick Junction in May. Life being what it is, he had to endure the not-so-good days as well before consolidating his reputation. A worrier, a perfectionist by nature — what else could produce grey hairs on a man's head before his fortieth birthday? — he had already gathered three Champion Hurdles (with Hatton's Grace), three Cheltenham Gold Cups (with Cottage Rake) when Royal Tan, ridden by his youngest brother, Alphonsus ('Phonsie'), came hacking up to the last fence in the 1951 Grand

National, with only Johnnie Bullock on the plodding Dorking-trained mare Nickel Coin to beat.

At least twenty of the thirty-six runners were left at the Start, and in the chaos which followed twelve never got beyond the first fence. Royal Tan and Nickel Coin survived however and went out clear on their own, half-way round the second circuit. 'Phonsie', always the impetuous member of the family, rode into the final obstacle 'like some cowboy at a rodeo' (said unkind friends) and came away out of control, his arms either side of the horse's neck.

By a stroke of poetic justice, as we shall see, this incident and the fall by Royal Tan at the same fence the following year, when getting on challenging terms with Mr. Harry Lane's Teal, were finally turned to profit. Vincent reviewed both defeats objectively. Attached as he was to 'Phonsie', a fearless and capable amateur rider, in future for big occasions he would employ only the top available professional talent.

'I attribute my success in the Grand National,' he says, 'in very large measure to those two great riders, Bryan Marshall and Pat Taaffe. All three of my winners differed significantly from each other, in character and in their mental attitude to jumping.'

Early Mist, the first of the Vincent O'Brien 'hat-trick', was bought by the trainer at the dispersal sale in 1952 of the late James V. Rank's horses.

Vincent went to 5,300 guineas to outbid Lord Bicester, on behalf of the young Dublin businessman, Joe Griffin. 'How ironical,' he commented, 'that I should win the 1953 Grand National at the first attempt for a new owner, after Mr. Rank and Lord Bicester had spent many years, and thousands of pounds, with this one object in view.'

The big chestnut horse caused Vincent some anxiety. 'He was not a natural jumper, and relied largely on his rider to make his mind up for him. I decided Bryan Marshall would be the ideal partner. He only sat on him once before the race, on the 17th March, when they jumped two fences.'

On dismounting, Bryan remarked: 'He's a hesitant sort. I agree with you — I'll have to do his thinking for him.' This uncanny intuition stamped Marshall's greatness in the saddle.

Continues Vincent: 'Bryan did exactly this with him at Liverpool, and the horse responded to his mastership. Valentine's was the only fence where he stood a bit far back, and brushed the fence hard. On the other hand, if Bryan

64

Opposite. XIII The Easter Hero (1928) and Foinavon (1967) débâcles, by Peter Biegel.

ANY PARIS 1928

ANON 1957.

Peter Biegel '67

had not asked him to take off when he did, he would probably have got too close, and fallen.'

After this great victory, the thirty-five-year-old newcomer to ownership and his pretty young wife (mother of his five children) were met with rounds of applause in the unsaddling enclosure, where Mr. Griffin danced a victory jig to cries of 'Well done, Mincemeat Joe!' This was the little man's nickname in the Irish canning trade, where his business appeared to be steadily prospering during the period of food scarcity following World War II.

It is no part of a trainer's job to enquire into the business efficiency of his patrons, and the Griffin cash was readily available when the purchase of Royal Tan and the hurdler Galatian was advocated for an overall figure of £5,000. During the winter of 1953 to 1954, Vincent turned a deaf ear to reports from Dublin business circles, and concentrated on the task of preparing the two horses for their Liverpool engagements.

The crisis which erupted in the Adelphi Hotel on 1954 National eve, as Vincent retired for the night, was left to be solved by brother Dermot, calmest and least volatile member of the family. Reports of the grave turn which had taken place in Joe Griffin's finances were, unhappily, well founded, and the balance of £500 still due to Bryan Marshall over his Early Mist victory remained unpaid, despite a number of promises. At Liverpool that very afternoon, Marshall had won the £515 Coronation Hurdle for Joe Griffin on Stroller, one of his three runners at the meeting.

Later that night the jockey squared up to the owner in the palm-tree lounge, requesting settlement. Griffin went to his bedroom, produced a bundle of notes from under the pillow, and handed them over. On counting, they amounted to £450. This short-change further infuriated Marshall, who threatened to physically assault Griffin, have the police summoned, and be placed in custody until after the Grand National. 'It will be the scoop of the year for your newspaper,' Bryan remarked to me.

In order to ease the way out of what seemed to be a senseless tragedy, the hotel manager was roused by Dermot, and persuaded to produce £50 from the safe. Bryan then insisted on an I. O. U. from Griffin for any further amount which might be due to him, whilst refusing to speak to him personally. It was nearly 4 a.m. before Dermot finally coerced Royal Tan's jockey into the lift and up to bed.

Within twelve hours, a cooled-down Bryan had ridden two of the greatest

Opposite. XIV Becher's 1969, by Michael Lyne.
      XV The Third Fence, 1970, by Michael Lyne.

finishes of his career, to bring off a triple in the Griffin colours on Galatian (at 6–1) in the Liverpool Hurdle by less than a length, following up with that epic duel between Royal Tan (8–1) and Tudor Line for the National. The owner, unable to obtain credit from the leading rails bookmakers, watched the races as if in a dream. The creditors in his £80,000 bankruptcy later that year included Bryan Marshall, with a claim for £2,781, a sad ending to this meteoric partnership.

It is an episode on which Vincent does not care to dwell, whilst remembering with affection the sterling qualities of the blaze-faced 1954 Aintree hero. 'He was so clever that he would stand for no dictation from his rider, and Bryan, when he first rode him, seemed unable to hit it off with him. Indeed, at Gowran Park in his final race before the National, Bryan fell off him at the open ditch. We were in a quandary, and it was my brother, Phonsie, who came up with the answer. On both occasions when he had ridden him in the Grand National on earlier visits, he had blundered his chance away. 'Phonsie reckoned that the mistakes were due to tactical errors on his part, and that had he allowed the horse his freedom, he would not have made them. Bryan returned to mount the horse in a school over fences, and rode him as Phonsie suggested. He came back grinning from ear to ear, confident that the solution had been found.'

The thirty-eight-year-old Irishman virtually coaxed him in the '54 race over the final obstacle, before sitting down to ride the finish, in style which he had learned when apprenticed to Atty Persse as a teen-ager.

The following year, Vincent O'Brien sent over a team of four for the race. Bryan Marshall reverted to Early Mist (now restored to soundness once more), Dave Dick took over on Royal Tan (bought by Prince Aly Khan at the Griffin dispersal) and Fred Winter was given the mount on Oriental Way.

Vincent chose Pat Taaffe for Quare Times, owned by Mrs. Cecily Welman, and winner the previous March of the National Hunt' Chase at Cheltenham. 'Quare Times was a free runner,' states Vincent, 'he galloped on boldly at his fences, jumped them clean, and Pat suited him ideally, as he rode short and sat up his neck.'

The evening before the race, the four jockeys were shown films of earlier Grand Nationals in Vincent's hotel sitting room. As usual, the riders were advised to set off on the outside. 'My reason? The chances of escaping trouble from loose horses were better on the outside, for the fallers invariably went towards the inside, where there were no rails, and naturally veered that way to avoid jumping the fences in front of them.'

Confidence in any one of the four winning had virtually sunk to zero, after a prolonged downpour during the night, which continued all morning. The stewards inspected the course at mid-day, to decide whether racing would be possible, and Lord Sefton favoured abandonment. It was finally decided to rail off the water jump entirely, and to erect 'dolls' restricting the width of the second-last fence, the two obstacles most severely affected.

Due to the national newspaper strike, few reports of the race were available, but the following is culled from the racing column of the *Liverpool Evening Echo.* 'It was a race which will not be forgotten. Indeed, many people considered that it should not have been run, as conditions have never been worse... even before the big event, the horses in the previous races were more than fetlock deep in mud and water.'

To the surprise of all intimately connected with him, Quare Times galloped lightly and carefully through the mud, and never put a foot wrong at any of the fences, to win with contemptuous ease by twelve lengths from the luckless Tudor Line.

As a training feat, this stands unique in Grand National annals. In saluting this masterly achievement, it is worthy of note that Vincent O'Brien followed, in his own way, the successful routine observed by Linde seventy years previously. 'I believe in schooling my Grand National horses twice a week, as part of their training schedules to keep the jumping muscles in trim, and their mental processes alert.'

★ ★ ★

The Grand National has been won by horses of all shapes, sizes and colours, from the gigantic Moifaa, to little 'uns such as Team Spirit and Battleship; the tubed Tipperary Tim, Quare Times, who was not put into training until six years of age; Jay Trump, Anglo and Specify, who were all raced hard as two-year-olds; the pale chestnut Shaun Goilin, and the coal black Reynoldstown and Royal Mail. How then to define that oft-used term 'a true Liverpool type'? Manifesto would certainly conform, and so, too, would Kellsboro' Jack, and in more recent years, Mrs. Lurline Brotherton's Freebooter.

Who should judge Aintree requirements more expertly than the keen-eyed Irishman Dan Moore, with his intimate knowledge of riding over fences at Liverpool, and preparing horses to race there? He first set eyes on this son of Steelpoint, running loose in a field in County Waterford as an unbroken three-year-old. That was in 1944, and Dan later bid 620 guineas for him, as a store-horse — a high price in those days — when he came up for sale in Dublin. Two years later, he mentioned his possibilities to Bobby Renton, the Yorkshire trainer, who still held an amateur rider's permit under both Rules, at the age of fifty-six, which he was to retain actively for another fourteen years. Bobby went over to Ratoath, rode him, liked the feel of him, and negotiated a deal for £3,000.

His bold eye, his length of rein, the slope of his shoulder, his sturdy gaskins and hocks, and the evident strength in the muscles over his quarters, all appealed alike to the spry little sportsman from Ripon. 'The best horse I ever trained, especially round Liverpool, and what a glorious individual!' he recounted when reminiscing about his training career, which had spanned fifty years, at Cheltenham last March. 'In his youth, he was inclined to flippancy, and it was not until he came to Liverpool in March 1949 to land the Champion 'Chase over the Sefton Course that he demonstrated his truly great ability.'

In the late autumn he came back to win the Grand Sefton 'Chase itself, under 12 st. 4 lb. and the following spring he dominated forty-eight rivals in the Grand National. The fearless Jimmy Power told the story many times afterwards of Freebooter's fantastic jump over the Chair Fence, when taking off a length too soon.

In all, he paid eight visits to Aintree. The malignant fate which seems to pursue all big-race winners in their bids for a second triumph dogged his footsteps in 1951, and again the next season. The only time when completing the course that he met defeat was in the 1950 'Sefton'. Short of prime condition due to his summer's rest, and set to carry 12 st. 7 lb., he was on offer at 20–1, and came a close second to Shagreen (one of those many magnificent jumpers from the Dreaper yard, all of whom failed to achieve Tom's most cherished ambition in the National itself).

Recovered after eighteen months from a severely strained hock, he made his final trip to Liverpool for the Becher 'Chase in November 1953. With 12 st. 7 lb. in the saddle, he was cheered to the echo, as he came away to win by three lengths.

If Freebooter belongs to the class of easily predictable winners, how could anyone have foretold the fame which would one day await Tipperary Tim (1928), Russian Hero (never able to win again anywhere after his 66–1 surprise in 1949), Ayala (1963), Fred Winter's pair, Jay Trump (1965) and Anglo (1966); or Foinavon who escaped solo from that incredible twenty-third fence melee, and kept on to his lead in 1967?

Books have already been published to celebrate the all-American triumph of owner Mrs. Mary Stephenson and rider Tommy Crompton Smith with Jay Trump, the cast-off from the half-mile flat-racing Charles Town track. It will always make an absorbing tale how Tommy came to dig out and buy this horse who, the previous season, as a two-year-old, had needed twenty-nine stitches to repair the jagged fifteen-inch cut in his off-foreleg after a racing mishap. He was trained for jumping timber and in the spring of 1964 beat all the best Maryland horses for the post-and-rails Triple Crown.

In September of that year the American seven-year-old gelding joined the Lambourn stables of Fred Winter, who had retired from race-riding after winning all the big races, including two Grand Nationals with Sundew (1957) and Kilmore (1962), and that ever-famous Grand Steeple de Paris on Mandarin. Aided by Fred's tuition and advice, by his own inspired will to win and by the cleverness and courage of a remarkable horse, the twenty-seven-year-old American Tommy Crompton Smith beat Freddie, the hope of Scotland, after a long tussle, so becoming the only amateur to succeed since Bobby Petre on Lovely Cottage in 1946.

It was a triumph which would have appealed hugely to Lord Mildmay, who showed equal determination in his Grand National ventures. He had, in Cromwell, a steeplechaser every whit as good as Jay Trump, but failed to command that so-essential Aintree luck or to conquer physical disability brought on by the spinal injury suffered in a 1947 Folkestone fall. A third and fourth place when racked with cramp, in 1948 and 1949 respectively, were the best he could achieve in his bid to avenge the luckless defeat of Davy Jones. He met his death by drowning in a tragic accident off a Devonshire beach in May 1950.

It was thought that Jay Trump's would be the last-ever race for Liverpool's historic prize. The crowds no longer flock to Aintree, but interest has increased a hundredfold by the millions who follow the running each year on their television screens. The congratulations for Eddie Harty after winning finally on the gallant Highland Wedding for the U. S. sportsman Thomas H. McKoy jnr., and his Canadian partner Charles Burns, in 1969, reached him not aurally but by letter and telegram. The thrill of John Cook's superb hands-and-heels drive to foil yet again Tom Dreaper's aspirations and beat Black Secret in the last fifty yards, with a suddenly brave Specify in the colours of Mr. Fred Pontin, was shared in April 1971 by millions of viewers in Britain and, linked by Eurovision, on the Continent.

The race itself, and the racecourse, have been entangled with all sorts of litigious processes and feuds over the past thirty years. (One super-zealous RSPCA official is on record for lodging the complaint that 'several jockeys were heard to be using obscene language to their mounts', in default of any objections to the nature of the course.)

No reference has been made to the legal and financial wranglings which have contrived to make each successive running laden with ever-increasing doubts for the future. Certainly more money has been spent on lawyers and accountants than on paint.

Can the difference of opinion between racing's Establishment and Tophams Ltd be ironed out? Will the development plan of architect Arthur Swift be supported with the £20,000,000 backing required? Or will the ghosts of Captain Becher, George Stevens and Manifesto find no better haunt to revisit than a grim acreage of high-rise council-flats, where the little stream which trickles between Becher's and Valentine's will be piped underground and where even the thin notes of the skylark will be heard no more?

I

From the birth of the race to 1915

2
1837

3
1838

4
1839

5
1839

8

1843

10
1844

11
1845

12
1845

13
1845

14

16

15

17

18
1856

19
1858

20

21

22
1862

23

24
1863

25
1867

Won by M? Studd's Salamander

28
1868

29
1869 & 1870

THEATRE ROYAL

PUSS IN BOOTS

Mr J M RICHARDSON
IN HIS ORIGINAL PART.

The Grand National
1873-74

The National Hunt
Steeplechase.

The Warwick
Grand Annual
Steeplechase (2)

The Scottish Grand
National (2)

United Kingdom
Steeplechase at
Croydon (2)

The Nottingham
Steeplechase

1874. Go along Reugny

Reugny's
price does
agree with
the Capstan

Owner of Rhysworth.

As Shakespeare
remarks —

Sir John Astley
and gentlemen

How to Pussy!
Hooray!

31 Mr James Barber
(late owner of Disturbance)

The Grand National 1873.

A Sketch at the last Hurdle.

"Back went Rhysworth's ears, and I knew
then my thousand to ten was all right."
J.M.R.

The Banquet to the Bold Harrow Boy
at Brigg. Sir John Astley MP in the chair
Password
for the night,
composed by the
matter, expressly
for the occasion

Disturbance.
But No
Row!

32
1883

The Grand National
March 1st
33
1884
Volligeur

34

36

35

37

38

40

H.S.H. PRINCE CHARLES KINSKY.

39

41

42

43

44

In CLOISTER DAYS

45
1882

46
1886

47
1891

The Grand National 1896

Alpheus leads over the Water

50
1893

51
1899

52
1895

53
1900

56
1900

57
1905

58
1900

59
1900

60
1903

61
1901

62

63
1903

64
1904

65
1905

Grand National 1905
The Start

66
1905

Grand National 1905
The Open Ditch

Grand National 1905
The finish

Kirkland

67
1905

Grand National - 190[...]

Mr. F. Bibby's — Kirkland after his victo[...]

68

69
1906

70
1906

71
1904

72
1908

Grief at the Canal turn.

Rathnally pecks at the water

Glenside is told there is no hurry, everything else fallen

Trianon III. the French crack fell early

Lutteur III. gets hung up at the fence after Beechers, &c

Caubeen and Glenside on Thursday morning

Beecher's first time round. Rathnally going strong

Glenside rolls home alone

Second round Caubeen baulks at the gap made by Lutteur III. and Rathnally collides with him

First time round, a loose
horse and Ballyhackle
make the field swing wide

me round
llyhackle unships his jockey

Jerry M
the winner - 12 st 7 lb

At the Canal Turn
Jerry M's
"National" 1912

79
1912

80
1912

86
1901

89
1902

87
1905

90
1907

88
1909

91
1910

I

BILL CURLING
RUNNING COMMENTARY

From the birth of the race to 1915

Lottery, winner of the Grand National of 1839, was the outstanding chaser in the early days of Aintree. Whether or not he should be first on the scroll of Grand National winners is a matter of opinion. The Victorians certainly considered that Lottery was the first National winner, and this was the view of D. H. Munroe in his history of the Grand National, published as recently as 1931.

Then T. H. Bird, a leading racing journalist between the two World Wars, did considerable research on the early years of steeplechasing at Aintree. He discovered that the first steeplechase run at Aintree was in 1836, and this had a clause that the winner was 'to be sold for 200 sovereigns, if demanded'. No race with a selling clause could possibly be considered a National.

In the following year, however, William Lynn, owner of the Waterloo Hotel near the course, and the man who organised the first steeplechase at Aintree, encouraged by the success of this 1836 race, persuaded the civic authorities of Liverpool to support a much grander steeplechase in 1837. He also persuaded Viscount Molyneux, eldest son of the 2nd Earl of Sefton, owner of the Course, to act as umpire, and the conditions William Lynn drew up were as follows:

A Sweepstake of 10 sovs each with £100 added by the Town of Liverpool for horses of all denominations, 4 years old, 11 st.; 5, 11 st. 7 lb.; 6 and aged 12 st., Gentlemen Riders. Over a country not exceeding five miles, to be chosen by the umpire or such other persons as he may appoint... The ground to be shown to the riders on the morning of the race, and the umpire to have the power of ordering them to start...

Bird considered this should be counted as the first National and persuaded Tophams, now owners of the course, that this 1837 race was certainly the precursor of the race with similar conditions of 1839. This was called 'The Grand Liverpool Steeplechase', and also had £100 added money, but the length was reduced to four miles, and all riders had to carry 12 stone. As a result, the 1937 National was known as 'The Centenary of the Grand National Steeplechase', and the first name on the National scroll became The Duke.

There is no doubt that the successful introduction of steeplechasing at Aintree owed much to the Molyneux family of which the present Lord Sefton is the head. The family have been associated with Aintree and the adjoining country for no less than 850 years, and when William Lynn, inn-keeper, started racing at Aintree in opposition to another flat racing course at neighbouring Maghull, Lord Sefton backed Lynn and the Maghull course died.

The 2nd Earl of Sefton, who played so vital a part in supporting William Lynn, was known as 'Lord Dashalong' and there is a delightful sketch (1) of him drawn and etched by R. Dighton at Lord Sefton's home at Croxteth' a few miles from the National course. The 2nd Earl died in 1838, so he saw only the start of jumping at Aintree, but his eldest son, the umpire in 1837, continued to support the project and when William Lynn gave up through ill health in 1839, the 3rd Earl was a leading member of a syndicate of local notabilities formed to see that racing at Aintree prospered.

The Duke (2) has gone down to National history as owned by Mr. W. Sirdefield, a local inn-keeper. In fact, it is more probable that he was jointly owned by Mr. Jonathan Williamson, a member of a Lancashire family, and Mr. Sirdefield. Colonel J. P. Stanton of Snelston Hall near Ashbourne in Derbyshire has a charming picture of The Duke, a bright chestnut with one white sock, who in this picture is clearly annoyed by the yapping of a terrier. Colonel Stanton inherited his picture of The Duke from his mother, a niece of Jonathan Williamson, who may well have bred The Duke. His mother, a Watson, came from County Carlow.

Ridden by the famous Captain Becher, The Duke won the first ever steeplechase at Aintree in 1836, but Captain Becher could not ride The Duke in 1837, owing probably to the fact that there was racing at St. Albans near London on the previous day. So, at the last moment, a hunting man from Chester, Mr. Henry Potts, took his place. Mr. Potts, a keen follower of the Cheshire Hounds, was apparently a friend of the Williamsons, who knew how well he rode, and prevailed on him to ride The Duke, although, as Mr.

Potts rather charmingly said later, he felt a bit ashamed of himself, since he rode unknown to his parents! He was 27 years of age at the time, and as yet unmarried.

Captain Becher was back at Aintree again in 1838, and rode The Duke in place of Henry Potts, The Duke starting a slightly better favourite than the Irish challenger Sir William, ridden by Mr. Alan McDonough, one of the best horsemen in Ireland.

Messrs. Weatherby in the first volume of *Steeplechases Past* incorrectly gave the second winner of the National as Sir Henry, but Bird's researches showed that there was no such steeplechaser as Sir Henry at the meeting, and Bird relied on local papers who reported Alan McDonough's Sir William as the winner with The Duke third. The Duke broke down when leading.

The picture of Sir William (3) is now in the possession of Mrs. A. G. McGregor of Halstead, Essex, who was born McDonough, and is a direct descendant of the brothers Alan and Willie McDonough. The latter was another fine horseman, who was said to be melancholy of aspect and was generally known as 'Ould Mick' or 'The Blazer', because of his exploits when hunting with the Galway Blazers. Sir William was described as a 'lightly made horse and almost unmanageable' except to Alan McDonough. In his picture, he looks a weed, but I cannot believe the artist has done him justice! His record showed that he could gallop, jump and stay.

The syndicate of hunting and racing notables who took over the Aintree course from William Lynn in 1839 included names still well-known in Lancashire today. The added money for the race was the same as in 1837, but it cost more to enter — a sweepstake of 20 sovereigns each — and, in fact, the race was so well publicised that there were 55 entries and 17 starters over the course of 29 jumps, including three brooks, and a stone wall which had been made in front of the stand and was only jumped on the first circuit of the course.

Posterity is lucky in that there are three sets of engravings of Lottery's great victory at Aintree on March 1st, 1839. The set I like best, published only eleven weeks after the race, was entitled 'The Liverpool Great National Steeplechase, 1839, under the special patronage of the Rt. Honourable The Earl of Sefton, to whom by express permission, this series of engravings from the original pictures by Mr. F. C. Turner are most respectfully dedicated.'

F. C. Turner painted well, with considerable eye for detail, and painted four scenes of the famous race — the first before the start in front of the five-tiered grandstand, the second at the first brook, which is being christened by

3

Captain Becher, the third at the Wall, again in front of the grandstand, and the fourth nearing the finish.

The jockeys looked then much as they do today, though they rode much longer, but not so the spectators in the grandstand.

The men all wore top hats, the women, bonnets. Lord Sefton, who as Lord Molyneux had acted as 'umpire' in 1837, is again responsible for starting **4** the race, and is shown on the left of the picture (4), mounted, wearing a top hat, and talking to the only other mounted man in top hat, William Lynn, who is riding a grey. In the middle of the picture in the foreground, there is one owner in top hat, covert coat, and long narrow trousers, clearly giving last minute instructions to his jockey. The owner is Sir G. Mostyn, his jockey is famous Black Tom Oliver, who was to ride in nineteen Grand Nationals, and win three of them, and the Mostyn horse is Seventy Four, who was destined to finish second in the race. Turner, no doubt exercising artistic licence, has put those due to play a prominent part in the race in the fore-front of his picture. In vertical striped colours on the left of the picture is Alan McDonough on Lord McDonald's The Nun, between The Nun and Seventy Four is Paulina, who was to finish third, and on the right of Seventy Four and Sir G. Mostyn is Conrad with Captain Becher's back to the artist, whilst the immaculate Jem Mason is next on the favourite Lottery, wearing the blue, black cap of his renowned owner Mr. J. Elmore, the leading horse dealer, whose stables were not far north of London at Uxendon.

When Lord Sefton sent the field away, it is recorded that Daxon, one of the Irish challengers, and Captain Becher on Conrad made the running and both **5** took off at the first brook together (5). The brook was guarded by a timber fence a yard from the bank on the take-off side, and was preceded by plough. Daxon got away with it, Conrad did not, throwing Becher over his head into the brook beyond. F. C. Turner shows the unfortunate Becher scrambling out of the brook below the boy waving on the runners from his vantage point up a tree. This again is artistic licence for it is recorded that the moment he realised the position, Captain Becher sought safety in the brook under the bank until the way was clear. He had faithfully christened the brook which was always to bear his name afterwards. Tom Oliver on Seventy Four and Alan McDonough on The Nun are shown, as the two leaders, and in the middle of the picture Lottery is clearing the brook well with his rider's right arm upraised, 'calling a cab' in a manner which hardly stamps him as the best horseman of his day!

Beyond Lottery is a horse landing head first in the ditch and beyond him is Charity from the Cotswolds, clearing the brook well.

Finch Mason in his sketch of the scene (Colour Plate I) shows Becher going head first into the brook with Lottery in the act of clearing it well. Another rider and horse are already in the brook. This is again artistic licence.

At the Stone Wall (6), the leaders include Lottery, Seventy Four and The **6** Nun, who is seen knocking a hole in it, whilst on the right of the picture Charity, although used to stone walls in his native Gloucestershire, surprisingly refuses.

In the last picture (7), Lottery, having jumped the final hurdle well, is **7** coming away to win by three lengths from Seventy Four, followed by Paulina and True Blue. The vertical striped silks of Alan McDonough on The Nun can just be seen as he clears the hurdle to finish fifth. It is to be noted that Captain Becher, after his ducking, caught and remounted Conrad, and continued in the race, but then landed in the next big brook — and this time his horse disappeared sensibly from the scene! Captain Becher was over forty at the time. He was not to ride in another National.

Lottery was bred by a Mr. Jackson of Riston Grange near Hull in the East Riding of Yorkshire, won as a four-year-old at the Holderness Hunt meeting of 1834, and two years later was sent by his owner to Horncastle in Lincolnshire, then one of the biggest horse fairs in the country. Elmore was there, decided to try him, liked him, and bought him on the spot for £120. Though he was the outstanding chaser of his day, he was never destined to win another National, as he was weighted out of the race in future with a prohibitive penalty. Nevertheless, he went on winning races all over the country.

The 1840s

The first few Nationals were either weight for age affairs or all horses carried 12 stone, with the exception of poor Lottery who in 1841 and in 1842 was asked to shoulder an 18 lb. penalty for winning the Cheltenham Steeplechase. In 1843, however, the race became a handicap, and has remained so ever since. In 1843, the race was called for the first time The Liverpool and National Steeplechase, and four years later, it became The Grand National Handicap Steeplechase, and so it has remained.

In 1845, an artificial water jump was made in front of the stands and this spectacular jump has remained in the same place ever since, whilst the Stone Wall, which had been used intermittently up to 1843, was never part of the course again.

The 1840s were, therefore, formative years. The spectacular success of Lottery's year meant enthusiasm for the race throughout the 1840s and in 1840 itself, Lottery, Seventy Four, and The Nun, all conspicuous in 1839, were again competing with newcomers of note in Jerry and the Irish-trained Arthur, who, in fact, was one of six Irish challengers.

Another of these Irish challengers was Mr. Power, riding his own horse Valentine, who backed his horse to be first over the Wall at the end of the first circuit, and therefore set a great pace. Valentine and Lottery raced side by side at the Wall at the head of the field. Valentine cleared it. Lottery came down, and so did Seventy Four and The Nun. In the end Valentine, after whom Valentine's Brook is named, finished third behind Jerry and Arthur, ridden by Alan McDonough.

The superb picture of Lottery and Valentine racing together by F. C. Turner (Colour Plate III) is in the Walker Art Gallery at Liverpool. Valentine in red is falling. Mason on Lottery has lost his cap.

C. B. Spalding, another horse painter of note of this period, painted a charming picture of Mr. Elmore's steeplechasers, Lottery, Jerry and Sailor in 1840 (8), and I think it probable that Elmore had a share in Jerry when he won the 1840 National. Bird believes that he may have belonged to a Norfolk landowner Lord Suffield, when he won at Aintree, although he ran in the name of another Norfolk squire Mr. Villebois. With both Villebois and Lord Suffield, Elmore in fact had frequent dealings. What is quite certain is that both Lottery and Jerry were much better looking horses than Sir William!

There can be few sporting events which have caught the popular imagination so quickly as the National. One realises it when one reads a report of the 1843 race:

> On Wednesday last, the town of Liverpool was filled by one of the most brilliant companies that ever graced a provincial meeting. Indeed the whole elite of the sporting circles of England, Ireland, and Scotland had made it their rendezvous... the grandstand and its enclosure were filled with fashionables...

The race was won by Lord Chesterfield's Vanguard ridden by Black Tom Oliver, who had been second on Seventy Four in 1839, had a bad fall on the same horse in 1840, had won the 1842 race on Gaylad and rode a very strong finish on Vanguard to win his second National in succession — the first man to do so.

The wall was part of the course for the last time this year, and the engraving (9) shows the top weight, the grey Peter Simple leading at the fence after the wall with Lottery about fifth, and Tinderbox falling at the wall. 9

The 1844 race went to Discount (10) owned by a well-known Piccadilly dealer, Mr. Quartermaine. 10

Then came the romantic victory of the rank outsider Cure-All in 1845. This race was run in very bad weather and it was touch and go whether it would take place on the appointed day. Said one reporter:

> Precisely at two o'clock, the Earl of Sefton, one of the stewards, came on the ground, driving his four chestnuts in a perfectly appointed barouche, attended by Mr. George Payne, the other steward, in a char-a-banc. It was hard upon three when the flat race was run and at 4.35, the runners for the great event drew to the post, and at the word from Lord Sefton, proceeded. Before the race was over, the sun's rays had lost their power and the ground became hard as a hearthstone. The race had only taken place after the stewards had discovered that the majority of the owners wished to run.

For the first half of the 1840s, horse-dealers had seemed to be connected with all five National winners. There was no such background to Cure-All, and it was perhaps the first real triumph of a true amateur, for Cure-All was owned, trained and ridden by William Loft, a Lincolnshire farmer, and had been walked and ridden to the course from Lincolnshire by Loft's diminutive groom 'Kitty' Crisp. I am indebted to William Loft's only living great grandson Mr. Wallis Loft for the picture of Cure-All (11), a son of Physician, 11 with his great grandfather up, and 'Kitty' Crisp in top hat, holding Cure-All's rug, also in the picture. It is the work of the Lincolnshire artist Bennett Hubbard of Louth, Lincolnshire.

How William Loft, son of Lieutenant-General J. H. Loft of Healing, Lincolnshire, came to win the National on Cure-All is a tale typical of many National winners. Cure-All was bred in Yorkshire and was bought by a horse coper Getting of Grantham who sold him to a sporting tailor of Northampton, Drage by name. Cure-All was too much of a handful for Mr. Drage the tailor, so he was sent to Horncastle Fair with a reserve price of £260 on him. The dealer in charge of him allowed him to be tried out over fences by a prospective buyer, as was then the custom, and poor Cure-All had a ghastly fall, came back to stable dead lame, and eventually was bought for £60 by William Loft, a well-known follower of the

Brocklesby Hounds who farmed his brother's estate at Healing near Grimsby.

Under the care of Loft's groom 'Kitty Crisp', Cure-All eventually became sound; Kitty believed in long walking and trotting exercise in as long grass as he could find. After carrying William Loft very well to hounds, it was decided to run Cure-All in a steeplechase at Lincoln. In spite of going the wrong side of a flag and losing much ground, Cure-All was with a well-known chaser Crocus at the last fence, came down, was remounted, and still only beaten a neck. It was decided that he would be entered in the 'Liverpool', provided a nomination could be obtained. Mr. W. Stirling Crawfurd's candidate going amiss, Cure-All was nominated in Mr. Crawfurd's name, and some weeks later Kitty Crisp and Cure-All set out together to make the journey from the banks of the Humber to the banks of the Mersey!

William Loft had little experience of steeplechasing, but had a good eye for a country and his quick thinking perhaps won him the race for, whilst his competitors went through some very heavy plough, he galloped up a 'narrow screed of stubble, a few feet wide near the side of the fence running parallel to the course.'

12	As they jumped the water in front of the grandstand (12), the grey Peter Simple is conspicuous, and Clansman has fallen. The leader is The Exquisite, and The Exquisite continued to lead until the straight with Loft riding a waiting race on Cure-All. At the last hurdle, there was little to choose between the two, but The Exquisite had done racing when he had done pulling, and Cure-All went away to win from another Lincolnshire horse, the grey Peter Simple.

When Kitty Crisp and Cure-All arrived back at Healing, the church bells were rung and there was great rejoicing for a Lincolnshire man and his talented little groom Kitty Crisp.

The 'Liverpool' had brought fame to steeplechasing, and in the year following, J. F. Herring painted his well-known picture 'The Steeplechase Cracks' (Colour Plate IV), which is now in the collection of Her Majesty Queen Elizabeth, The Queen Mother, at Clarence House, London.

Herring took great trouble over his picture and did sketches of the riders to be portrayed, and four of these sketches are reproduced in this book.

14	(14) The Queen Mother's great uncle, the 12th Earl of Strathmore, who rode in two Nationals.

15	(15) Alan McDonough who won on Sir William.

16	(16) Jem Mason of Lottery fame, and

17	(17) P. P. Rolt.

The three leaders in Herring's picture are Captain Powell, who won the 1841 National on Charity, Tom Oliver on Discount, winner of the 1844 National, and Captain Broadley on the grey, Cigar, who was second to Charity in 1841. Jumping the fence from left to right are Lord Strathmore on Switcher, which he rode in the 1848 National, P. P. Rolt on the grey Peter Simple, who was second to Cure-All in 1845, Alan McDonough on the brilliant Irish mare Brunette, sixth in 1847 after being nobbled, Mr. Rowlands on Culverthorpe, winner of the Paris Steeplechase, Captain William Peel on Pioneer, winner of the 1846 National from Culverthorpe, P. Barker, who rode True Blue in 1839, and J. Bradley on Tramp, conspicous in 1847. Last in the foreground and about to take the fence is Jem Mason on Lottery. It is worthy of note that it was only a bare ten years since the first steeplechase with its selling clause had been run at Aintree in 1836.

Cheltenham

From 1842 to 1872 may be said to be the period in which riders from Cheltenham and the surrounding Cotswolds made their biggest impact on the National. If one includes the Warwickshire rider Johnny Page along with the leading Cheltenham jockeys Black Tom Oliver, George Stevens, Thomas Pickernell, William Archer, and the Holman family, there was hardly a year in which a rider from Cheltenham or its neighbourhood did not make his mark in the National, and owners and trainers from in and around Cheltenham had equally successful records.

The amateur riders' heyday may be said to be the twenty-five years from 1873 onwards but, of course, there were successes for the real amateurs in the 1840s too. The Lincolnshire farmer William Loft was certainly of that breed and so was Captain Josey Little, a pupil of Black Tom Oliver, the first cavalry soldier to win the National, and victorious in 1848 on Chandler, which he owned in partnership with Captain William Peel, one of the steeplechase cracks of the day who had won the Paris Steeplechase on Culverthorpe, runner-up to the 1846 winner, Pioneer.

13 The Littles were small of build and dark of countenance as the picture (13) of Chandler shows. Their motto was 'Multum in Parvo', and they were all cavalry soldiers at the time. Josey's eldest brother Cosmo was a 5th Lancer, another brother Malcolm commanded the 9th Lancers, and Josey was in the King's Dragoon Guards till he lost his money in a bank failure and joined a less expensive regiment — the 81st Regiment of Foot!

In spite of the bank failure, Captain Little had enough money to buy a half share in Chandler from Captain Peel, who bought him almost out of a gig after he had had a day's hunting on him when his own hunter had failed to appear!

Captain Little, who was usually known as The Captivating Captain — I believe he died a bachelor — was very short of money one day when he went out at Worcester to ride Chandler. A bookmaker thought he looked green and called out 'Twenty Ponies, Chandler'. The Captivating Captain took the bet, won his £500, and was less hard-up in future!

He was twenty-seven years of age when he came from behind to win the 1848 National from twenty-eight opponents, narrowly beating Black Tom Oliver on The Curate. As I have said, Tom Oliver had been coaching Little, so it was a question of pupil beating teacher!

Whilst Chandler had in effect been bought out of a gig after a day's hunting, Abd el Kader, who was the first horse to win the race two years running, owed his existence, as Clive Graham narrates, to the fact that an Irishman, returning from England to Ireland, took a great fancy to the mare running as leader in the Irish Mail from Shrewsbury to Holyhead and took her back to Ireland, where in due course, she became the dam of Abd el Kader. The man who picked out the leader on the Irish Mail was the father of Mr. Joseph Osborne of Dardistown Castle, Co. Meath, who was born in 1810, and at the time of his death over ninety years later was the oldest Irishman who went racing.

34   Mr. Osborne (34) conspicuous with his white beard, owned, bred and trained Abd el Kader when he won his two Nationals. His horse stood little more than 15.2 hands, and was said to be the smallest chaser to win the National before The Lamb in 1869. Mr. Osborne was a gambler and it is on record that in 1850, he backed Abd el Kader with the leading bookmaker Davies to land the double for the Lincoln Steeplechase and the Grand National — the bet being £10,000 to £150 the double. The Lincoln Steeplechase was lost through the horse swerving and going the wrong side of a post, but Mr. Osborne was very impressed at Lincoln by the riding of Christopher Green, the son of a Norfolk farmer, and forthwith engaged him for Aintree. Abd el Kader had only a featherweight at Aintree, and, with Green up, won comfortably from a big field, which included the two previous winners — Chandler, ridden by the Captivating Captain, and the top weight and favourite, the bay Peter Simple. Mr. Osborne had backed his horse at £4,000 to £100 just before the off. The following year the handicapper was very lenient with Abd el Kader, and, this time, Mr. Osborne took £10,000 to £500 about his horse, who in fact, only won by a whisker. Two years later, Mr. Osborne had great hopes that his little horse would win again, but his rider could not hold him minus the noseband he usually wore, and he was out-stayed by the bay Peter Simple, admirably ridden by Black Tom Oliver in his third and final victory in the race, and carrying the colours of none other than Captain Josey Little.

Black Tom Oliver was about to depart from the National stage. The Cheltenham trainer William Holman who had finished fourth to Peter Simple on Sir Peter Laurie at the age of forty-two, had ridden in the National for the last time, but George Stevens and William Archer were about to come on the scene, and Freetrader, trained by Holman and owned by a Cheltenham man, Mr. W. Barnett, who built the stables on Cleeve Hill, overlooking the Cheltenham course, was just beaten in 1855. His turn, how-ever, came in 1856, when George Stevens gained the first of his five victories in the race. Freetrader (18) was only a seven-year-old when he won. I cannot **18** believe that the picture of this horse does him justice! Nor, in fact, was Freetrader fancied as much as his stable companion, Sir Peter Laurie, who to the mortification of his rider Sam Darling 'bolted up Proceeds Lane in the direction of his corn bin during the race, and was stopped and walked home'.

Two years later William Holman saddled the winner again in Little Charley (19) owned by Mr. Christopher Capel of Prestbury House near the **19** Cheltenham course. He was ridden to victory by William Archer, father of Fred Archer, and another inhabitant of Prestbury. William Holman trained the winner again two years later when Mr. Capel's Anatis, the Cheltenham amateur Mr. Thomas Pickernell up, just got the better of a desperate finish with The Huntsman (22), who was to win the race two years **22** later for the Frenchman Vicomte de Namur. Sixth to finish behind Anatis was Bridegroom, ridden by Mr. Ekard (23), who in reality was the Rev. **23** Edward Tyrwhitt-Drake, one of the finest horsemen of his day who became Rector of Amersham in Buckinghamshire near the family home of Shardeloes. I think it is the only occasion on which a parson has ridden in the National! Over half a century later another of the same family, Jack Tyrwhitt-Drake, who was killed in the First World War, was the leading amateur rider, and finished third in the 1913 race on Carsey after falling at the last when in front. A half century later again another Tyrwhitt-Drake was to marry a champion National Hunt jockey in Terry Biddlecombe. I think Parson Ekard, so amusingly portrayed in our picture on a rocking horse, would have been well pleased!

Mr. Thomas Pickernell (35), who was always said to ride under the nom **35** de course of 'Mr. Thomas' because of his family's clerical associations, was a Worcestershire man by birth, but went to school at Cheltenham where he was a friend of the poet Adam Lindsay Gordon. Pickernell, in his first National, had finished fifth on Anatis in the previous year. Before he had finished with Aintree, he had ridden in seventeen Nationals, had won three, had finished in fifteen of them, and had only fallen in two — a wonderful record, unsurpassed by any other amateur rider.

'Mr. Thomas', however, had to wait eleven years before his second National winner, and he had no ride in the years 1863 and 1864 when George Stevens won both Nationals for Lord Coventry on the full sisters Emblem

24 and Emblematic. Emblem (24), the elder of the two, and winner of the race in 1863 was a very moderate mare on the flat, and only won one of her thirteen races as a three-year-old — and that a handicap at Cardiff! The 9th Earl of Coventry, who lived at Earls Croome in Worcestershire, then bought her and sent her to Tom Golby at Northleach near Cheltenham to be taught to jump fences. She was actually trained for the race by Edwin Weever at Bourton-on-the Hill in the Cotswolds. Lord Coventry is seen standing by Emblem in Harry Hall's picture of the 1863 National winner — George Stevens up. Lord Coventry was a young man in his twenties when he won the National with Emblem and Emblematic. He was a very old man when his great mare Verdict won the Cambridgeshire of 1923 sixty years later!

The Cheltenham brigade were much in evidence in Emblem's race, for George, one of William Holman's six sons — riding in the race for the first time, was fourth on the family horse Fosco, and Mr. 'Fogo' Rowlands, the founder of the National Hunt Chase, was conspicuous for a long way on his own mare Medora, the topweight, on which he won many races. William Holman's sons George, John and Alfred were all to ride in Nationals in the next ten years, but none of them won it — Cheltenham, from a race riding point of view, was their happy hunting ground. In the first Holman family

20 group (20), William is seen with two of his sons. William Holman (1810) himself rode five Cheltenham Grand Annual winners, and so did his second son George, the best jockey amongst the Holman brothers. Next to William Holman in the first picture is his youngest son Frederick (1857), who hunted with the Cotswold, and only rode as an amateur. He is the grandfather of Brigadier W. R. Holman, who finished sixth in the Grand National of 1955 at the age of forty-one, and of Mrs. H. C. D. Nicholsen, wife of the trainer 'Frenchie' Nicholson, and mother of the present jockey and trainer David Nicholson, who has so far had no luck in the National. On Frederick Holman's

84

right in the picture is John Holman (1844), the third son, who rode in three Nationals.

In the picture below (21) are the other four Holman brothers, and their sister Louie in the grotto of the garden of their father's Cleeve Hill Racing Stables above the present Cheltenham Course, William (1835), the eldest, who became a vet, is on the left, next to him George (1842), the second son, who rode in eleven Nationals, Alfred (1846), the fourth son, who became a trainer after riding in a couple of Nationals, and then manager of Cheltenham Racecourse, and, on the right, Walter (1855), the fifth son, who rode only as an amateur — a splendid Cheltenham racing family. **21**

George Stevens had now won three Nationals. He had two more to come, both on The Colonel (29), owned in partnership by Mr. John Weyman of Ludlow, his breeder, and Mr. Matthew Evans. Stevens was married to Mr. Evans's niece. In 1869, The Colonel won decisively. In 1870, he had a tremendous duel with The Doctor, trained by William Holman and ridden by his son George, The Colonel winning by a neck. Stevens rode The Colonel again in 1871, but with 12 st. 8 lb. on his back, he was beaten into fourth place, and a few months later, Stevens was killed by a fall near his home on Cleeve Hill. A very simple notice in the grandstand at Aintree recalls the fact that Stevens rode in fifteen Nationals, won five and none of his mounts fell. His record speaks for itself. **29**

Amateur Riders' heyday

Amateur riders had little success in the National in the 1850s. There was, however, a battle royal between two soldier riders in 1865, Captain 'Bee' Coventry (36), a Grenadier Guardsman, riding Alcibiade, and Captain A. C. Tempest of the 11th Hussars, riding Hall Court. There was nothing in it at the last hurdle, as the Finch Mason picture (26) graphically shows, and Alcibiade finally got home by a head. Both were real Liverpool horses, for Hall Court, Captain Tempest up, was second four years later to The Colonel, and Alcibiade, ridden by another guardsman Colonel 'Curly' Knox of the Scots Guards, was third in 1868. **36** **26**

Another outstanding soldier rider of this era was the 6th Earl Poulett, who before inheriting his title, was in the 22nd Regiment, and rode a large number of winners whilst serving in the army in Ireland and in India. Soon after succeeding to the title, he bought an Irish chaser called Cortolvin who, (25) ridden by Johnny Page, the son of a Warwickshire farmer attached to Mr. **25**

E. Brayley's Wroughton stable, was second to Salamander in the National of 1866. Poulett then sold Cortolvin to the 12th Duke of Hamilton, 'The Red Duke', and again, ridden by Page, Cortolvin won the National of 1867.

At the time, Lord Poulett had a big stable of horses at Droxford in Hampshire, and at Tedworth House, Hampshire, near the Wiltshire border, Mr. Edward Studd had another stable of chasers. Mr. Studd, a retired indigo planter, liked to buy his own horses, and had bought Salamander and two others very cheaply from Mr. John Hartigan of Limerick Horse Repository fame as a 'job lot'. Salamander had a crooked foreleg, and was thought unlikely to stand training, but after a time, Mr. Studd realised that he had bought something out of the ordinary in Salamander and backed his horse to win £40,000 at 40–1 in the National. He engaged as jockey, Mr. Alec Goodman, a successful farmer from the Fen country, as well as a successful steeplechase rider. Mr. Goodman had won the National of 1852 on Miss Mowbray, when he was approaching the age of thirty, and when he appeared in the parade ring at Aintree, conspicuous with his grey side-whiskers to ride Salamander fourteen years later, the public looked askance at the veteran in his forties. Finch Mason who brought alive so many Nationals of the nineteenth century with his vivid pictures, has (27) a delightful sketch of Mr. Studd running out onto the course to greet Mr. Goodman and his winner Salamander, but this National lives pictorially through the painting of the race by Ben Herring (Colour Plate V) called 'Silks and Satins of the Field'. This was in fact a composite picture to be compared to J. F. Herring's 'Steeplechase Cracks' of 1835, and brought in many of the leading owners of the day — Edward Studd, Lord Poulett, Mr. F. Hughes, Count Furstenberg, Mr. W. R. H. Powell, Mr. E. Brayley, Mr. T. Parr, the leading trainer Mr. B. Land, and Mr. A. W. Clayton, all of whom had runners in the 1866 National, and Lord Sefton, Prince D. Soltykoft, and Lord Drogheda who were leaders of the sport at the time.

Salamander, in the opinion of Mr. Joseph Osborne was an exceptionally high-class National winner, but Mr. Studd was too greedy. In the following week, Salamander ran in the Grand Annual at Warwick and won in a canter, and then in April was brought out again to run for a small stake at Crewkerne in Somerset, where he injured himself badly in a fall and had to be put down. Mr. Studd came near to winning two more Nationals with Shangarry and Despatch, and indeed Despatch would have done so, but for a little grey horse belonging to Lord Poulett called The Lamb.

Lord Poulett, in fact, leased The Lamb from an Irishman after seeing him run at Aintree as a five-year-old, and he chose his Hampshire friend Mr.

George Ede (37) as his rider at Aintree. Mr. Ede, who with his twin brother
Edward Ede was largely responsible for founding the Hampshire County
Cricket Club, learnt his steeplechase riding under Ben Land, and very nearly
won the first National he rode in, on Weathercock, in 1858. He finished
unplaced on horses of Lord Poulett's in 1866 and 1867, and then apparently
rode a superb race on The Lamb, who looked like being crowded out by
two loose horses at the Water. He hit one of the loose horses, with his whip,
changed his whip hand in a trice, hit the other likewise, and then had The
Lamb balanced to jump the fence perfectly. He had over 300 winners to his
credit when he was killed at Aintree. In the picture (28) by Ben Herring of
the 1868 National, The Lamb, the only grey, is lying tenth at Bechers.
When, therefore, Lord Poulett required a jockey for The Lamb in 1871, he
had to look elsewhere. He was helped by a vivid dream three months before
the race, when he saw Mr. Thomas Pickernell winning on the grey. He
accordingly wrote without delay from his London Club:

My dear Tommy,
Let me know for certain whether you can ride for me at Liverpool on
The Lamb. I dreamt twice last night I saw the race run. The first dream he
was last and finished amongst the carriages. The second dream I again saw
the Liverpool run. He won by four lengths, and you rode him, and I stood
close to the winning post... I saw the cerise and blue sleeves and you...
Let me know as soon as you can, saying nothing to anyone...

Needless to say, Mr. Thomas Pickernell, with ten Nationals already behind
him, accepted the ride and won on The Lamb, who had to jump over fallen
horses as he cleared one of the fences. It was an immensely popular victory.
The story of the dream had spread far and wide before the race was run!

The amateurs were very hopeful of winning the race again in 1872 with
Pickernell on The Lamb again. Mr. Arthur Yates of Bishop's Sutton,
Hampshire on his own horse, Harvester, Mr. W. R. Brockton on his mare
Primrose, previously third on The Colonel, Mr. J. M. Richardson (38) on the
National Hunt Chase winner Schiedam and the Irishman Mr. Garrett Moore
on a favourite horse called Scots Grey. They were all beaten by a little
chestnut mare called Casse Tête, who only stood 15 h. 3 in., and was ridden by
John Page, who rode with much success on the continent and had already
won the National on Cortolvin. Mr. Brayley, a big name in the theatrical
world, had started life with a Punch and Judy show. Old Boots, as he was
known, had bought Casse Tête out of a seller for little more than £200, but

39 she was probably a lucky winner. The great amateur rider Arthur Yates (39) who trained a big string of horses at Alresford, always reckoned Harvester about the best chaser he trained, but the horse, coming to win his race, two from home, overjumped, wrenched off a racing plate, broke down, and had to be pulled up.

42 Mr. Maunsell Richardson, a gifted player of games and a fine horseman, did no good on Schiedam, but he was to win the two following Nationals on Disturbance and Reugny for the remarkable Captain James Machell (42). Richardson trained both winners for Machell at his Lincolnshire home Limber Magna, after buying both horses very cheaply on Machell's behalf. Richardson was always known as The Cat, so lithe and agile was he, and he was a neighbour of Mr. Henry Chaplin, for whom Machell had won the Derby with Hermit, and who was represented in the 1873 National by Rhysworth. Chaplin had sent Rhysworth to be schooled at Limber Magna. He was a top class horse who had finished fourth in the Derby, but Richardson knew

30 he was shifty, and when Richardson brought Disturbance (30) (nearer camera) to challenge Rhysworth at the last hurdle, the latter's ears went back as Finch Mason shows, and he refused to struggle.

Later at a banquet at Brigg in Lincolnshire with its M. P. Sir John Astley, the Mate, in the chair, the inscription on top of the menu was 'Disturbance but No Row'! It was said to be a hilarious evening. Machell had backed his horse to win £10,000 on a £200 outlay. Richardson had had on £10 at 100–1.

A year later, Richardson was training Disturbance, Reugny and Defence for Machell, and after a gallop, Richardson informed Machell that he ought to back Reugny straight away. He dithered and failed to do so, but Richardson's Lincolnshire farmer friends backed Reugny which caused his price to topple. This infuriated Machell, who was then unwarrantably rude to Richardson. As a result, Richardson vowed he would never ride in races again after the National. Again as on Disturbance 'The Cat' rode a waiting race, coming from behind to beat Lord Marcus Beresford's old charger Chimney Sweep. Alas, The Cat, disgusted at Machell's behaviour, kept to his word and never rode at Aintree again. Had he done so, he might well eventually have had a record to compare with George Stevens.

31 Finch Mason's cartoon (31) of the two Richardson winners, shows Puss in Boots in the top left hand corner, below, Mr. Henry Chaplin, the owner of Rhysworth, and the theatrical figure of Mr. James Barber, the former owner of Disturbance. In the middle, the chief successes of Richardson are listed — the National Hunt Chase, two Scottish Grand Nationals, and two Warwick Grand Annuals amongst them. In the centre is a good picture of

Disturbance with ears pricked about to get the better of Rhysworth with ears aback, on the right Reugny winning, Captain Machell scowling because he has not got a better price for his money, and the bearded 'Mate' Sir John Astley at the banquet in Brigg to Richardson 'the Bold Harrow Boy'.

Machell sold his three National horses at an enormous profit after Reugny's victory, but two years later was back in the National picture running two — the favourite Chandos and the five-year-old Regal, and Regal, the outsider, was the winner, ridden by the professional Joe Cannon; but the amateurs were back in the picture again in 1877. Thomas Pickernell had gained his third and final victory in the National of 1875 on Pathfinder in the colours of Mr. Hubert Bird, but the senior partner in the horse was really the Marquess of Huntly, 'the Cock of the North'. Mr. Pickernell outrode another amateur to win the race, whilst John Page was third on the crack French mare La Veine, winner of the Grand Steeplechase de Paris.

Thomas Pickernell by this time had more experience of Aintree than any of the contemporary professionals, but not so Mr. Freddy Hobson, who won on his own horse Austerlitz in 1877 (Colour Plate II). Squire Hobson, a life-long friend of Mr. Arthur Yates, had headed the list of amateur riders in 1867 above George Ede and Yates, but owing to his well-known trick of hanging on to the back of his saddle when taking his fences, few people thought he would ever win a Grand National. The stable connections were anxious that Robert I Anson should ride the horse, but Mr. Yates persuaded his friend to do so. Finch Mason's sketch of Becher's Brook, second time round, 1877 with the sub-title 'What price Mr. Hobson and Austerlitz' shows the squire (claret, white sash) leaning back and catching hold of the cantle of his saddle. It was not graceful, but it was effective! Hobson belongs to the very small band of owners who have ridden their own horse to victory in the National, and what is even rarer, Austerlitz was only a five-year-old, and an entire.

Finch Mason in 1887 published in cartoon form some of his Grand National recollections (44) from 1860 to 1877, and it is amusing to see the races he chose — Mr. Thomas Pickernell on Anatis winning the National for the first time in 1860 from Huntsman ('All right Mr. Thomas — you've got 'em safe'), a jaunty picture of The Lamb's owner Lord Poulett in top hat on left ('What'll win? — why The Lamb to be sure'), third and last appearance of The Colonel in 1871, when George Stevens up, with 12 st. 8 lb. to shoulder, he could only finish fourth to The Lamb ('"too much weight this time old boy", — The Sporting Public give the old horse a cheer as he goes down the course'). On the top right, Captain Machell in top hat is giving

44

instructions to his rider Richardson before he goes out on Reugny (1874). It is Captain Machell's horses again bottom left, for, in 1876, he started both Chandos, the favourite, and Regal, the outsider. Regal won and Chandos fell 'But he could fall though, so it seems. — How did he d(J)ewitt?'). Jewitt was Machell's trainer at Newmarket!

In the next five years, three other owner riders were to join the small band of owners to win on their own horses at Aintree — Mr. Garrett Moore on The Liberator in 1879, Lord Manners on his six-year-old Seaman in **40** 1882 (45), and the Austrian Prince Charles Kinsky (40) on his own mare **45** Zoedone in 1883.

There was a very Irish flavour about this 1879 National for four of the five Beasley brothers rode in the race — Tommy, Harry, Willie and Johnny. The fifth, Jimmy, though a good horseman, too, spent most of his life in India, and never rode in the National. The Beasleys as a family were to have a staggering record in the National, for in the sixteen Nationals from 1877 to 1892, the brothers between them were to win four, finish second six times and third twice, and have a total of thirty-four rides.

In 1879, Tommy, the oldest, was third on the mare Martha, Willie eighth, and Harry ninth and only Johnny failed to get round. Garrett Moore and The Liberator won easily that year, and as the same combination was second with 12 st. 7 lb. a year later, their victory was no fluke.

Tommy Beasley won the next two Nationals on the Linde-trained Empress and Woodbrook, and expected to complete the hat trick on Cyrus in 1882, but in one of the most thrilling finishes in the history of the National, Cyrus was caught and beaten on the post by Lord Manners, riding his own horse Seaman, whom he had bought a few months previously from Linde. This was certainly one of the most amazing victories in the history of the race for Lord Manners, though a great man to hounds, had practically no experience of race riding, was at the time a serving soldier in the Grenadier Guards, and had only decided to have a cut at the National a few months beforehand, and had accordingly bought a couple of chasers in the autumn of 1881. With one, Lord Chancellor, he won the Grand Military Gold Cup at Sandown at the beginning of the following March, and the second horse he bought was a horse of considerable quality called Seaman, who had originally been sent into training with Linde and had been fired on both forelegs as a two-year-old long before he saw a racecourse. Linde managed to win the Liverpool Hunt Chase with Seaman in 1881, and a month later, the four miles Conyngham Cup at Punchestown watched by Lord Manners. In the summer, he won the Grand Hurdle race at Auteuil, but there was the risk that he might break down at any moment. Linde and his breeder Mr. J. Gubbins had no hesitation in selling him that autumn to Lord Manners for £2,000. He was then put under Captain Machell's care at Newmarket, but he went to Aintree short of work and little fancied by Machell. Linde saddled the favourite Mohican, ridden by Mr. Harry Beasley, and the second favourite Cyrus. Mohican fell and it looked any odds on Cyrus at the last. Although Seaman broke down landing over the hurdle, Lord Manners and Seaman slowly wore down Cyrus and caught him on the post, a staggering performance on the part of his rider against the best amateur of his day. Seaman never ran again, and Lord Manners rarely rode in another race. He later became Master of the Quorn.

Lord Manners' success must have inspired many amateurs to have a ride in the National since Seaman's thrilling triumph. It almost certainly inspired the Austrian Prince Charles Kinsky to try his luck. Like Lord Manners, Prince Charles Kinsky, a member of a noble family with estates in Bohemia — then a part of the Austro-Hungarian empire — was a follower of the leading packs of hounds in Leicestershire. The Prince was at Newmarket in Cesarewitch week six months after Seaman's victory, and won £1,000 on the Cesarewitch winner Corrie Roy. Highly excited, he met Mr. E. C. 'Uncle' Clayton on his way to the unsaddling enclosure and suddenly decided to make him an offer for his mare Zoedone, who had been third to Seaman and Cyrus. He bought him on the spot from 'Uncle' for 800 guineas with a contingency of 200 guineas more if the mare won the Grand National — and win the Grand National she did after she and The Prince had won a steeplechase at Sandown first. Finch Mason has a splendid sketch (32) of her **32** jumping the water, just behind the favourite Zitella (Mr. T. Beasley) with Lord Yarborough's Montauban (Mr. E. P. Wilson) on Zoedone's heels.

If Mr. Tommy Beasley was the outstanding Irish amateur of the 1880s, Mr. E. P. Wilson was perhaps the outstanding English amateur. No amateur has ever had a record to equal his in the National Hunt Chase, in which he was only out of the first three thrice in eleven rides, whilst he won two Nationals on Voluptuary and Roquefort, and rode altogether in seventeen! Mr. Wilson was often known as The Farmer either because he 'farmed' the National Hunt Chase, or because he was a countryman, bred and reared in Warwickshire where he lived most of his days.

Voluptuary's success in 1884 (33), Mr. Wilson up, portrayed by Finch **33** Mason, was certainly remarkable for he had never before jumped fences in public. When Voluptuary's racing days were over, he appeared regularly in a melodrama on the Drury Lane stage where he had to jump The Water, ridden by the actor Leonard Boyne. Voluptuary was trained by Farmer Ted Wilson's brother W. Wilson at the family home at Ilmington, as was Roquefort on whom Wilson won the following year. Roquefort had been third to Voluptuary in the colours of Captain Fisher-Childe of the 10th Hussars, but this cavalry soldier, who won the Grand Military, broke a leg badly when schooling with Arthur Yates, and put his horse up for auction. At Wilson's suggestion he was bought by Mr. A. Cooper and sent to his brother to train, and thus Ted Wilson naturally rode him. He was a very hard puller, given to running out, and the view was that very few men would have been equal to winning a National on him.

46   Roquefort was expected to win again in 1886 but this time he fell when going well and the race went to Old Joe (46), bred in Cumberland, trained in Cumberland at Burgh-by-Sands by George Mulcaster, and owned by a Cumbrian Mr. A. J. Douglas, who called his chaser Old Joe as a compliment to Old Joe Graham, former huntsman of the Dumfriesshire, from whom he bought him. He was ridden by a professional, Tom Skelton at 10 st. 9 lb., in all probability because one of the leading soldier-riders of the day, Captain 'Wenty' Hope-Johnstone could not do the weight. It was at Burgh-by-Sands the year before Old Joe's victory that Hope-Johnstone won the first five races one afternoon, and missed riding the winner of the last race, because he could not do the weight! In the picture of Old Joe, Hope-Johnstone is up, Mulcaster holds Old Joe's head, and Mr. Douglas in bowler hat is talking to Mr. Ned Heron Maxwell, who had an interest in the horse and for whom Hope-Johnstone often rode.

One of the Beasley brothers had been on the runner-up in 1885, 1886 and 1888, so they were due for a change of luck and it came in 1889, when Mr. Tommy Beasley won on the gallant mare Frigate from the border country amateur, Mr. Charlie Cunningham on Why Not. Mr. Harry Beasley had been second on Frigate both in 1884 and in 1885, and Mr. Willie Beasley second in 1889. It was Frigate's sixth appearance in the National, so for once, consistency had its due reward. Without much doubt, Frigate is the best mare ever to have won the National.

47   The Beasley brothers era was nearly at an end, but there was one more triumph to come in 1891, when Come Away (47), ridden by Harry Beasley for Mr. W. G. Jameson won a thrilling race from Cloister, Captain Roddy Owen up. Come Away was a high-class horse, but an unsound one. When he won the National, he already had two Conyngham Cups at Punchestown and the Valentine Chase at Aintree to his credit, but he broke down when winning the National, and would probably have been beaten by Cloister if

Roddy Owen on Cloister had not tried to squeeze through on the rails instead of challenging on the outside. Beasley quite rightly, in the view of the stewards, closed the gap, and overruled Owen's objection for jostling.

Captain Roddy Owen's day was still to come, and so was that of Cloister, who was trained at Bishop's Sutton by Arthur Yates. The mount on Cloister, the favourite for the 1892 National went to Mr. J. C. Dormer, who rode out regularly for Yates at Bishop's Sutton. Owen rode Father O'Flynn (48), **48** owned by a then subaltern in the Household Cavalry, the future Colonel Gordon Wilson, who, as a boy at Eton, had attracted the attention of Queen Victoria, when dashing out to try to stop an attempt on her life. Owen was also an Etonian, and later a very keen soldier in the Lancashire Fusiliers. He had few opportunities for race riding in England until 1885, when he was nearly thirty. For the next seven years, however, he was the most sought after soldier-rider in the country, and rode over 250 winners including several races for the then Prince of Wales, the future King Edward VII, who was taking a keen interest in steeplechasing. Father O'Flynn was only a small horse, under 15–3, but he was receiving nearly two stone from Cloister, and over two stone from the 1890 winner Ilex, and, Owen up, he won, easily. Shropshire bred, he had actually won a two-year-old seller at Aintree, for Lord Cholmondeley, and was of little worth on the flat.

Two days after winning the National, Captain Roddy Owen was at the War Office in London, applying for foreign services. He had ridden in his last race in England, and four years later he died in Egypt of cholera during the Dongola expedition. A patriot, and, as a contemporary said, 'a fearless and peerless horseman', Roddy Owen would doubtless have held high rank in the Army had he lived.

We are nearly at an end of the heyday of the amateur riders at Aintree. Mr. John Dormer (41), later to take the name of Upton, had been second on **41** Cloister to Father O'Flynn, but he then had a ghastly fall at Sandown, losing an eye.

In the picture of the 1892 National by G. D. Giles (Colour Plate VI), Tenby is leading at the Canal Turn from Flying Column (W. Beasley), with Billee Taylor (H. Beasley) third, and a grey falling. Almost in line the favourite Cloister (J. C. Dormer green, pink cap), the 1890 winner Ilex (A. Nightingall, vertical stripes), and Father O'Flynn (horizontal stripes) jump the Canal Turn together. Owing to his accident, Mr. Dormer in 1893 had to stand down for Dollery, Arthur Yate's stable jockey, when Cloister, carrying 12 st. 7 lb. won in a canter after making practically all the running. It was held at the time to be the most brilliant victory in the history of the

National, and Cloister was the first horse to win with so big a weight. Sir Charles Assheton-Smith (43) who was then Mr. C. Duff, is seen holding his horse. (50) He had apparently commissioned another artist to do a portrait of Cloister (Dormer up) in 1892. When he won with Cloister the following year, he asked the artist to paint out the face of Dormer and substitute that of Dollery! Captain P. J. Upton, the present trainer, who has the scrapbooks of his Dormer grandfather, later to train with success under the name of Upton, says that his grandfather commented as follows on Assheton-Smith's request to the painter. 'He (Assheton-Smith) can have my face painted out, but my backside has been left where it was, and not painted out!'

Two more amateurs were to win the race in the 1890s — the Irishman Mr. Joe Widger from County Waterford, and the Englishman General Sir David Campbell, who, as a subaltern in the 9th Lancers won on The Soarer in 1896. The Widgers at the time were the biggest horse dealers in the South of Ireland — old Tom Widger had a family of nine, including six boys, and the two youngest, Mick and Joe were the best horsemen, and five of the six went into the family horse coping business. Nevertheless, it was Joe's ambition to win the National, and in 1893, he bought a chaser called Wild Man from Borneo (52) on which he finished third behind Why Not in the National of 1894. Joe Widger thought he ought to have won this race, and he and his brother Mick decided to 'lay themselves out' for the National of 1895, taking up their quarters at Alfriston in Sussex with the trainer J. Gatland to whom they had sent Wild Man from Borneo. The scheme worked, for Wild Man from Borneo, a chestnut with three white socks, won well. Fourth, making his first appearance at Aintree was a very good-looking chaser called Manifesto.

Gatland ran two horses in the 1895 National — Wild Man from Borneo and Father O'Flynn, of which he fancied the 1892 winner Father O'Flynn the more. In 1896, his belief in Father O'Flynn was nearly rewarded for the old horse after being baulked two from home finished very fast — his owner Mr. C. Grenfell up, but just failed to catch The Soarer, ridden by David Campbell. This race was a personal triumph for Campbell, for he had bought The Soarer unbroken out of a field in Ireland, he had ridden the horse in practically all his work in training with Willie Moore at Weyhill in Hampshire, he had ridden him in all his races in public until after his victory in the National, but he had sold him for £500 a few weeks beforehand to Colonel W. Hall Walker — the future Lord Wavertree — on condition that he retained complete control of the horse, rode him himself, and if he happened to win the National, he kept the Cup and half the Stake. Lord Wavertree, who was to present his thoroughbred stud to the nation to found the National Stud nearly twenty years later, had great local interests and was a tremendous all-round sportsman. The painting (49) by W. V. Longe of the National field jumping the water that year, shows how open the race was at the half-way stage with Mr. Vyner's Alpheus leading from the favourite Rory O'More (R. Nightingall), who is immediately behind Alpheus, with the 1892 winner Father O'Flynn just jumping the water on the stand side, and The Soarer next to him, but two or three lengths behind (light jacket with spots). Moments after jumping the water Alpheus in fact ran out. **49**

Coming on to the racecourse for the last time, Rory O'More cracked, and two fences from home, the mare Biscuit was passed by The Soarer with Barcalwhey and Father O'Flynn next, but Father O'Flynn met with interference and was only fourth at the final hurdle. He finished very fast but just failed to catch The Soarer, who was beginning to tire. Campbell had already won the Grand Military Gold Cup that year for Major J. A. 'Weasel' Orr-Ewing of the 16th Lancers on Nelly Gray, so he was completing the same double Lord Manners had brought off in 1882. It was ten years before another amateur was to win the National. In future, their successes were to be few and far between.

Two of the three Nationals at the end of the century were, in fact, to be dominated by the greatest of all Liverpool horses, Manifesto (Colour Plate VII), winner both in 1897 and 1899, the latter occasion in the colours of Mr. J. G. Bulteel, father of the late Sir John Crocker Bulteel, the outstanding clerk of the course of his day. At this point too, Mr. J. G. Bulteel's brother Walter was a highly successful amateur, on one occasion winning nine races out of eleven rides at a Torquay meeting of 1905. This colour plate of Manifesto going down to the post is by A. C. Havell.

Photography of racing was just starting at this time, and the earliest racing photograph we have in the book is of Manifesto (51) (on left) jumping the preliminary hurdle in 1899, when he won for the second time. W. V. Longe painted a picture of the water in 1899 (Colour Plate VIII), showing Manifesto (lying fifth, blue jacket, red sleeves, white cap) jumping the water on the far side, just in front of the then Prince of Wales's Ambush II (royal blue, red sleeves, black velvet cap). The leaders at the water were Mum, Trade Mark and Sheriff Hutton. Manifesto won eventually from Ford of Fyne and Elliman, who, as Finch Mason shows (55), are not far behind him at the last. **55** **51**

In between the two successes of Manifesto, the 1898 National was won in the midst of a snowstorm by Drogheda owned in partnership by Mr. C. G. Adams and his trainer Dick Dawson of Whatcombe fame. Dick

54 Dawson is one of the few people to have trained both a Derby and a Grand National winner, and Finch Mason (54) vividly portrays Drogheda coming away from the final hurdle in the snow pursued by Cathal, ridden by his owner Reginald Ward.

1900 — Ambush II's year

Manifesto made a very gallant attempt to win the race with 12 st. 13 lb. and at the final obstacle, there was little to choose between Mr. J. G. Bulteel's great chaser and H. R. H. The Prince of Wales's Ambush II, who was getting 20 lb. from Manifesto. In the long run-in the weight told on Manifesto, and Ambush drew clear. In the last twenty yards, Manifesto was eased and the lightweight Barsac beat him on the post for second place. The Prince of Wales was given a great reception by the crowd, and afterwards he asked Mr. N. Arthur Loraine, known to many racegoers as the clerk of the course

59 at Sandown, to paint Ambush, A. Anthony up (59). With its dark background, it was a striking picture of the royal winner of the National and his royal

56 owner. The Prince of Wales watched his horse going on to the course (56),

58 53 and leading the parade (53). Afterwards he came out on to the course (58) to welcome his winner. He is seen in dark overcoat, bowler hat in hand, greeting Ambush.

1901 — Grudon's year

This race was run in a snowstorm despite the protests of owners and jockeys. There was no parade, and the race itself started a quarter of an hour late.

86 The winner was Grudon (86) owned, bred and trained in Northamptonshire by Mr. J. B. Bletsoe, with Arthur Nightingall up. Arthur, with his brothers Robert, John, and William, were all steeplechase jockeys. Arthur was an outstanding jockey at Aintree, and was winning the race for the third time. His owner apparently filled Grudon's feet with butter in the parade ring to prevent the snow balling, and this may well have helped to win him the race.

61 In the picture by John Beer (61), with the snow falling, Grudon is seen in left

62 foreground before the start. Finch Mason portrays Grudon (62) leading at the final obstacle. Mr. H. Nugent was second on Drumcree and Buffalo Bill, owned by Mr. J. E. Rogerson was third.

1902 — Shannon Lass's year

Manifesto was in the field again, fourteen years of age, with 12 st. 8 lb. to weigh him down. He ran a gallant race to finish third being beaten only by two lightweights to whom he was giving over two stone. The winner was the mare Shannon Lass (89), owned by Mr. Ambrose Gorham, a bookmaker, who then had Jem Hackett as his private trainer at Telscombe near Brighton on the Sussex Downs. The mare would have had more to do if the lightweight Detail, ridden by Arthur Nightingall had not blundered at the final fence.

89

1903 — Drumcree's year

Ambush II was in the field again and the King came to see his chaser attempt to win under top weight. Manifesto was trying again, at fifteen, and the favourite was Drumcree, trained by Sir Charles Nugent at Cranborne on the borders of Dorset and Hampshire. Drumcree (63) was to have been ridden by Sir Charles's son Hugh Nugent, who was injured in a fall and his place was taken by the then eighteen-year-old Percy Woodland. There were five in it, coming to the last fence where Ambush II fell, and in the run-in, Drumree was 'seized with a fit of the staggers', and fell on the flat rather in the same way as the Queen Mother's Devon Loch was to do half a century later. Manifesto, Drumcree, Detail, again ridden by Nightingall, and Kirkland remained, Drumcree just getting the better of Detail with Manifesto beating Kirkland a head for third place.

63

    King Edward VII watched this race from a temporary balcony in front of Lord Derby's box (60). The Royal Party from left to right were: Lord Derby, Lord Roberts, Lady Gerard, Lady Alice Stanley, H. M. The King, Mrs. Leopold de Rothschild, Lord Lurgan, H. M. The Queen.

60

1904 — Moifaa's year

Ambush II was favourite but fell at the third fence, and there was a lot of grief. The winner was the New Zealand horse Moifaa who jumped magnificently and won easily from Mr. Frank Bibby's Kirkland. Only six horses completed the course, the last to finish being Manifesto, who, at the age of sixteen, was at last really feeling his years. Moifaa stood over 17 hands, and afterwards, he was bought by King Edward VII, but Moifaa went in his wind and did no good for his royal owner.

64   The picture by John Beer (64) shows him winning decisively from Mr. Frank Bibby's Kirkland (green, yellow sleeves and belt) and Mr. Widger's The Gunner (scarlet), who was nearer the stands.

71   W. V. Longe's picture of the Canal Turn (71) painted in 1904, was probably not an actual scene of this year's race, but it shows the hazard of loose horses, as the leader desperately tries to ward off the attention of a riderless horse before he jumps Valentine's Brook.

1905 — Kirkland's year

Fourth to Drumcree in 1903 and second to Moifaa in 1904, Kirkland on form had an obvious chance, though Moifaa in the royal colours started favourite. John Beer, who caught the atmosphere of Aintree so well in his paintings of the great race, has a charming series of sketches of this 1905 National. This was a highly popular victory, for Kirkland's owner Mr. Frank

87 Bibby was a Liverpool man, and his jockey Tich Mason (87) pictured on the horse, was born at Wavertree near Liverpool, so that there could not have been a stronger local flavour to Kirkland's success.

65   In one of the sketches (65) we see the start by flag with Kirkland getting well away and lying second. Moifaa in the royal colours is in the rear group

66 on the nearside. In another (66) we see Kirkland with his white blaze and two white hind socks in the act of jumping the Chair — the Open Ditch John Beer called it. A stand is seen in the background and the head and neck of a riderless horse with dangling reins is just appearing in the picture. In a

67 third scene (67), we see Kirkland approaching the winning post preceded by the riderless Ascetic's Silver, a future winner, and Timothy Titus, and

68 pursued by Napper Tandy, ridden by Percy Woodland. Finally (68), we see Kirkland returning to the unsaddling enclosure, with the bowler-hatted watchers hurrying to greet him. I should add that the race was preceded by a special parade for the King's benefit at the back of Lord Derby's box, in which we see the King in bowler hat watching the parade headed by Aubrey

57 Hastings on Deerslayer (57).

1906 — Ascetic's Silver's year

In John Beer's picture of Kirkland winning in 1905, I have mentioned that the riderless Ascetic's Silver had preceded him past the post. He had actually

98

fallen at the third fence and then jumped riderless almost twice round the course. He had run then in the colours of an Irishman Mr. P. J. Dunne, who died soon afterwards, but his jumping and appearance had impressed Aubrey Hastings who rode Deerslayer for the German Prince Hatzfeldt in the race. Hastings had recently come to train at Wroughton near Swindon where Black Tom Oliver and Tom Leader had trained the Derby winner George Frederick thirty years before. Hastings had recently taken over the training of the Hatzfeldt horses and when Ascetic's Silver was sold with the rest of Mr. Dunne's horses, he bought him for Prince Hatzfeldt, Lord Coventry of Emblem and Emblematic fame being the underbidder.

Nearly all the jockeys riding in the National were now professionals. The exceptions included Walter Bulteel on the top weight Drumcree, Atty Persse on the mare Aunt May and Captain Percy Whitaker on Prince Hatzfeldt's Deerslayer. Both Persse and Whitaker were destined to be successful trainers. Walter Bulteel was on the second string of his owner Mr. J. S. Morrison, who expected to win with the favourite John M. P., a brilliant horse on Park courses, but unproven at Aintree. There were many fallers this year. John M. P. fell, Bulteel on the second string Drumcree got round to finish eighth, but Ascetic's Silver came to the last fence with the race in his pocket bar a fall with Atty Persse on Aunt May and the outsider Red Lad the dangers.

John Beer captured the scene (69) well of the field jumping the preliminary **69** hurdle on the way to the start. Its use was about to be discontinued. Ascetic's Silver (Aubrey Hastings up), who was painted by Emil Adam (70), was the **70** first Wroughton National winner — more were to come — Ally Sloper in 1915, Ballymacad in a substitute race at Gatwick in the First World War, Master Robert in 1924, Kellsboro' Jack in 1933, and Royal Mail in 1937. This Wiltshire stable, first under Aubrey Hastings and then after his death under his widow and Ivor Anthony were for over thirty years part and parcel of the National scene.

1907 — Eremon's year

Though Eremon, Alf Newey up, (90) had only 10 st. 11 lb. to carry when he **90** won the National, he might well have proved in the top class of chasers if he had not got loose at exercise a few months after his win and had to be put down. He was trained at Hednesford in Staffordshire by Tom Coulthwaite, a Lancastrain, and undoubtedly a brilliant trainer of chasers, and he won in the colours of Mr. Stanley Howard, a Worcestershire man by birth and amazingly lucky as an owner of racehorses.

Eremon won under great difficulties. His rider Alf Newey, another Worcestershire man, broke a leather at the beginning of the second round and Eremon was constantly worried by a loose horse. Lionel Edwards, whose sporting pictures are to be found in homes all over the British Isles, captured the hazards of Aintree in his picture of the race at the Canal Turn (Colour Plate IX) with Patlander, the third, just landing safely, Buckaway II (red, green cap) in mid-air, Bouchal Ogue (blue and yellow jacket, red sleeves) about to fall, whilst Loop Head in Mr. Frank Bibby's well-known colours of green, yellow sleeves, belt and cap is definitely coming to grief as his jockey is thrown over his head.

At Valentine's second time round, Eremon was no less than twenty lengths in front of the second Tom West, and the pair finished first and second. Eremon was only the second horse to carry Mr. Howard's colours. He bought him on the recommendation of James Daly, a well-known Irish dealer, for only £400. He was thick-winded and others had turned him down, but Daly, a fine judge, thought he would make good, and he was right.

1908 — Rubio's year

Rubio, H. B. Bletsoe up, was the first American-bred horse to win the National, and his victory was one of the most extraordinary in the history of the race. Bred in California by Mr. J. B. A. Haggin, who used to send yearlings to Newmarket Sales, Rubio was knocked down to Major Frank Douglas-Pennant — the future Lord Penrhyn — for fifteen guineas, as a potential hunter. He was hunted as a four-year-old, showed he had some speed, but was sent to Leicester repository for sale with a reserve of sixty guineas. He did not sell so he was put into training, won races and broke down, and was then lent by Douglas-Pennant to the landlord of a Towcester hotel to run in harness in the hope that plenty of road work would get him sound again. This worked and three years later, he was back in training with Mr. Fred Withington at Danebury, near the old Stockbridge racecourse where Tom Cannon had trained Playfair to win the 1888 National.

Fred Withington, a fine amateur rider at the end of the century, had only just started to train at Danebury, and his patrons included Sir William Cooper and his son-in-law the then Major Douglas-Pennant. Sir William Cooper had a very good mare called Mattie Macgregor who had been bought on the recommendation of the ubiquitous James Daly and was much fancied for the National, whilst Rubio, who was useful, was thought highly unlikely to stay, and also likely to break down! The stable jockey L. W. N. Bissill, chose to ride Mattie Macgregor, and Bernard Bletsoe, son of the owner of Grudon, was engaged for the 'cabhorse' Rubio on whom he had won as a five-year-old.

John Beer has done another series of paintings of the race. The King was represented this year by Flaxman, who is lying third at the second fence (73) **73** — which, in those days was usually known as Fan's fence, because the steeplechaser Fan consistently refused there. Johnstown Lad (near the rails) and Rubio are the two leaders, Mattie Macgregor is jumping the fence (near the flag), and just behind her is Roman Law. Behind Flaxman (A. Anthony), Extravagance is blundering, and Kirkland is jumping the fence. At Becher's (74), **74** Roman Law and the second favourite Tom West led, Lora (Walter Bulteel) is seen falling, and Flaxman is leading Mattie Macgregor and Rubio (white face) on the near side. At the water (75), Rubio (far side) leads from Dathia, **75** The Lawyer III (dark jacket, white sleeves), Major Percy Whitaker up, and Springbok (stand side). Anthony on Flaxman broke a leather early in the second circuit, and blundered badly at the Canal Turn second time round (76), **76** where Rubio led from Flaxman, Mattie Macgregor (near flag) and Springbok with The Lawyer just behind. Rubio and Mattie Macgregor were the leaders two from home and stayed there to the finish.

Mr. Withington thus had the distinction of saddling both first and second in the National — probably the first trainer to do so, though the early records are far from complete. Major Douglas-Pennant as Lord Penrhyn lived to a great age — he topped the century. His son, the present Lord Penrhyn has the charming picture of Rubio by A. C. Haigh (72). **72**

1909 — Lutteur III's year

In 1862, a French owner, Vicomte de Namur, had won the National, but the horse was Irish-bred and was trained for most of his racing life in England. Conversely, Alcibiade, the winner of 1865, was French-bred, but was sent to race in this country and claimed out of a seller. Occasionally, a top-class French chaser was sent direct from France to run at Aintree, La Veine who was third to Pathfinder in 1875, and Wild Monarch, twice winner of the Grand Steeplechase de Paris, being two to come to mind. The French, however, had had little luck, and were much handicapped by the fact that the Aintree course with its drop fences was very different from anything encountered in France. In 1909, however, M. J. Hennessy decided to send his brilliant five-year-old Lutteur III to take his chance in the National, and took the sensible course of sending him over from his French trainer George Batchelor well before Aintree to give him experience of English fences in a preliminary race. Lutteur III won his preliminary race at Hurst Park, most impressively, and then completed his preparation for Aintree with Harry Escott at Lewes.

There was a field of over thirty strong in 1909 and Lutteur III was helped by the fact that the two previous winners in the field Rubio and Ascetic's Silver both broke down when going well. Lutteur III, however, was taken to the front by his French jockey G. Parfrement soon afterwards, and the only danger to him in the final mile was the runner-up Judas. Although **88** Lutteur III was rather a washy chestnut, his portrait (88) with G. Parfrement up, shows that he was a horse with quality and with more good looks than many National winners.

1910 — Jenkinstown's year

In Lutteur's year, most of the field had got round safely. In 1910, although the race was run on perfect going in a good light, only eight were still in the race at The Chair, as Alfred Bright shows in the centre piece to his story of **81** the race in pictures (81). The winner was Jenkinstown, like Eremon, owned by Mr. Stanley Howard, trained by Coulthwaite, and bought in Ireland on the recommendation of James Daly. The story goes that at one Sandown meeting in 1908 Daly's son met Mr. Howard and told him his father wanted him to buy Jenkinstown, as he would win another National with him. The price was £600, and when Mr. Howard said that it was more than he could afford, young Daly replied, 'My father said in case you answered like that, I was to say: "Damn the money, I'll send the horse to Coulthwaite for you!"' So the horse went to Coulthwaite and two years later won the National! Although he won, the honours of the race, as Bright shows, went to the top weight Jerry M, who was giving Jenkinstown 30 lb., was with Jenkinstown at the last (third sketch on left), and was only beaten by three lengths. Jenkinstown and Jerry M had been clear of the remainder coming on to the race-course, both hampered by three loose horses. (Top sketch on right). R. Chadwick is up on Mr. Stanley Howard's second National winner in this **91** picture of Jenkinstown (91).

102

This was the first National in which only one horse completed the course without mishap. The winner was Mr. Frank Bibby's Glenside, the stable second string, who was ridden at the last moment by a young Welshman Jack Anthony in place of Tich Mason, who broke his leg a few days before the race. Jerry M, the star of 1910, was on the sidelines with leg trouble, but it was a high-class field, the best-backed being Lutteur III, Mr. Bibby's first string Caubeen, who had been third two years previously, and Rathnally from the Coulthwaite stable. At the first fence, the grey Trianon III fell — the French crack — as Alfred Bright calls him (77). At Becher's, Bright depicts **77** Rathnally, 'who pecks', and Glenside. Precentor II fell at the second fence Lutteur III 'got hung up at the fence after Becher's', and as Bright shows, caused considerable havoc. Bright shows more 'Grief at the Canal Turn'.

By the time the leaders came to The Chair, only eight of the twenty-six starters remained in the race, with the Bibby first string Caubeen the leader, followed by Precentor II, owned by the American Mr. Foxhall Keene, and Rathnally. Bright shows Caubeen leading at the water from Precentor II, Rathnally, 'who pecks', and Glenside. Precentor II fell at the second fence going away from the stands and Mount Prospect's Fortune at the next. The race now lay between Caubeen, Rathnally, Shady Girl and Glenside. At the fence, after Becher's, where havoc was to be caused by a loose horse fifty-six years later in Foinavon's year, Caubeen 'baulks at the gap made by Lutteur III, and Rathnally collides with him'. It was now a duel between Shady Girl and Glenside, but Shady Girl fell at Valentines and Glenside, now very tired, alone remained. Rathnally and Shady Girl were remounted and set off in pursuit of Glenside, just as Honey End, Red Alligator, and others were remounted in Foinavon's year. Jack Anthony, however, just managed to get Glenside over the last fence and keep him going up the long straight. 'Glenside rolls home alone', as Bright puts it in a little sketch below his picture of the stable companions Caubeen and Glenside on the eve of the race. The picture of Glenside, Anthony up and No. 13 on the race card (78) **78** shows him to have been a chaser with plenty of bone. Both Caubeen and Glenside were trained by Captain R. H. Collis at Kinlet. Bright called them 'the Kinlet pair'.

Sir Charles Assheton-Smith as Mr. C. Duff had won the National of 1893 with Cloister, and was to win his second National this year with the great Jerry M already winner of the Grand Steeplechase de Paris of 1910 after finishing second to Jenkinstown at Aintree. Jerry M then had leg trouble and only had one outing between Auteuil in 1910 and Aintree in 1912, and many doubted whether he would be at his best.

They reckoned, however, without his trainer Bob Gore of Findon, an Irishman by birth, who was with the leading Irish trainer Linde for a time at The Curragh, and was associated with Garrett and Willie Moore, and in the last years of the nineteenth century rode on the continent with great success. Now in his late forties, he was a highly experienced trainer, and when the public saw Jerry M in the paddock at Aintree, they hurried to back him. Jerry M had top weight of 12 st. 7 lb. The minimum weight had been raised this year from 9 st. 7 lb. to 10 st.

79 Glenside and Rathnally, the first two in 1911, were soon amongst the fallen (79). At the Canal Turn first time round, Bright shows a loose horse and Ballyhackle 'making the field swing wide'. At this point, second time round, Ballyhackle can be seen 'unshipping his jockey' with Jerry M in the picture below, jumping the Canal Turn perfectly on the inside. Bright, who painted these Aintree scenes so deftly, was uncle of Colonel 'Babe' Moseley, one of the best amateur riders of the 1930s. Bright managed the Duke of Westminster's stud at the time, and had a fine eye for a horse.

Bloodstone, trained like Rathnally by Coulthwaite, led over the last, but he was caught in the run-in by Jerry M, ridden by Ernest Piggott, father of Keith, trainer of the 1963 National winner Ayala, and grandfather of Lester. Ernest Piggott had served his apprenticeship with Tom Cannon at Danebury, and was a very strong finisher. Bloodstone was ridden by a Lincolnshire man Frank Lyall. Nineteen years later, Coulthwaite engaged his nephew Bob Lyall to ride Grakle in the 1931 National, and Bod Lyall succeeded where his uncle narrowly failed.

Gore had bought Jerry M through the Widgers in County Waterford, and the horse was named after Jerry Mulcair, a well-known Irish horse-breaker. Jerry M was only nine when he won with 12 st. 7 lb., but he became a roarer and never raced again. He was undoubtedly one of the greatest National **80** winners, and the picture of him by W. A. Rouch (80), with E. Piggott up, shows him on looks to be a real Aintree horse.

This year was very nearly a triumph for the Tyrwhitt-Drake family of Shardeloes in Buckinghamshire — but not quite. Mr. William Tyrwhitt-Drake and his son Jack, then the leading amateur rider, trained more than a dozen horses at Shardeloes, and owned a useful chaser called Irish Mail. Jack had finished fourth in the 1912 National on Carsey, had won the Grand Sefton at Aintree on him, and was committed to riding him in the 1913 National. His father therefore engaged Owen Anthony for Irish Mail.

The leader for much of the first part of the race was The Rejected IV, ridden by Mr. Gilbert Cotton, who had won the previous year's National Hunt Chase on this horse. John Beer (82) in his picture of the field at the **82** Canal Turn shows the leaders as Blow Pipe (W. J. Smith), Merry Land (R. Trudgill), the favourite Ballyhackle, ridden by the Irishman Harry Ussher, Rejected IV, the previous year's runner-up Bloodstone, Carsey, Irish Mail, and Covercoat ridden by Percy Woodland in place of the injured Piggott, who had to stand down at the last moment. They were followed by Fetlar's Pride, who is jumping the fence, Lord Derby's Axle Pin (No. 14), the grey, Trianon III, and Black Plum (No. 13). The picture by John Beer gives an unusual impression of the sharpness of the Canal Turn, which is only realised if one walks the course.

The American challenger Highbridge and the Austrian Jamagata had been early casualties, and the fancied French horse Trianon came down at Valentines, soon after the scene portrayed here. Only three were standing, coming to the last, Jack Tyrwhitt-Drake leading on Carsey with the race in his pocket if he stood up, followed by his father's horse Irish Mail and Covercoat in the Jerry M colours of Sir Charles Assheton-Smith. Then poor Carsey fell, leaving Covercoat to win at his ease from Irish Mail. Drake remounted Carsey, jumped the last fence, and was the only other to finish. Two years later he was a casualty in France. Covercoat, like Jerry M, was trained by Gore, and had been bought at Dublin Sales, but he was not in the same class as Jerry M.

This was the only appearance in the National of Mr. Gilbert Cotton, who was to become part and parcel of the Aintree scene for fifty years as the inspector of the course, from 1920, until he retired at the age of ninety in 1970! Gilbert Cotton's father Frank Cotton had also been inspector of the course and had also finished first in the National Hunt Chase, and Gilbert Cotton was rightly proud of the fact that his grandson Sir William Pigott-Brown, twice the leading amateur, had also won the National Hunt Chase of 1961 on Superfine. At the time of his death in 1971, Gilbert Cotton was still the alertest nonagenarian in the country. Quietly, in the background, he had been responsible — or partly responsible — for the various improvements of the last half century to the Aintree Course — the filling in of the open ditch at the Canal Turn, following the Easter Hero débâcle, and the sloping of the fences to make it easier for horses to measure them. The change which this modest remarkable nonagenarian advocated, but did not see adopted, was the removal of the fence between Becher's and the Canal Turn, as he thought horses needed longer to recover their balance after Becher's. This was the fence where the shambles recurred in 1967 in Foinavon's year.

1914 — Sunloch's year

Sir Charles Assheton-Smith, with three Nationals to his credit, tried to buy Sunloch from his owner trainer Mr. Thomas Tyler before the race, but this sporting Leicestershire farmer had no wish to sell his horse. Sunloch's rider W. J. Smith, who had made the running on Blow Pipe in the previous year, decided on similar tactics on Sunloch, and was soon clear of his field with a lead of up to forty lengths. There were two fancied French runners this year — Trianon III and Lutteur III, but their jockeys had given Sunloch too much rope. He was never caught, as the picture shows (83), as he passes the post with ears pricked. Sir Charles Assheton-Smith bought Sunloch after this race, but he never did much good again.

83

1915 — Ally Sloper's year

Ally Sloper won in the colours of Lady Nelson, widow of Sir William Nelson, who won the Ascot Gold Cup with Tangiers. Lady Nelson was the first woman owner to win the National. Trained at Wroughton by Aubrey Hastings, Ally Sloper (85) owed much to the jockeyship of his rider Jack Anthony, who is seen on the horse in the picture by T. P. Earl. Bred in Lincolnshire, Ally Sloper once changed hands at Doncaster Sales for twenty-five guineas, and was later bought by the former jockey Herbert Randall of Sceptre fame. He sold him for £700 to Lady Nelson. It was war-time, and the stands were half empty, and soon afterwards the course was requisitioned by the army and there was no more racing at Aintree until after the end of the war. In the picture of the 1915 finish (84) Ally Sloper is seen winning all out from Mr. C. Bower Ismay's Jacobus (A. Newey).

85

84

Three so-called substitute races were run at Gatwick near London on a course bearing no resemblance to Aintree. Steeplechasing in the middle of a desperate war and grave shortage of food did not seem appropriate to many. The 1916 and 1917 races were not of great interest, but the 1918 substitute race was won by a very high-class chaser called Poethlyn, and Poethlyn was very much in the public eye when Aintree opened its gates again in the spring of 1919.

II

Between the two World Wars

93
1920

94
1921

95
1921

96
1921

97
1921

98
1921

99
1923

100
1922

101
1922

102
1923

103
1923

104
1924

105
1924

106
1925

107
1925

108
1925

109
1926

110
1926

III
1926

112
1926

113
1927

114
1927

115
1927

116
1927

117
1928

118
1928

119
1928

120
1928

121
1927

122
1928

123
1929

124
1929

125
1929

126
1929

127
1929

128
1930

129
1930

132
1930

133
1930

134
1930

135
1930

136
1931

137
1931

138
1931

139
1931

140
1932

141
1932

142
1932

143
1932

144
1933

145
1933

146
1933

147
1933

148
1934

149
1934

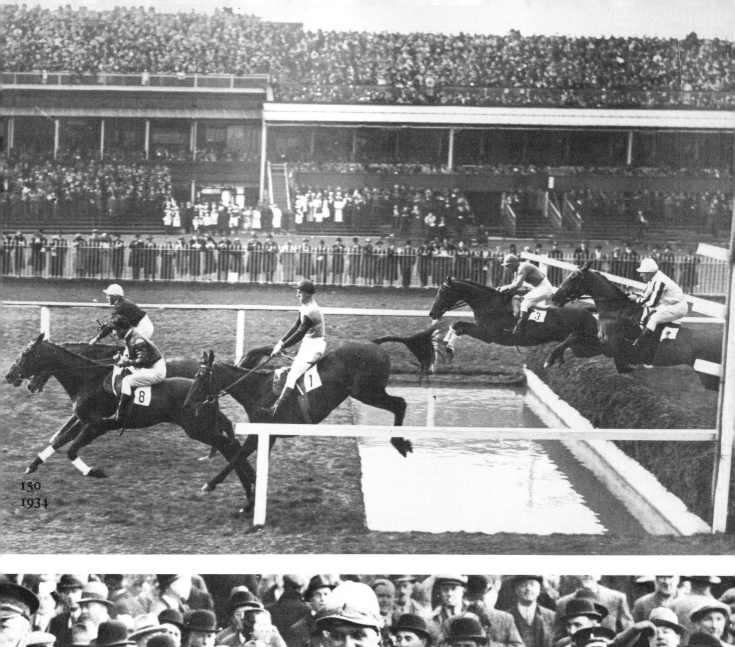

150
1934

151
1934

154
1935

155
1935

157
1935

158
1935

159
1936

161
1936

160
1936

162
1936

163
1936

164
1937

105
1937

166
1937

167
1937

168
1937

169
1937

170
1937

173
1938

174
1938

175
1939

176
1939

177

178
1940

II

BILL CURLING
RUNNING COMMENTARY

Between the two World Wars

1919 — Poethlyn's year

Poethlyn, owned and bred in Wales by Major and Mrs. Hugh Peel, had top weight in 1919. Ridden by Ernest Piggott, he won comfortably in spite of dropping his hindlegs in the water. The Grand National of 1919 was Poethlyn's ninth victory in succession. If one counts his victory at Gatwick in 1918, he is one of only seven horses to have won the National twice. He was trained by H. Escott at Lewes, in Sussex.

In the composite picture of the race (92), now in the possession of Lester Piggott, Poethlyn can be seen lying about fifth at 'The Stand Water'. Bottom left there is a list of Ernest Piggott's ten National rides up to 1919 and a reminder of the fact that he twice rode the great Manifesto. Above, is a picture of the crowd on the rails braving the snowstorm which preceded the race. Sir Alfred Munnings, a friend of the Peels, painted a picture of the scene in the paddock with the storm threatening, and a picture of Poethlyn at their home in Wales (Colour Plate X) with an old forest oak very much a part of the picture in which Major and Mrs. Peel are seen with their son Captain Owen Peel (on right).

92

1920 — Troytown's year

Poethlyn had top weight again in 1920, started favourite, and fell at the first fence. Cecil Aldin has depicted the scene at the Canal Turn (Colour Plate XI), where the second favourite Troytown (No. 2) and Turk II (No. 22) were disputing the lead from Sergeant Murphy (No. 10), another horse hidden, Turkey Buzzard (No. 7, brown and blue colours), Bonnie Charlie (No. 19, owned by Captain Willoughby Norrie, now Lord Norrie), and Silver Ring (No. 3), ridden by the famous hurdle race jockey George Duller. Troytown led at the water and made most of the rest of the running. It was the third and last victory of his Welsh rider Jack Anthony in the National. The picture (93) shows Troytown, Jack Anthony up, being led in with the future successful trainer Ivor Anthony, in bowler hat, on his left. Troytown was one of the outstanding National winners between the two wars, and might well have been a second Manifesto had he not broken a leg in a race in France.

1921 — Shaun Spadah's year

Shaun Spadah eventually finished alone as the picture (96) shows. He was the only horse which did not fall. Easy to pick up with his white blaze, Shaun Spadah would have been hard pressed if the favourite The Bore, owned, trained, and ridden by the leading amateur Harry Brown had not fallen at the second last. Harry Brown had had £500 each way on The Bore, and in spite of a broken collar bone, remounted him, jumped the last fence to finish second, and won money on his bet. Over The Chair first time round, The Bore (left), Shaun Spadah (centre) and All White (right) had been close together (94). All White and Turkey Buzzard later both came to grief and were remounted by their jockeys R. Chadwick and Captain G. H. Bennet to finish third and fourth. Turkey Buzzard, owned by Mrs. H. M. Hollins actually fell twice, and on his return Mrs. Hollins chased Captain Bennet round the paddock with her umbrella for daring to continue in the race on her darling horse. (No picture available!) King George V and Queen Mary were welcomed by an enormous crowd on their arrival (98). The Prince of Wales (bowler in hand) and the Princess Royal can be seen behind the King and Queen. After the race (95), the King, in bowler and spats, sent for the winning jockey, Fred Rees, to congratulate him. Lord Derby is on the King's right hand.

Shaun Spadah was owned by a Scot, the future Sir Malcolm McAlpine, trained at Lewes in Sussex by an Englishman, George Poole, the son of a trainer, was ridden by the champion jockey Fred Rees, son of a Welsh vet, and was bred in County Meath in Ireland. Fred Rees was the first steeple-chase jockey to ride a hundred winners in a season (97). The winner is seen with Sir Malcolm McAlpine (in spats), his trainer George Poole, and Fred Rees up.

112

Only three completed the course without a fall. Music Hall, the winner, was ridden by Lewis Bilbie Rees, brother of Fred Rees, and father of the present jockey Bill Rees. He was trained by Owen Anthony, brother of Ivor and Jack. Music Hall, in the colours of Mr. Hugh Kershaw, came over the last fence leading from Mr. Joe Widger's Drifter (100). The race was marred by the death of Awbeg at Becher's and the spectacular fall of Wavertree who ended up wedged in Becher's Brook (101). Taffytus, who finished third in the Manifesto colours of the future Sir John Crocker Bulteel, was ridden by Ted Leader, one of the best Aintree jockeys of the 1920s.

100

101

1923 — Sergeant Murphy's year

Ridden by Captain G. H. 'Tuppy' Bennet, the leading amateur rider who was also a vet, Sergeant Murphy was thirteen in his year of triumph. He won from the 1921 winner Shaun Spadah, who was carrying 12 st. 7 lb. Third was Conjuror II, owned by Major C. Dewhurst and ridden by his amateur son Mr. C. Dewhurst.

Captain Bennet believed in a middle course at Aintree, and (103) he is seen taking Becher's in the middle of the fence second time round, whilst (102) three fences later at Valentine's, he has swung rather wide after the Canal Turn and taken Valentine's on unpoached ground on the far side of the fence. Note how far back he leans. Note also Lord Sefton's private stand in the background.

103

102

At the end of 1923, Captain Bennet had a fall in a four horse race at Wolverhampton on Boxing Day, and was kicked in the head by a horse following, had his skull smashed, and died a fortnight later. This dreadful accident, following other serious head injuries to steeplechase riders, at last led the National Hunt Committee, over half a century after its foundation to make skull caps compulsory equipment for National Hunt jockeys. Captain Bennet, whose father Geoffrey Bennet trained jumpers near Newmarket at one time for King Edward VII, rode many winners for his trainer brother Sam Bennet in the three years before his death. Sergeant Murphy was trained at Newmarket by George Blackwell, one of the small band of trainers to saddle both a Derby winner and National winner. He won the Derby with Rock Sand in 1903. Sergeant Murphy's owner, Stephen Sandford, a former Cambridge University undergraduate, was the first American to win the National (99). He and Captain 'Tuppy' Bennet were congratulated by King George V after the race. The King is shaking hands with Bennet, and Sanford is on Bennet's left, whilst Lord Derby is just behind the King on the right of the picture.

1924 — Master Robert's year

Owned in partnership by Lord Airlie and Major Sidney Green, Master Robert (R. Trudgill) was the last of four Grand National winners trained by Aubrey Hastings at Wroughton (104). The joint owners (Green on left) are seen in the picture with Hastings standing by Master Robert's head. Considered useless for flat racing, Master Robert was bought in Ireland as a potential point-to-pointer by Harry Fordham, one of the outstanding point-to-point riders of his day, who lived near Royston in Hertfordshire. When he got him to England Fordham soon realised that he was out of the ordinary, though he was what is known as a 'high blower'. He was easy to ride, and in fact his daughter Betty, then a girl of ten — now Mrs. W. Faure-Walker — used to ride him in morning work with her father on Royston Heath, where a quarter of a century later Willie Stephenson was to train both a National and a Derby winner. When Master Robert ran in the Nomination race at the Hertfordshire Point-to-Point he won by 'the length of two fields' from strong opposition, and he was bought immediately after the race by Mr. W. Walker, then Master of the Hertfordshire. Three weeks later Walker asked Fordham to take him back as he considered erroneously that he was 'wrong in his wind'. Fordham naturally did so, and Colonel Sidney Green and Lord Airlie, having heard of his prowess, came to see him with Aubrey Hastings, and bought him as a horse likely to do well in military races. Lord Airlie won on him, and then in March 1923 he ran third in the Liverpool Fox-hunters and in the autumn won the Valentine Chase for amateur riders at Aintree, ridden by Peter Roberts, a well known amateur of the day. Master Robert had however developed navicular, and his racing days were numbered. In the National Hastings asked Roberts to ride him again, but Roberts turned him down in favour of another, and the mount went to Bob Trudgill, a gallant West Countryman, who had a bad fall the previous day and was barely fit to ride. Trudgill returned to the Aintree unsaddling enclosure with one leg covered in blood. He was scarcely able to stagger to the weighing room, for the stitches he had had in his injured leg had burst. The joint owners gave him a present of £2,000 for his victory, which he thoroughly deserved.

Master Robert in the race (105) was helped by the fact that the favourite Conjuror II was brought down by a loose horse at Becher's, where the runner up, Fly Mask (No. 13, J. Moylan), was leading from the 1923 winner, Sergeant Murphy (No. 6, J. Hogan), with Lord Woolavington's Eureka II (No. 9, A. Robson) just behind. Master Robert was also helped by the fact that his feet were specially treated before the race, which helped him to show his true form.

One further postscript. The joint owners did not forget Harry Fordham after their triumph, and Harry Fordham did not forget his daughter Betty. Not many girls of ten have ridden a National winner in work.

1925 — Double Chance's year

Amongst the amateurs who rode in this race were the future Colonel Bill Whitbread, founder of the Whitbread Gold Cup, Major Jack Wilson, and Pat Dennis. Top weight was Silvo, third in 1924. Silvo (No. I, Fred Rees) and Double Chance (Maj. Wilson) were (108) out in front at Becher's second time round, as the picture shows, but the weight told on Silvo, and at half way in the run-in (106) there was little to choose between Double Chance (on the rails), Old Tay Bridge (Jack Anthony) in the centre and Fly Mask on the outside, with Sprig (white blaze, half hidden by Double Chance) fourth and the fading Silvo (behind Old Tay Bridge), fifth. Double Chance, receiving 17 lb. from Old Tay Bridge, drew clear in the last 100 yards (107).

Major Wilson, a Yorkshireman from the East Riding, served in the Air Force in the First World War, and it was said that his hair went white in the night after being one of the first to jump successfully by parachute from a balloon. Double Chance was bred by Mr. Anthony de Rothschild and given by him to the trainer Fred Archer, grandson of William Archer, who won the 1858 National on Little Charlie, and a nephew of the great jockey Fred Archer. The trainer Fred Archer sold a half share in Double Chance to a Liverpool cotton-broker Mr. D. Goold in whose colours he ran. Nine horses finished, including Jack Horner, ridden by the American Morgan Blair, who had backed himself to get round.

1926 — Jack Horner's year

Fired by the victory of Mr. Sandford's Sergeant Murphy in 1923, and the exploits of Morgan Blair, the American A. C. Schwartz arrived in England with almost a blank cheque in search of the National winner, and Jack Leader, the Newmarket trainer, bought on his behalf, for 4,000 guineas, Jack Horner, who had finished seventh in 1925.

Schwartz was also prepared to pay a big fee for the services of a top class jockey, but Ted Leader, due to ride Sprig for his owner Mrs. M. Partridge and father Tom Leader, loyally turned down an enormous offer, and the mount was given to the experienced W. Watkinson, an Australian by birth, who had come near to winning the 1922 National on Drifter.

109 Jack Horner was always amongst the leaders (109). He jumped Becher's (spotted jacket, dark cap) first time round with Bright's Boy (No. 5) and just ahead of Old Tay Bridge, whose jockey Jack Anthony is visible behind No. 5.

110 At the water (110), Sprig (white blaze) on the inside was followed by Jack Horner (spotted jacket, dark cap), with Bright's Boy (E. Doyle) jumping the water by the flag ahead of a group including Ben Cruchan (W. H. Whitbread) nearest the stands, and Old Tay Bridge. At Becher's second time

111 round (111), the blinkered Darracq led from Jack Horner (spotted jacket) and Lone Hand (T. Morgan), who is in the act of falling. Bright's Boy still

112 looked dangerous coming to the last, but (112) tired in the run-in to finish third behind Jack Horner and Old Tay Bridge (Jack Anthony). Sprig was fourth.

One of the few not to see the finish was Jack Leader, trainer of the winner, who was slapped on the back so hard by Charlie Schwartz that he fell off his perch on the stand. Schwartz wanted to give Watkinson a present of £4,000, but it was then decided to give him £1,000 a year for four years. Three weeks later, poor Watkinson was killed in a fall at Bogside in Scotland.

1927 — Sprig's year

The Grand National was broadcast for the first time this year. Bright's Boy, third in the race in 1926, was top weight, and T. P. Earl, whose pictures adorn many houses in Newmarket, caught the scene well at Becher's Brook

121 first time round (121) with the riderless Marsin (No. 7, P. Powell) being led out of the way of the runner-up Bovril III (on the outside of the picture), and near the rails Grecian Wave (No. 6, J. Meaney) is leading from Hawker (black cap) ridden by Capt. A. E. Grant, Sprig (No. 4), Knight of the Wilderness (W. Gurney), Keep Cool (J. Goswell) in the Silvo colours of W. H. Midwood with white cross bands, and behind Keep Cool by the flag just landing is the top weight Bright's Boy (vertical stripes, Jack Anthony).

116

In the centre of the picture between the leader No. 6 and No. 7, the future trainer Stewart Wight, riding Colonel R. W. Tweedie's Mr. Jolly, has lost an iron, and behind him is Lord Glanely's Shaun Or, (light cross band, W. Madden) and between Shaun Or and Keep Cool is J. B. Balding on Lord Queenborough's Drinmond, who was to finish fourth.

At Becher's second time round (114), the field was much depleted with the three leaders Keep Cool on the inside (white cross belts), Master Billie (F. Rees) in the centre, and Bovril III on the outside next to the loose horse. Behind Master Billie and half hidden is Sprig and next to him is Bright's Boy with his prominent blaze. In the middle of the picture, about to land, are Lady Helen McCalmont's Amberwave (halved jacket, J. O'Brien) and on the extreme outside Drinmond. **114**

Three fences from home, there was little to choose between Sprig on the right (113), Bright's Boy on the left, and Bovril III (approaching the fence on the outside). The weight began to tell on the two leaders in the long run-in and Mr. G. W. Pennington, now Sir William Pennington-Ramsden, on his own horse Bovril III (bandaged forelegs) nearly caught Sprig on the post, Sprig winning by one length with Bright's Boy third (115). **113** **115**

Sprig's victory was perhaps the most popular of the 1920s. His owner, seventy-four-year-old Mrs. M. Partridge (116), is seen leading him in with Tom Leader, the trainer, and father of the winning rider. The head of Jack Anthony and Bright's Boy are in the background and a delighted stableman in large cap, bow tie, breeches and leggings is on the right. Mrs. Partridge's son, killed shortly before the Armistice, had bred Sprig, and, nine years later, this was in effect the fulfilment of his dream. **116**

1928 — Tipperary Tim's year

This was the year in which the brilliant Easter Hero was stuck on top of the Canal Turn fence, putting most of the field out of the race. The scene is well captured by Peter Biegel in his picture comparing it to the similar débâcle in Foinavon's Year nearly forty years later (Colour Plate XIII). In the 1928 race Darracq (on the inside), Easter Hero, Soldier's Joy, Tipperary Tim, and Billy Barton are the horses caught by the artist.

There is no hint of the débâcle to come, in T. P. Earl's picture (122) of the first fence, with Easter Hero (No. 3) leading and Tipperary Tim (No. 52) lying about fifth on the outside. Easter Hero led at Becher's, then made the mistake at the Canal, straddling the fence, baulking those behind, and putting half the field out of the race. **122**

117   Only nine were standing at the water at halfway (117), Mr. Howard Bruce's American challenger Billy Barton (T. Cullinan nearest camera), then leading from De Combat (F. Croney, spotted jacket), May King (on outside — blaze prominent), and Great Span, ridden by the then seventeen-year-old

118   Bill Payne. At Becher's second time round (118), there were only five in it, Great Span on the inside by the flag, Billy Barton (next), May King (white blaze) and Tipperary Tim on the outside with his amateur rider Billy Dutton almost calling a cab. The French challenger Maguelonne (Bedeloup) is approaching the fence. She was a brilliant mare, and winner of the Grand Steeplechase de Paris.

     Two from home, Great Span looked to be going best, but his saddle began to slip, he blundered, and gave Payne no chance to stay in the saddle.

119   Tipperary Tim (119), who is nearest the camera, Great Span (with his saddle invisible) and Billy Barton jumped the last in line, but Billy Barton fell and

120   Tipperary Tim, at 100–1 (120), finished alone followed by the riderless Great Span. Cullinan remounted with difficulty to finish second on Billy Barton — the only two to finish.

     Billy Dutton, a qualified solicitor from Cheshire, and later to become a highly successful trainer, had won the Foxhunters' Chase at Liverpool three years previously on his father's Upton Lad, and was one of the best amateurs of his day. He steered clear of trouble in the National by keeping to the outside, as Pennington had done on Bovril III the previous year. The tubed Tipperary Tim had changed hands as a yearling for fifty guineas, and was trained in Shropshire by J. Dodd, and owned by H. S. Kenyon of Manchester.

1929 — Gregalach's year

At the suggestion of Gilbert Cotton, the inspector of the course, the ditch on the take-off side of the Canal Turn had been filled in this year as a result of the Easter Hero disaster of 1928. There was a record field of sixty-six, which

123   are pictured just after the start (123). Easter Hero, in spite of top weight, was a hot favourite and beat all but one of the sixty-six. At Becher's first time round T. P. Earl has captured the scene (Colour plate XII) with Easter Hero setting a cracking pace and with the field already well strung out, Sandy Hook and Richmond II prominent, and the eventual winner Gregalach in

125   tangerine colours, light cap, jumping the fence. At the water (125), a third of the field were still standing, where, however, the immense crowd saw R. Thrale, the rider of Ardoon's Pride bite the dust. Ardoon's Pride was owned by Captain T. H. Bird, whose *One Hundred Grand Nationals*, published in 1937, added to the history of the race. Easter Hero (J. Moloney) led at Becher's (124) second time round, followed by Sandy Hook (F. Fish, dark cap) and Mr. R. McAlpine's Richmond II (W. Stott) with the 100–1 outsider Gregalach lying seventh, nearing the fence. The three leaders jumped the Canal Turn together, but Easter Hero spread a plate soon afterwards and in the end (126) was beaten by Gregalach, ridden by R. Everett, a former sailor, and trained by Tom Leader of Sprig fame. Richmond II, the mare Melleray's Belle (J. Mason) and May King (F. Gurney) were third, fourth and fifth, well behind Easter Hero. Ted Leader rode his father's more fancied runner Mount Etna who collided in mid-air with Darracq early in the race. In the picture (127), Ted Leader is seen congratulating the winning owner Mrs. Gemmell and Everett. Billy Stott on Richmond is on the right of the picture, J. Mason on Melleray's Belle on the left. Leader and Thrale were both to become successful trainers.

1930 — Shaun Goilin's year

This was a memorable National on two counts. First it was the most exciting finish for nearly fifty years, between the winner Shaun Goilin, Melleray's Belle, and Sir Lindsay in the colours of Jock Whitney, owner of Easter Hero. Secondly, it produced one of the most spectacular falls in the history of the race, when the then Mrs. H. Mond's May King fell at Becher's second time round. I am indebted to Mrs. Mond's son, Lord Melchett, for the reproduction of pictures of this remarkable fall, in which fortunately, May King and his rider Gordon Goswell, escaped little the worse. Goswell was one of three Cheshire jockey brothers, sons of George Goswell, a fine rider at the beginning of the century, and Goswell had had a lot to do with the making of Shaun Goilin in his early days at the home of his owner, W. H. Midwood in Cheshire. Midwood, a famed Master of the Cheshire Hounds, had tried to win the National with Silvo and other horses. At Becher's first time round (128), the two greys Mr. R. K. Mellon's Glangesia (J. Browne) and Gate Book (T. Morgan) were the leaders with Gregalach lying about sixth after landing in the centre, and Merrivale II (F. Brookes) leading those near the camera. May King is just jumping the fence and to his right (nearer the camera) the striped sleeves of Dudley Williams on Mr. Jock Whitney's Sir Lindsay are clear. The leaders at the water (129) were Shaun Goilin (No. 4), Lord Westmorland's Merrivale II (No. 40), Toy Bell (D. Morgan), May King, who is just jumping the fence after meeting it wrong, Sir Lindsay (striped sleeves) and Melleray's Belle, ridden by J. Mason (nearest guardrail). A second later, May King's off fore is splashing the edge of the water (130) as Toy Bell clears it, and Melleray's Belle and Sir Lindsay take it together. At Becher's second time round (131), the grey Glangesia, who had been hunted in Pennsylvania by Mr. Mellon, then Master of the Rolling Rock Foxhounds, led from Toy Bell, who pecked. Grakle (white cross belts) is jumping the fence on the right and Sir Lindsay on the left, and on the right of Sir Lindsay can be seen the white face of May King as he approaches the fence. The fall of May King was about to come (132 and 133).

Two fences from home, the race lay between the mare Melleray's Belle, owned by Mr. William Wilson from Castlehill, Ayrshire, Sir Lindsay, and Shaun Goilin. Melleray's Belle led at the last (134) from Sir Lindsay who hit it hard, his rider Dudley Williams losing both irons and thus probably the race. In a desperate finish (135), Shaun Goilin, strongly ridden by the Irishman T. Cullinan, is seen wearing down the gallant Melleray's Belle to win by a head, with Sir Lindsay third. The winner was chance bred, his dam Golden Day being served in the night by an unknown colt in a paddock in Co. Limerick. Shaun Goilin was trained by another Irishman Frank Hartigan, who succeeded his uncle Willie Moore as trainer at Weyhill, near Andover. Willie Moore trained The Soarer and Manifesto to win Nationals, and his brother Garry Moore won the race on his own horse The Liberator in 1879. Hartigan, who had previously twice saddled a National runner-up in Old Tay Bridge, was a most versatile trainer and one of the few to saddle over 2,000 winners.

1931 — Grakle's year

The brilliant Easter Hero, who had had to miss the 1930 race through leg trouble, was favourite and at the water (136) was going well in third place just behind the 1929 winner Gregalach (No. 4) and Great Span (No. 17), who had been so unlucky in 1928. Solanum (J. Hamey) was lying fourth. As they came to Becher's second time round (137), Gregalach, ridden by J. Molony (white cap) was leading from Great Span (G. Hardy), with Solanum on the floor and his rider Hamey beside him, and Easter Hero to his left as Fred Rees is thrown towards Solanum. The riderless Tamasha (in the foreground) had in fact brought Solanum down. Grakle is third behind Great Span, and in fact is 'landing on all fours' — the only mistake he made.

At the last, Grakle, ridden by Bob Lyall, led from Gregalach, and the race lay between the two. Grakle disliked the whip and was inclined to hang, and Lyall had orders not to use it till the last moment, and as a result Gregalach drew level in the run-in. Lyall kept his head and only showed Grakle the whip in the last hundred yards, and went clear (138) to win a fine race by one and a half lengths in fast time. Bob Lyall is the youngest son of the Lincolnshire trainer J. G. Lyall, who had five steeplechase jockey sons, the eldest, Frank, being just beaten in the 1912 National on Bloodstone. He now lives at Newmarket.

138

Grakle had been bought by Mr. Cecil R. Taylor, a leading Liverpool cotton broker for 4,000 guineas from Irishman T. K. Laidlaw and was trained by that great character Tom Coulthwaite, who is seen walking beside his horse after the race (139), whilst Robinson, a well-known Nottingham farrier, congratulates Lyall. Coulthwaite was in his seventieth year when Grakle won. He had previously trained the National winners Eremon in 1907 and Jenkinstown in 1910 for Mr. Stanley Howard.

139

1932 — Forbra's year

This race became a duel in the second circuit between Forbra and Egremont (140) after K. C. B. had fallen at the water when leading Forbra, the blinkered Near East (No. 14), and Egremont (white jacket, dark sleeves). At Becher's second time round (141), Forbra (nearer camera) and Egremont were neck and neck. At the fence after Valentine's (142), Forbra (No. 30) led perhaps by half a length, and at the finish (143), there was still little between them. It had been a marvellous duel. Forbra, trained by T. R. Rimell at Kinnersley, near Worcester, was ridden by J. Hamey, and owned by Mr. W. Parsonage of Ludlow, a retired bookmaker. Egremont was ridden by an amateur, Edward Paget, a stockbroker, who had had a £4,000 to £1 spring double on Jerome Fandor, the 40–1 winner of the Lincolnshire Handicap, and his own mount Egremont, 33–1 outsider in the National!

140

141

142

143

There were three past National winners in the field. Grakle, running for the sixth and last time, Gregalach, who was brought down by a loose horse, and Shaun Goilin, who finished a remote third.

1933 — Kellsboro' Jack's year

Kellsboro' Jack won in record time from a field which included Golden Miller for the first time. Lord Mildmay, whose name was to be writ large in the story of the race, also appeared in it for the first time but came to grief at the first fence on Youtell.

144   At the water, Kellsboro' Jack (No. 7) (144) is leading from Delaneige (No. 14), Forbra (nearest camera) and Holmes, whilst Southern Hero (No. 19) is just clearing the water, and Golden Miller is in the act of jumping it behind him. The riderless Apostasy (No. 22) is in the foreground, after avoiding the

145   fence. The two Jacks, (145) Pelorus Jack (nearest camera), ridden by the champion jockey W. Stott, and Kellsboro' Jack (Dudley Williams) came to

146   the last together, but Pelorus Jack hit it hard and (146) collapsed on landing, leaving a crestfallen Stott standing helplessly by his horse.

147   Kellsboro' Jack (147) was left to follow the riderless Apostasy past the post, followed by Frank Furlong on his father's horse Really True and the blinkered Slater.

1934 — Golden Miller's year

148   Martin Stainforth's picture (148) of Golden Miller leading at Becher's is full of action. He is followed by the grey Uncle Batt, Thomond II, in the striped sleeves of his owner Jock Whitney, is just landing, and in the foreground is the 1932 winner Forbra.

150   At the water (150), Delaneige (No. 8) and Gregalach (dark jacket, white cap) are disputing the lead ahead of Forbra, who is followed by Golden Miller (No. 3), who is wearing bandages, and Thomond II.

149   Charles Simpson captures the thrill of the duel (149) between Golden Miller (Gerry Wilson) and the American-owned Delaneige (J. Moloney) as they rise at the last almost together, but Golden Miller in the long run-in shows the better finishing speed, and wins in the end decisively.

151   A couple of minutes later, Golden Miller is being led in (151) by his owner Miss Dorothy Paget with her father, Lord Queenborough holding her arm, Mick Boston, Golden Miller's lad, next to Lord Queenborough, and two behind the mounted policeman is Clive Graham, joint author of this book, in bowler hat with race glasses in left hand. The Miller's trainer, Basil Briscoe, is not yet in view.

    It was Golden Miller's finest hour, and he was hailed as 'the horse of the century'. (Frontispiece by Peter Biegel).

122

This was a family triumph for the Furlong family, the winner being ridden by Frank Furlong, and owned and trained by his father, Major Noel Furlong. Golden Miller came to Aintree this year as the winner of four consecutive Cheltenham Gold Cups. Though carrying 12 st. 7 lb., he started the hottest favourite for eighty-eight years, but the horse made a bad mistake at the fence after Valentine's first time round dislodging Gerry Wilson.

At The Chair fence, in front of the stands (152), the grey, Uncle Batt (No. 27), ridden by T. Isaac, led from a group including, on the far side of the picture, Reynoldstown (light jacket and cap), and the Whitney pair, Thomond II (striped sleeves, white cap) and Royal Ransom (striped sleeves, black cap), whilst, in the foreground Alexena (Colonel Peter Payne-Gallwey) is followed by Blue Prince (white, dark sash and cap).   **152**

Mr. W. H. Harrison of Wychnor, long a supporter of racing, with horses in training with Rufus Beasley, went to his first National this year in a party of sixteen, and had two vivid dreams before the race. In the first, he saw No. 4 winning the race ridden by a woman. At first the number 4 did not co-incide with the colours of the rider he saw winning, but he had a second dream on the night before the final acceptances, and this time, the colours of No. 4 co-incided with those of Reynoldstown. What is more, in his dream, he saw the colours of Golden Miller fall at the fence at which in fact he did fall, and he also saw only six colours pass the post — and only six horses were destined to finish! The other members of the party fortunately interpreted the woman winning as an amateur beating a professional, and they all backed Reynoldstown, ridden by the amateur Frank Furlong.

Bill Harrison with part of his winnings commissioned Algernon Thompson to do two pictures of the race which are reproduced. In the first at the water (154), the grey, Uncle Batt (No. 27) is leading from Thomond II with Royal Ransom (No. 3) in the same ownership lying third, Alexena (No. 11) fourth, Reynoldstown (No. 4) fifth, Blue Prince (No. 12) partly hidden by Alexena, sixth, and Emancipator (No. 14) ridden by his owner Peter Cazalet, seventh. In the second (155), Reynoldstown (No. 4) and Thomond II (No. 2) are coming over Becher's, Reynoldstown leading by a length.   **154**   **155**

A moment later (153) Reynoldstown is pecking on landing, but finds a leg, and W. Speck with his legs short in comparison with Frank Furlong, leans back on Thomond II.   **153**

Reynoldstown and Thomond II, who had just been beaten by Golden Miller in the Cheltenham Gold Cup, were still locked in battle at the

156   last (156), with grim endeavour on the faces of both riders in this marvellous picture, but Thomond II was very tired, and in the run-in Blue Prince (W. Parvin) took second place behind the winner Reynoldstown. A moment

157   later (157), Major and Mrs. Furlong had dashed out on to the course to greet their son, then a subaltern in the 9th Lancers. Major Noel Furlong, an Irishman, had come to live in Leicestershire, where he trained Reynoldstown and Really True, the runner-up of 1933. He bought the horse as a five-year-old from his breeder Dick Ball, after whose home at Reynoldstown, Co. Dublin, the horse was named. The Prince of Wales (in bowler hat) watched the race

158   this year (158), and beforehand walked round the course with Lord Sefton (bowler hat and furled umbrella), the senior steward.

1936 — Reynoldstown's second year

Frank Furlong had trouble with his weight, had retired from the Army, and decided to give up his ride on Reynoldstown this year to Fulke Walwyn, another subaltern in the 9th Lancers.

     Golden Miller fell at the first fence this year, and the running was made by a rank outsider Davy Jones, who had been bought for £650 by Lord Mildmay of Flete for his son Anthony Mildmay to ride. The tubed Davy

159   Jones (159), a 100–1 outsider (No. 20) led at Becher's from Kiltoi (No. 18, T. F. Carey), Double Crossed (No. 5), and the favourite Avenger (No. 3,

160   F. Rimell). At the Chair (160), Davy Jones (No. 20) still led from Avenger, Double Crossed (D. Morgan, striped sleeves), and Emancipator (No. 24, P. Cazalet), racing between Avenger and Double Crossed. Reynoldstown was well placed just behind Double Crossed, and is just rising at the fence with Lady Lindsay's Blue Prince following.

161   At the water (161), Davy Jones led from Avenger, Inversible (S. McGrath) half-hidden by Avenger, Double Crossed, Emancipator, Keen Blade (T. Elder), following Emancipator, and half-hidden by the guard rail — Reynoldstown.

162   Davy Jones and Reynoldstown then drew clear (162), Davy Jones just leading at Becher's second time round. At the second to last fence, with his race in his pocket, Davy Jones pecked, the buckle of the reins snapped, and Davy Jones, rudderless, ran out at the last fence, leaving Reynoldstown a very lucky winner.

     Nevertheless, Reynoldstown had humped 12 st. 2 lb. to victory and thoroughly deserved to join the small band to have won the National twice.

163   As he returned to weigh in (163), a delighted Frank Furlong in bowler hat,

Major Noel Furlong (behind his son), and Reg Hobbs (behind Major Furlong) greet their hero. Mrs. Furlong is to the right of her son.

Frank Furlong was keen on flying, joined the Fleet Air Arm in the Second World War, torpedoed the German battleship Bismarck, and was killed in a crash-landing later. He was one of three 9th Lancers to win the National, — Sir David Campbell, who won on The Soarer, Furlong and Walwyn.

1937 — Royal Mail's year

This was celebrated as The Centenary Year of the National, and King George VI and the Queen graced Aintree with their presence, and were accompanied on the course by Lord Sefton (165), for long an admirable **165** Senior Steward at Liverpool, and by the King's Racing Manager Captain Charles Moore. The Queen is seen walking with Captain Moore, and the King with Lord Sefton (with carnation in buttonhole). As usual, at this period, a number of people used an Aintree excursion train as a grand-stand (164). **164**

Golden Miller was once again in the field, but again showed his dislike for Aintree by refusing. At the water (167), the mare Pucka Belle, owned, **167** ridden and trained by E. W. Bailey, led from the riderless Drim, the blinkered Flying Minutes, ridden by sixteen-year-old Bruce Hobbs, and Royal Mail, trained at Wroughton by Ivor Anthony and ridden by another Welshman Evan Williams. Royal Mail is followed by Ego ridden by the future Colonel Harry Llewellyn of show jumping fame (white jacket with black diamond, black spots on cap), with Cooleen in the J. V. Rank colours just behind.

Flying Minutes led Royal Mail at the first fence on the second circuit, but Royal Mail then went on and is seen taking Becher's superbly (166). **166** A moment later, he is landing safely (168) followed by the riderless Drim **168** with Cooleen (Jack Fawcus, blue and primrose quarters) just behind Drim, and next to Cooleen Ego (primrose jacket, black diamond) and Flying Minutes (blinkers), who is meeting it wrong. Drim later attempted to savage Cooleen, and impeded her badly, but the mare was still in touch with Royal Mail at the last, with the riderless Drim giving Evan Williams on Royal Mail cause for anxiety and making him glance over his right shoulder (169). **169** Cooleen could, however, make no impression on Royal Mail in the run-in, as the picture (170) shows. Drim splits the two. **170**

Royal Mail, one of the few black horses to win the great race, was a second National winner for Ivor Anthony and the sixth for Wroughton —

Ascetic's Silver, Ally Sloper, Master Robert, Ballymacad (in a substitute race at Gatwick), Kellsboro' Jack, and Royal Mail, who won in the colours of Hugh Lloyd Thomas, a member of the Diplomatic Service and formerly on the staff of the Duke of Windsor when Prince of Wales. After the war, Evan Williams was to become a successful flat race trainer at Kingsclere and then a M. F. H. in Ireland.

1938 — Battleship's year

This was the first victory of a horse both owned and bred in the United States.

Lord Penrhyn's Rubio (1908) had been American bred, Sergeant Murphy (1923), Jack Horner (1926), and Kellsboro' Jack (1933) had been American owned. Now the diminutive entire Battleship (No. 5, blinkers) (174) on the stands side, ridden by seventeen-year-old Bruce Hobbs, and trained by his father Reg Hobbs, just got the better of a desperate duel with the Irish-trained Royal Danieli (No. 6, far rails), ridden by Dan Moore, who was to become a successful trainer at The Curragh.

The unusual head-on view of the field jumping the water (171) makes the distance between The Chair and The Water and similarly, the last fence and The Water appear deceptively short. At the water, Mr. J. B. Snow's American owned Delachance (J. Moloney, black cap with orange spots) is leading Lough Cottage (R. Black, horse with star), whilst Battleship is just behind Lough Cottage in mid air. Sir Warden Chilcott's Dunhill Castle (H. Nicholson) is next to Lough Cottage, and Royal Danicli is on the far side of Delachance. Blue Prince has come a cropper at the open ditch (172) and his jockey, W. Parvin, straddles the fence which Drim (No. 33, B. K. Tighe), who had given endless trouble in 1937, is seen jumping.

On the second circuit, Battleship (No. 5, blinkers), moved up on the inside and led at Becher's (173) by nearly a length from Royal Danieli (No. 6) in the middle and Delachance (No.11), nearest the camera as the picture shows. Battleship made a mistake two out which, in the view of his rider, helped him to win his race, for the little horse had to be brought from behind in a finish. Royal Danieli, as a result, led at the last from Battleship and Workman, but (174) in a thrilling finish, Battleship, racing wide of Royal Danieli, got up to win on the post.

Bruce Hobbs, now a successful flat race trainer, remains the youngest rider ever to win the National. Mrs. Marion Scott with her film actor husband, Randolph Scott, came from America to see the race, but she was too overcome with excitement to lead her horse in.

1939 — Workman's year

The race was overshadowed by Hitler and the threat of War, but there was still a big crowd for the great race, as is shown by this picture (175) of the field jumping the Water. The leader on the inside to the left of the flag is Miss Dorothy Paget's Kilstar, the favourite, (George Archibald), who is leading from Lord Derby's Underbid, (black, white cap). West Point (No. 25, J. Brogan, light colours) is taking the jump ahead of Workman (on the inside).

175

Colonel W. E. Peel's Inversible (M. Hogan), is level with West Point and two behind him, J. V. Rank's quartered colours of blue and primrose are clear on the blinkered Bachelor Prince (No. 24). The top weight Royal Mail (No. 1), now owned by Mrs. C. Evans, has just come into the right of the picture.

At the final fence (176), the race lay between Workman, owned by Sir Alexander Maguire, an Irishman with Liverpool connections, and Mac Moffat, the hope of Scotland, owned and trained by Captain L. Scott-Briggs, as the picture shows. Workman was just in front, and he kept his advantage to the end. Once owned by an Irish doctor and sold for £26 on his death, Workman was bought for Sir Alexander Maguire by his trainer Jack Ruttle after the latter had seen him point-to-pointing. The first Irish-trained horse to win the National since Troytown in 1920, he was ridden by Tim Hyde, who was equally at home in the show ring.

176

1940 — Bogskar's year

Steeplechasing, somewhat surprisingly, was allowed to continue in spite of the nation being at war. Uniforms were in evidence and the crowd was smaller. At the water (177) Away (No. 9, Kim Muir) was leading with the winner Bogskar (No. 20) lying fourth, Miss Paget's fancied Kilstar (No. 8) approaching the jump, and Symaethis (No. 14, M. Feakes) behind Bogskar. Dominick's Cross (No. 6, vertical stripes) lay second to Away, and beyond him and half hidden is Lazy Boots, ridden by his naval owner Sir Geoffrey Congreve.

177

MacMoffat was in front two from home in spite of being worried by a loose horse. There was (178) little between the loose horse, Mac Moffat (in centre) and Bogskar as they rode to the last, but again Mac Moffat found one too good for him in the run-in.

Bogskar was owned and trained by Lord Stalbridge at Eastbury in Berkshire. Lord Stalbridge's only son, H. Grosvenor, won the 1927 Cheltenham Gold Cup on his father's Thrown In and then rode him in the National but was tragically killed in an accident in Australia soon afterwards. Bogskar was ridden by Mervyn Jones, a nephew of Ivor Anthony. Jones was killed in the R. A. F. two years later. Kim Muir was another to lose his life, and a race at the National Hunt meeting at Cheltenham commemorates him. His sister married Evan Williams of Royal Mail fame.

This was the last National for six years.

III

The last quarter of a century

179
1946

180
1946

181
1946

182
1946

183
1947

185
1947

184
1947

186
1948

187
1948

188
1948

189
1949

190
1949

191
1949

192
1949

193
1949

194
1949

195
1949

196
1950

197
1950

198
1950

199
1950

201
1950

200
1950

202
1951

203
1951

204
1951

205
1951

206
1951

207
1951

208
1951

209
1952

210
1952

211
1952

212
1952

213
1953

214
1953

215
1954

216
1954

217
1953

218
1954

219
1954

220
1955

221
1955

222
1955

223
1953

224
1954

225
1955

226
1956

229
1956

227
1956

230
1956

228
1956

231
1956

232
1956

233
1956

234
1956

235
1956

236
1957

237
1957

238
1957

239
1958

240
1959

241
1959

242
1959

243
1960

244
1960

245
1960

246
1960

247
1960

248
1960

249
1961

250
1961

251
1961

252
1962

253
1962

254
1962

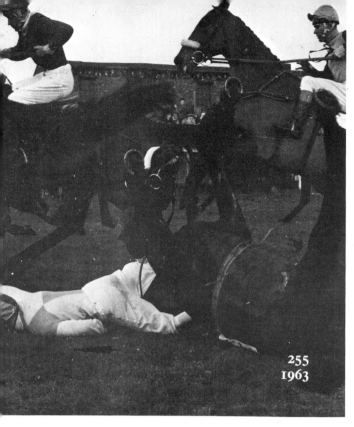

255
1963

256
1963

257
1963

258
1964

259
1964

260
1964

261
1964

262
1964

263
1965

265
1965

264
1965

266
1966

267
1966

268
1966

270
1967

271
1967

272
1967

273
1967

274
1967

275
1968

276
1968

277
1968

278
1969

279
1969

280
1969

281
1969

282
1969

283
1970

284
1970

285
1970

286
1970

287
1970

288
1970

289
1971

291
1971

290
1971

291
1971

293
1972

294
1972

295

298

296

299

297

300

301

304

302

305

303

306

THE FOLLOWING ARE TO BE SEEN ON THE TOUT'S ILLUSTRATION

Harry (Mr. H. A. Brown), Pay Only (Mr. Filmer Sankey), Humphrey (Captain Humphrey de Trafford), Super Man (Mr. W. A. Bankier), Hugo (Lord Londesborough), St. Louis (Lord Queenborough), Golden Myth (Sir George Bullough), Hugh (Lord Molyneux), Knowsley (Lord Derby), Croxteth (Lord Sefton), Taffytus (Mr. J. C. Bulteel), Buck (Captain Buck Barclay), The Handicapper (Mr. E. A. C. Topham), Percy (Mr. Percy Whitaker), Charlie (the Hon. C. J. Coventry), Duke's Walk (Mr. Reid Walker), Emblem (Lord Coventry), Champion (Sir Claude Champion de Crespigny), Hughie (Lord Lonsdale), F. B. (F. B. Rees), L. B. (L. B. Rees), Aubrey (the Hon. Aubrey Hastings), Burghie (Lord Westmorland), The Major (Major Doyle), Jack (Jack Anthony), The Croucher (George Duller), Teddie (Mr. Teddie Gwilt), Shaun Spadah (George Poole), Willie (Lord Wavertree), Patsey V. (Mr. Lemon), The Admiral (Sir H. Meux), Jimmie (J. Hogan), George (Colonel G. Paynter), Tom (Tom Coulthwaite), Sergeant Murphy (George Blackwell), Bob (Bob Gore), Silvo (Sir E. Edgar), Wiggy (Captain M. Weyland), Frank (F. Wootton), Weyhill (Frank Hartigan).

III

BILL CURLING
RUNNING COMMENTARY

The last quarter of a century

1946 — Lovely Cottage's year

The outstanding horse in this field was James V. Rank's Prince Regent, trained by Tom Dreaper in Ireland and ridden by Tim Hyde, who had won the 1939 National on Workman. Bogskar and Mac Moffat who had fought out the 1940 finish, were also in the field.

Prince Regent had 12 st. 5 lb. and was giving 21 lb., or more, to all but two of his opponents in a field of thirty-four, which included three runners in the Golden Miller colours of Miss Dorothy Paget.

Those at Becher's saw (179) the spectacular fall of Largo, ridden by J. Cook and trained at Beverly in Yorkshire by Captain J. C. Storie. Fortunately Cook and Largo were none the worse. **179**

At the water, as shown in the picture (181), the field was led by the riderless **181** Heirdom, followed almost in line by Miss Paget's Housewarmer (No. 16, nearest camera), Prince Regent, the riderless Alacrity (No. 38), Limestone Edward in the colours of Clifford Nicholson, for many years a strong supporter of steeplechasing, and Lord Bicester's Silver Fame (nearest stands). Tulyra, ridden by his owner D. Jackson, was just behind Prince Regent and Schubert (Cliff Bechener) last of the group.

At Valentine's second time round, Tim Hyde on Prince Regent, harried by loose horses, decided to push on ahead of Limestone Edward, who made a bad mistake. Passing the Anchor Bridge turn, Prince Regent was so far in front that he looked unbeatable, but he was very tired as he took the last fence (180) four lengths ahead of Lovely Cottage, the winner, who is **180** seen (182) passing the post clear of Jack Finlay. **182**

Lovely Cottage was admirably ridden by Captain Bobby Petre, then recently demoblised from the Scots Guards. Petre, the leading amateur rider in the 1937-38 season, was winning the National exactly 11 years after his old friend Frank Furlong. The two were at the same small preparatory school, St. Neots, Eversley in Hampshire. The winner had been bought by John Morant of Brockenhurst, Hampshire, four months before the race, and was trained by Tommy Rayson near Winchester.

1947 — Caughoo's year

This race was run in rain and mud and poor visibility. It looked to be an outsider's year beforehand, and so it proved, the winner Caughoo starting at 100–1 followed by little Lough Conn and Kami, ridden by the amateur John Hislop, who 24 years later was to own and breed the 2000 Guineas winner Brigadier Gerard.

184   At Becher's first time round (184), Lough Conn was followed (from left to right) by the grey Kilnaglory, Bricett (vertical stripes), Gormanstown, and Domino (on inside) as can be seen in the picture. Behind Domino was Prince Regent, just landing, and behind Prince Regent, the black cap of Luan Casca, who was to come to grief. Tulyra was jumping the fence behind Kilnaglory whilst Lord Bicester's Silver Fame (Capt. R. Petre, black jacket, light sleeves) is about to jump it. The field of 57, the second biggest in the history of the race, was already well spread out. Lough Conn led at the water and is disputing the lead with Musical Lad at the first fence on the second

183   circuit. The picture (183) shows the battering this fence received first time round from the 57 starters.

At Becher's second time round, Lough Conn is clear but attended by four

185   riderless horses (185). Then came the winner Caughoo (nose band — on left of picture), Bricett (vertical stripes), Musical Lad (nose band — on right) and the grey Kilnaglory. Prince Regent is in the next group. Lough Conn failed to stay, and, in the end, Caughoo won easily.

It was a victory for the Irish family McDowell — J. J. McDowell, a Dublin jeweller, as owner, and his veterinary surgeon brother as trainer, and their mother and sister who debated beforehand whether to try to win the Ulster National for the third time or bring their only racehorse to Aintree. Luckily they chose to come to Aintree! They had bought Caughoo for 50 guineas as an unbroken two-year-old.

The field of 43 can be seen giving the first fence hard punishment in the picture (186). Miss Dorothy Paget's Happy Home (No. 2) is leading, and behind **186** him on the inside is the runner-up, First of the Dandies (No. 25, with nose band). Immediately behind is the winner Sheila's Cottage (No. 22, dark jacket, light sleeves, just landing). Revelry (No. 8, Dan Moore) is just ahead of First of the Dandies, and Lord Bicester's Parthenon (No. 39) is level with Sheila's Cottage. Mrs. John Rogerson's grey War Risk is taking off at the fence, and the last two in the picture are Bricett (No. 11, Tim Moloney) and Rowland Roy (No. 4, Bryan Marshall).

At the water, as can be seen from the picture (187), the blinkered mare **187** Zahia (Eddie Reavey) led from Happy Home (Gene Kelly), the blinkered Le Daim, and Sheila's Cottage (Arthur Thompson). Two fences from home, First of the Dandies, trained by Gerry Wilson and ridden by J. Brogan led, but Zahia appeared to be going much the better. Reavey on Zahia, instead of following Brogan, thought Brogan had mistaken the course, which was not then dolled off, and missed the last fence, which was cruel luck on her owner E. N. Gee and trainer Major Geoffrey Champneys. Gee had had £100 each way on Zahia at 100–1!

With Zahia out of the race, First of the Dandies (nose band), was well clear at the last (188) and led from Sheila's Cottage (black and white halved **188** jacket) and the fading Happy Home (jockey's head just visible). Sheila's Cottage caught First of the Dandies in the last fifty yards, whilst Lord Mildmay's Cromwell came from behind to take third place. As a result of breaking his neck in a fall, Lord Mildmay was apt to be attacked by sudden cramp and had ridden Cromwell almost blind, unable to lift his head, in the last mile.

Sheila's Cottage was trained at Middleham in Yorkshire by Captain Neville Crump, a former cavalry soldier, who was frequently to have a fancied runner in the National in the 25 years after the Second World War. He had bought Sheila's Cottage on New Year's Day from Sir Hervey Bruce for 3,500 guineas for John Proctor of Brigg, Lincolnshire, farmer, trawler-owner and hotelier, who started life as a half-a-crown a week errand boy. Sheila's Cottage was the first mare to win the National since Shannon Lass in 1902. If Reavey had not taken the wrong course, two daughters of the stallion Cottage would almost certainly have been first and second.

Lord Sefton, whose family had owned the site of the Grand National from before the founding of the race, was persuaded by Messrs. Tophams, the lessees, to sell the course to them for under £300,000, but there was a covenant which seemed to guarantee the future of the National: that the land should not be used for 'purposes other than racing or agriculture.'

189 Lord Mildmay and Cromwell started favourite. As usual, there was plenty of incident at Becher's (189), where Southborough (No. 37), in the colours of the Contessa di Santa Elia, led from Ulster Monarch (R. Curran, blaze, three white socks showing), whilst on the extreme left of the picture, Bryan Marshall is well placed on Miss Paget's Happy Home, L. Vick is falling on Magnetic Fin, and D. Ancil on Perfect Night. Monaveen (blinkers, black jacket, white stars, near flag) is seen near the inside just ahead of the half-hidden winner Russian Hero, whilst in the centre, approaching the fence, is Cromwell (prominent blaze).

190 At the water (190), the Crump-trained Wot No Sun (No. 32, G. Kelly) is leading from Russian Hero (nearer the stands) with San Michele (J. Boddy, black jacket, white cap and sash), just behind, and taking the jump is the third Royal Mount (P. Doyle — checked cap). On the right of the picture is Ulster Monarch followed by Cromwell in Lord Mildmay's light blue and white hoops.

191 At Becher's second time round, there were more than a dozen still in the race with a chance as the picture (191) shows, Royal Mount (nose band) leading from Lord Bicester's top weight Roimond (black jacket), Southborough (just landing), Astra (on inside with hooped cap), Russian Hero, just jumping the fence with Cromwell (prominent blaze) and San Michele (white sash on jacket) on either side, Wot No Sun on inside behind Astra, followed **192** by Miss Paget's Happy Home. Earlier in the race, at Becher's, Jimmy Power, **193** a top class Aintree jockey, made a marvellous recovery on Clyduffe and **194** these four pictures show what is possible! (192, 193, 194, 195).

195 Although it looked an open race at Becher's second time round, there was much grief at the Canal Turn and Valentine's, and two fences out Russian Hero passed the tiring Royal Mount, jumped the last well clear, and drew away to win easily. The race was a triumph for Cheshire, for the winner was owned and bred by Mr. Fernie Williamson of Aldford, Cheshire, a tenant farmer of the Duke of Westminster, and trained for him at Malpas in Cheshire by George Owen, the former steeplechase jockey. Williamson had £10 on his horse at 300–1 — a nice bet!

For the first time since King Edward VII's death in 1910, Royal colours were seen in the National field. Monaveen, (No. 18, blinkered) (196), owned in partnership by Queen Elizabeth and Princess Elizabeth, and racing in Princess Elizabeth's colours of scarlet, purple hooped sleeves, and black cap, is nearly down at the first fence but his jockey Tony Grantham makes a good recovery. Level with Monaveen at the first is one of the top weights, Lord Bicester's Roimond (No. 2), and next to him, Freebooter (star on forehead), as Stockman (No. 14) and Inchmore (No. 42) clear the fence.

196

(197) At Becher's first time round, Freebooter (No. 5) is seen leading from Monaveen, who hit it hard, with Roimond (nearest camera No. 2 — Dick Francis), taking it superbly. At the Chair fence (198), Freebooter made his one mistake and had Power clinging to his neck, but he recovered well as Acthon Major (No. 13) and Column (No. 32) led him, with Inchmore (No. 42) just behind.

197
198

Freebooter (No. 5) jumped Becher's superbly the second time round (200) and he came away from the fence lying second to Mr. J. V. Rank's Shagreen with Cloncarrig (Bob Turnell) third and the blinkered Monaveen going for a gap in the fence behind a riderless horse. Shagreen fell soon afterwards and two from home the race lay between Cloncarrig and Freebooter. Cloncarrig fell, leaving (199) Freebooter and Jimmy Power to jump the last on their own. In the unsaddling enclosure, Freebooter's Yorkshire owner, Mrs. L. Brotherton is being congratulated (201) by Bob Wood, the Surrey farrier, bowler hat in hand, watched by the late Lord Grimthorpe (by Freebooter's right ear) and Mr. Clifford Nicholson (by Freebooter's left ear). Bobby Renton, Freebooter's trainer, a clergyman's son, and an outstanding trainer of Aintree horses, is not yet in the picture but Mr. Tony Herbert, formerly clerk of the course at Chester, is in the top left hand corner in bowler hat, surveying the scene.

200
199
201

The King and Queen, Princess Elizabeth, Princess Margaret, and the Duchess of Kent, saw Monaveen lose his chance when he blundered badly at the fence before the Chair. Lord Mildmay on Cromwell, riding in his last National before his tragic death by drowning, had been brought down earlier. It was said of Lord Mildmay, 'There never was a harder rider, a better loser, or a more popular winner'. Freebooter was widely acclaimed then as the best National winner since Golden Miller, an opinion with which I fully agree.

A very high class field, but the starter let them go before a number were ready, and perhaps partly because of this, there was a débâcle at the first fence where eleven of the 36 fell. Two scenes recapture the pile up at the first.

202 The top scene (202) shows a fallen horse bringing down Stockman (No. 24, G. Vergette), whilst Revealed (No. 38), and Cadamstown (No. 18, Jack Dowdeswell) also come to grief. Fred Winter on Glen Fire (No. 27) just avoided trouble at this fence but came down later. Column (No. 35) was another first fence casualty.

203 The bottom scene (203) shows five horses and their jockeys on the ground, and J. Seely, the rider of his own horse Parsonshill (No. 41) about to join the others. R. Carter, the rider of Queen of the Dandies (No. 32) and A. S. O'Brien, the rider of Royal Tan (No. 10) are trying to take avoiding action. Eight of the fallen jockeys, crest-fallen, are little the worse as can be seen in

204 the picture (204) — from left to right P. Fitzgerald, Bryan Marshall, Dick Francis, P. Taaffe, M. O'Dwyer (bending), R. McCreery, J. Dowdeswell and M. Scudamore — some of the best riders of their generation.

By the time the survivors reached the fence before the Chair, there were only half a dozen standing and here Russian Hero was baulked and brought

205 down (205), leaving his jockey McMorrow looking back to see Dog Watch refusing and his rider Tim Brookshaw landing over the fence, still clinging to the reins! Royal Tan is beyond McMorrow.

206 At Becher's second time round (206), the mare Nickel Coin (on right of picture) leads from Gay Heather (R. Curran), who is about to fall, Royal Tan (white face) is on the outside, Derrinstown is to the right of Gay Heather, and fifth and last is Broomfield (dark hoop on sleeves) on the inside. A

207 moment later (207) Gay Heather has fallen and is about to bring down Derrinstown, whilst Royal Tan makes a bad mistake. From then onwards it

208 was a duel between Royal Tan and Nickel Coin. Royal Tan (208) is seen making a ghastly blunder at the last, and this lost him the race. Derrinstown was remounted and finished third. Nickel Coin, well ridden by ex-paratrooper and prisoner-of-war Johnny Bullock, was the second mare to win in three years. Her owner Jeffrey Royle, a Surrey farmer, originally bought her for 50 guineas as a yearling from her Hampshire breeder Richard Corbett at Newmarket in 1943, but subsequently sold her, and his son Frank used part of his war gratuity to buy her back. She was trained near Royle's home by Jack O'Donoghue near Reigate in Surrey, and was the 13th mare to win the National.

Again there were too many casualties at the first fence including Russian Hero. At the third (209) the ex-point-to-pointer Teal, trained at Middleham by Neville Crump and ridden by Arthur Thompson (No.13, white spots on dark jacket) is followed by Freebooter (Bryan Marshall — No. 1), and Brown Jack III, ridden by his sporting Spanish owner the Duque de Albuquerque.

209

Behind Brown Jack III was Whispering Steel who gave R. Morrow a most spectacular fall as he came head first over the fence. Arthur Thompson in contrast to George Stevens, the outstanding National jockey of the 19th century, always believed in forcing tactics, and was in the leading group throughout on Teal.

At Becher's second time round (210) he made a mistake, as a result of which Freebooter took the lead from him with Miss Dorothy Paget's Legal Joy (M. Scudamore) now third, and Crump's second string, Wot No Sun, fourth (nose band, just landing), followed by Derrinstown approaching the fence.

210

Teal led Freebooter by a length going to the Canal Turn, causing Freebooter to take off too soon and come to grief, and the race now lay between Legal Joy, Teal, and the improving Royal Tan. Legal Joy (right) (211) and Teal (spots on jacket) jumped the last together with Royal Tan about six lengths behind, but as in 1951 Royal Tan blundered. In the run-in Teal wore down Legal Joy to win decisively for his ebullient owner Mr. Harry Lane, a Stockton-on-Tees engineering contractor who had brought 600 of his employees to see his horse run and win. Lane, white haired and hatless (212), is seen leading in his horse, followed by Neville Crump, similarly hatless, with two mounted policemen clearing a gangway for them.

211

212

Teal had once been offered for sale by his Irish breeder Mr. G. Carroll of Clonmel for £2. 10s. 0d with no takers! He later sold him with another horse for £35 the pair! He found his way to England and changed hands at Stockton Sales at 32 guineas when known as Bimco, and eventually came into the possession of Mr. Ridley Lamb, a hunting farmer from Thornaby-on-Tees, who won two nomination races at point-to-points and then the United Border Chase at Kelso, whereupon Lane bought him for £2,000. A few months after the National Teal died of a twisted gut.

1953 — Early Mist's year

Two of the men who tried hardest to win the National after the Second World War were Mr. J. V. Rank and Lord Bicester. Both just failed. Early Mist, carrying the Rank colours, fell at the first in 1952. On Rank's death Lord Bicester tried to buy him at the dispersal sale, but was the underbidder at 5,300 guineas to the Irish trainer Vincent O'Brien, acting on behalf of Mr. J. H. Griffin, an Irishman often referred to as 'Mincemeat Joe'. Early Mist wore the Griffin colours in the 1953 National.

213   There were only two fallers at the first this year (213) Quite Naturally (Tim Molony) and Grand Truce (No. 36, D. Leslie). Quite Naturally's fall did not worry Ordnance (No. 19, Scudamore) but Jimmy Power on the favourite Little Yid (black and emerald checks) can be seen taking avoiding action, whilst P. B. Browne on his own horse Knuckleduster (No. 15) avoids the fallen Grand Truce (No. 36).

At Becher's Ordnance (No. 19) jumped it just ahead of Early Mist (No. 7, **214**   Bryan Marshall) — a superb picture (214), showing the modern seat of two crack riders as they go over the most dreaded fence on the course. Before the First World War they would have looked very different!

Ordnance was still in front at the water but fell two fences before Becher's second time round, and Little Yid was very tired when he refused two fences after Valentines.

At the Canal Turn Early Mist led from Miss Paget's top weight Mont **223**   Tremblant (No. 1), as Peter Biegel's picture graphically shows (223), but the weight told on Mont Tremblant, leaving Early Mist, out clear, to take the **217**   last fence on his own with Bryan Marshall a study in concentration (217).

1954 — Royal Tan's year

This was a second successive victory in the race for Bryan Marshall as rider, Vincent O'Brien as trainer, and 'Mincemeat Joe' Griffin as owner. Not since the amateur E. P. Wilson in 1884 and 1885 on Voluptuary and Roquefort had a jockey won the National two years running.

Early Mist had broken down, and Vincent O'Brien was represented by Royal Tan and Churchtown (Toss Taaffe). Royal Tan had not won a race for over two years, and a short time beforehand O'Brien asked Marshall to go over to Ireland to ride Royal Tan in his final gallop over fences with Churchtown. In the gallop Marshall twice tried to give Royal Tan the 'office' when to take off and twice the horse bungled his fence, and Marshall realised he must leave it to Royal Tan. Churchtown appeared to go the better in the gallop, but Marshall had got to know his horse.

In the race Royal Tan (No. 2) was nearly brought down when his stable companion Alberoni fell at the first (215) and struggled to his feet like a stag at bay. Minimax (Capt. Mike MacEwan, No. 32) and Martinique (E. Green-way) also avoid Alberoni. **215**

At Becher's second time round (216) the blinkered Samperion (D. Leslie, No. 17) who finished fifth, is leading from Churchtown (No. 12) and Tudor Line (checked silks, George Slack), who is nearest to the camera in the picture. **216**

At Valentine's Peter Biegel (224) depicts Royal Tan leading from Tudor Line and Churchtown, but between the Anchor Bridge turn and the second last, Churchtown faltered and it transpired that he had broken a blood vessel. Tudor Line in spite of being specially 'bitted' was always inclined to jump to the right. As he tired he jumped to the right more noticeably, led at the second last but was then passed by (218) Royal Tan. At the last, Tudor Line again jumped to the right. This cost him the race, for although he finished gallantly he failed by a neck (nearest camera) in a desperate finish (219) to catch Royal Tan. Two game horses ridden by two top jockeys in Marshall and Slack, trained by two Aintree specialists in Vincent O'Brien and Bobby Renton! It was a pity it could not be a dead heat. **224** **218** **219**

1955 — Quare Times' year

The race was run in deep going after heavy rain, and as a result the stewards decided to cut out the water jump — believed to be the only occasion this has happened since its introduction. Vincent O'Brien had four runners — his two previous winners Royal Tan and Early Mist, Quare Times (No. 12, Pat Taffe) and Oriental Way (F. Winter).

At Becher's first time round as seen in the picture (222) Steel Lock (J. Bullock, No. 28) is seen leading from Moogie (J. Neely, No. 27, nearest camera) with the hooded E. S. B. (T. Cusack, calling a cab) about to fall, and next to him Quare Times (No. 10). Roman Fire (J. Dowdeswell — on right of picture) is brought down by E. S. B. **222**

At Becher's second time round Peter Biegel (225) depicts Sundew (P. J. Doyle) on the inside just leading from Quare Times (with hooped silks) with Steel Lock on his outside and Queen Elizabeth the Queen Mother's M'as-tu-vu (A. Freeman, black cap) just behind Sundew. M'as-tu-vu in fact blundered **225** at this fence. Quare Times sailed over the Canal Turn majestically with Taaffe perfectly balanced (220) and came to the last (221) with Tudor Line for the second year running in second place. Tudor Line again veered to the right, losing his chance, but Quare Times was in fact the faster horse and won easily. It was Vincent O'Brien's third successive victory. The Taaffe family from Co. Dublin had a memorable day — Pat Taaffe rode the winner, whilst the third Carey's Cottage was ridden by his younger brother Toss Taaffe and trained by his father T. J. Taaffe. Quare Times was a brilliant jumper but an unsound horse. For jumping ability Freebooter and Quare Times must rank amongst the best of the National winners since 1946.

1956 — E. S. B.'s year, and Devon Loch

This should have been Devon Loch's year, but the Queen Mother's brilliant jumper came down on the flat with the race at his mercy fifty yards from the post — the saddest moment in the history of the race. What really happened will never be known, but, though this is not the opinion of his rider Dick Francis, the pictures suggest that Devon Loch tried to jump an imaginary fence, slipped, and 'pancaked' to the ground.

The Queen, Queen Elizabeth the Queen Mother, and Princess Margaret (232) were in the paddock beforehand to watch Dick Francis and Arthur Freeman (hidden by Francis in picture), mount Devon Loch, and the Queen Mother's second runner M'as-tu-vu. Lord Sefton is on the right of the Queen. The Queen Mother's racing manager Lord Abergavenny has turned to talk to Peter Cazalet, the Royal trainer. Jim Fairgrieve, travelling head lad to Peter Cazalet for many years, is on the left of the picture.

At the Water (233) Sundew (F. Winter) led from Eagle Lodge (No. 25, A. Oughton), E. S. B. (No. 7, D. V. Dick), and Devon Loch (No. 5, R. Francis). At Becher's (234) Winter is seen falling from Sundew with E. S. B. (No. 7) just behind and Devon Loch (No. 5, nearest camera).

Devon Loch (on right) took the last fence just ahead of E. S. B., (235), but he was going much the better of the two, and quickly drew into a commanding lead. Dick on E. S. B. had ceased to persevere when the unbelievable happened, as the pictures (226-231) show. Devon Loch originally drew up to the guard-rail protecting the water jump with ears pricked. When he 'pancaked', E. S. B. swept by to victory. (226) Devon Loch pricks his ears. (227) Guardrail of water jump comes into the picture. (228) He takes off. (229) As the whole of the guardrail becomes visible, he

pancakes. (230) With the water jump visible, he is almost down. (231)   **230**
E. S. B. passes Devon Loch with Francis on Devon Loch's neck.   **231**

The Queen and the Queen Mother gave no sign of their intense disappoint-ment as they congratulated Mrs. Leonard Carver, owner of E. S. B. Poor Devon Loch broke down the next autumn and never ran in the National again. He had jumped absolutely superbly on that sad March day at Aintree.

1957 — *Sundew's year*

This was a first success in the National for Fred Winter, ex-paratrooper, and champion jockey four times in the 1950s. Sundew had fallen on his two previous appearances in the National, both times on the second circuit when with the leaders. Horses with such credentials have rarely won a National.

At Becher's first time round (238) Sundew (not in picture) was the leader   **238**
closely followed by Colonel W. H. Whitbread's Athenian (D. Ancil, No. 15), Merry Throw (Tim Brookshaw, No. 12), China Clipper II (Major W. D. Gibson — half hidden by Athenian and almost down), Red Menace (L. Whigham), and Mr. E. R. Courage's gallant mare Tiberetta (No. 30, A. Oughton, just behind China Clipper). The hooded Cherry Abbot (G. Underwood — on the right of the picture) is about to fall.

Second time round E. S. B. still led Athenian at Becher's with Athenian going apparently the better of the two, but Athenian fell at the fence after Valentine's, and at the second last (236) Sundew led from a tiring E. S. B.   **236**
(hoop on dark jacket). The Scottish-trained Wyndburgh, Tiberetta, and the grey, Glorious Twelfth, all came from behind to pass E. S. B. and fill the minor placings. China Clipper II (No. 23) had no chance when Major Gibson took a crashing fall at the last fence (237).   **237**

Sundew was the only jumper in the small Warwickshire stable of ex-jockey Frank Hudson. His owner, Mrs. Geoffrey Kohn, had sent him up to the Newmarket December Sales, but fortunately for her he did not reach his reserve of £2,500, and she kept the horse. The National in 1957 was worth nearly £9,000 to the winner! A few months later Sundew broke his back in a minor race and had to be put down.

1958 — *Mr. What's year*

The Irish Hospitals Sweep organisation added £5,000 to the prize money this year, but the race was run in very heavy going and ended in an easy victory for one of the bottom weights Mr. What on whom A. Freeman put up six pounds overweight.

239   At the last Mr. What is well clear (239), but he hits it hard and a less accomplished jockey than Freeman might well have parted company. The gallant mare Tiberetta, Green Drill, and Wyndburgh, followed in procession. Wyndburgh, the favourite, was never at his best in the mud. It was a disappointing National. Mr. What, trained for the race in Ireland by T. Taaffe, never won another steeplechase in over thirty attemps.

1959 — Oxo's year

The 1959 National, run on good going, was much more dramatic than that of 1958. There was little grief until Becher's first time round when S. Mellor took a spectacular fall on The Crofter (No. 36), who had run well in the

240   previous year (240).

At Becher's second time round Wyndburgh, ridden by Tim Brookshaw, leading National Hunt jockey at the time, was disputing the lead with the ex-point-to-pointer Oxo when a stirrup iron broke without warning. Brookshaw slipped the other foot free and henceforth rode without irons.

241   Coming to the last Oxo was clear but hit it hard (241). Michael Scudamore, a farmer's son, who first rode in point-to-points, sat tight, but Brookshaw was in hot pursuit — irons or no irons. He never gave up, as this superb

242   picture of him at the last fence shows (242). In the end Oxo had only one and a half lengths to spare. A lost iron probably made the difference between victory and defeat for this gallant horse, in effect trained for the race by Mrs. Rhona Oliver, who, as Miss Wilkinson, had in turn bred hunted and point-to-pointed Wyndburgh herself before her marriage to Kenneth Oliver, a leading auctioneer from Hawick in Scotland and himself a good amateur rider. Mr. and Mrs. Oliver were to run together a highly successful jumping stable in the years ahead.

Oxo was trained at Royston in Hertfordshire by the former flat race jockey Willie Stephenson, who eight years previously had saddled the Derby winner Arctic Prince. Stephenson thus joined the very small band of trainers to have saddled both a Derby and a National winner — amongst them Dick Dawson with Drogheda (1898 National) and Derbys with Fifinella, Trigo and Blenheim, George Blackwell with Sergeant Murphy (1923) and the Derby with Rock Sand, and Vincent O'Brien, with three Nationals and three Derbys. Stephenson had paid 3,000 guineas for Oxo on behalf of Mr. J. E. Bigg after Oxo had shown great ability as a point-to-pointer.

The B. B. C. televised the Grand National for the first time this year and ever since a vast audience in Britain, Europe, and elsewhere has watched the most spectacular horse race in the world. Mrs. Topham realised quickly that the television rights were very valuable and that television would affect the size of the National crowd.

Those who watched the first televised National saw some highly spectacular falls. At the Chair (243) the Irish trained Belsize II came to grief as the picture shows and his rider P. Shortt is seen coming to earth head first, but seventeen of the field of 26 went into the country on the second circuit, and at Becher's second time round (245) Tea Fiend (No. 30, P. Madden) was leading from Lord Leverhulme's Badanloch (No. 11, S. Mellor) and Merryman II (No. 8, G. Scott). It was at Becher's, however, that the field began to dwindle seriously. Here the 1958 winner Mr. What fell, almost bringing down Green Drill. Seconds later little Team Spirit (No. 9, G. W. Robinson) tried to refuse but cleared the fence and (246) fell on landing almost at the same moment as the hooded Cannobie Lee (No. 13, D. Nicholson) succeeded in refusing, and the hooded Sabaria (No. 19, M. Roberts) landed beside the prostrate Robinson. At the same time the unfortunate Nicholson appeared on the top of Becher's ahead of Cannobie Lee (247)! Finally (248) Nicholson reaches the shelter of the ditch, the prostrate Robinson prays that Arles (No. 24, A. Moule) and Skatealong (No. 25, R. Harrison) will miss him, and the hooded Cannobie Lee looks on as parts of the fence fly through the air!

The stable companions Badanloch and Tea Fiend, both trained by G. Owen, were the two leaders at Valentine's, but then Merryman II, full of stamina, drew away to win unchallenged. It was a third National success for his trainer Neville Crump, and a first victory in the National for a spinster. In the picture (244) Crump has his arm round Merryman's owner Miss Winifred Wallace from Edinburgh, as she leads in the winner (Gerry Scott up) with Mellor on Badanloch following. Miss Wallace hunted and point-to-pointed Merryman herself, after buying him from Lord Linlithgow as a potential hunter, before sending the first Scottish-bred winner of the race to Crump to train.

243

245

246

247
248

244

1961 — Nicolaus Silver's year

For the first time there were two challengers from Soviet Russia — Reljef and Grifel, who were automatic top weights as they had not previously raced in this country and the handicapper had no means of assessing their ability. The Russians had no experience of such fences, and Grifel fell at Becher's first time round and Reljef at Valentine's. It was a sporting project, but not so far repeated. At Becher's Kingstel (No. 33, G. Slack) falls dramatically

249 with Slack's feet still in his stirrups as he nears the ground (249). At the same time Taxidermist (No. 7, John Lawrence) is heading for disaster, thanks to a loose horse, whilst Imposant (No. 11, R. Couetil) is hitting the fence hard, and the head and shoulders of Bill Rees on Scottish Flight II are just visible.

250 At Becher's second time round (250) Derek Ancil on Merryman (No. 3), riding in place of the injured G. Scott, is leading fractionally from the grey, Nicolaus Silver (No. 22, H. Beasley). Nicolaus Silver pecks on landing and is nearly down but recovers. The weight told on Merryman in the final mile and

251 at the last Nicolaus Silver (251) leads from Merryman and O'Malley Point, and then runs on well under pressure. Nicolaus Silver was the first grey to win since The Lamb in 1871. His rider Bobby Beasley was a grandson of Harry Beasley who won on Come Away in 1891, and son of Harry Beasley, junior, who rode on the flat for Atty Persse.

1962 — Kilmore's year

There was an outstanding young horse in this year's field Frenchman's Cove, who started favourite, was going well at the water but was brought down soon afterwards. In this National age and experience prevailed, the 12-year-old Kilmore winning in the mud from the 12-year-old Wyndburgh and the 12-year-old Mr. What — a combined age of 36 years — reminding some of Sergeant Murphy's National of 1923 when 'The Old Sergeant' at the age of 13 won from the then 12-year-old Shaun Spadah and the 11-year-old Conjuror II — likewise a combined age of 36.

252 At the Chair as the picture (252) shows, Taxidermist (No. 6, John Lawrence) is well placed, jumping beautifully, disliking the mud, but ahead of Kilmore, (No. 15, F. Winter), who is on the inside, as was usual with Winter. Superfine (No. 11, Sir William Pigott-Brown), Fortron (R. Langley), on outside, and behind Kilmore D. Bassett on Politics are also in the picture.

253 As they go over Becher's (253), Solfen (No. 3) blunders and loses his chance but Kilmore goes on, followed by Clear Profit (T. Ryan, perpendicular stripes). Winter bided his time on Kilmore, took the lead after the second

254 last and, (254), is leading at the last from Mr. What (No. 8, J. Lehane, on left), the fading Gay Navarree (A. Cameron, in centre of picture) and Wyndburgh

(T. Barnes), behind Kilmore. The gallant Wyndburgh passed Mr. What and Gay Navarree in the run-in but he could make no impression on Kilmore. It was Wyndburgh's sixth and last appearance in the National, second thrice, fourth once and sixth in 1962, and winner of the Grand Sefton. If ever a horse deserved to win the National he did. It was Fred Winter's second success in the National and a first victory for Kilmore's trainer Ryan Price, previously noted as a highly successful trainer of hurdlers.

1963 — Ayala's year

After the 1960 National, at the instigation of Gilbert Cotton, the Inspector of the Course, with the active support of the senior National Hunt Steward at the time, Wing-Commander Peter Vaux, the fences had been sloped on the take-off side to make them easier for horses to measure, and the results of the 1961, 1962, and 1963 Nationals went to show that this modification of the fences was a decided success. Many more horses got round safely.

There was a desperately exciting finish to this National between John Lawrence, amateur rider and racing journalist, now Lord Oaksey, riding Carrickbeg for another leading amateur Gay Kindersley, and Ayala, owned in partnership by his trainer Keith Piggott and hairdresser Mr. 'Teasy Weasy' Raymond, in whose colours he won. There was little grief at the early fences though Good Gracious rolls over legs in air after falling at Becher's, throwing his rider P. Connors clear (255). The favourite, Springbok (No. 6, G. Scott), **255** is seen avoiding Good Gracious, as does Vivant (R. Hamey, hooped cap) just in front of Springbok.

Springbok was leading at the Anchor Bridge turn second time round but weakened, and Lawrence on Carrickbeg went past him and Ayala, and was level with Hawa's Song at the second last. At the last (256) Carrickbeg **256** (No. 19) was nearly a length in front of Ayala (No. 40, P. Buckley) with Hawa's Song (P. Broderick) close behind, half hidden by Ayala. In the first part of the run-in Carrickbeg increased his lead and was clear at the elbow but in the last fifty yards he weakened, changed his legs, and was caught and beaten by Ayala in the last 15 yards (257). Pat Buckley, attached to Neville **257** Crump's stable, was only 19 when he won on Ayala, who broke a small bone in a foot in his next race and never won again.

1964 — Team Spirit's year

Little Team Spirit, fourth to Ayala in 1963, was trying again at the age of 12 for the fifth year in succession.

Over 20 of the field of 33 were still in the race at Becher's second time round, when the cameras caught Michael Scudamore making a most remark-
258 able recovery on one of the joint favourites Time. In the first picture (258) Purple Silk (No. 15, J. Kenneally) is just ahead of Time (No. 33, Scudamore) as his head comes to the ground, whilst Team Spirit (No. 14, G. W. Robinson) is hitting the fence and Springbok (No. 4, G. Scott) is jumping beyond Team Spirit.

A second later Scudamore's predicament on Time looks desperate, Purple
259 Silk is away, and Team Spirit is propping as he lands (259). Another second later Scudamore has gathered up Time, and continues in the race, and Willie
260 Robinson is doing likewise on Team Spirit (260). Time was baulked and brought down four fences from home when still in the race and at the Anchor Bridge fence three from home the pacemaker Peacetown is still
261 leading. At the last (261) Peacetown (No. 17, Roy Edwards) jumps it first, clearly dead tired, followed by Purple Silk (No. 15), Eternal (No. 16, S. Davenport — right of picture), whilst the head of Robinson on Team Spirit is just visible. Peacetown and Eternal weakened in the run-in, and
262 Robinson (262), avoiding the riderless Lizawake, got up in the last few strides to catch Purple Silk. The winner was owned in partnership by three Americans J. K. Goodman, Gamble North, and R. B. Wood — the first American-owned winner since Battleship in 1938. Willie Robinson, a beautiful horseman, was second in the 1958 Derby on Paddy's Point, and the victory of Team Spirit was a great triumph for him.

1965 — Jay Trump's year

In the previous year the sporting world had been shocked to hear that Mrs. Topham intended to sell Aintree to a property company for housing development, but Lord Sefton stepped in at the last moment to save the race. As a result it was thought that 1965 might be the last National, and enormous crowds came to Aintree, and were not disappointed.

263 At Valentine's first time round (263) Freddie (No. 2, P. McCarron), the favourite, is going well, followed by Jay Trump (No. 5, C. T. Smith), Kapeno (No. 13, D. Dick) is between the pair with Leedsy (G. W. Robinson, check cap) half hidden by Kapeno, whilst the former Polish cavalry soldier John Ciechanowski, who became one of the leading amateurs in France, is half hidden by Freddie on his own horse L'Empereur (vertical stripes). More than half the field cleared the water, but (264) at the second fence on the second circuit Leedsy fell when well placed leaving Robinson in peril, as he fully realized! Meanwhile Freddie (No. 2), Rondetto (next to him), the hooded L'Empereur (gold and black stripes) and Kapeno (on outside) gallop on.

Two fences from home Freddie and the American Jay Trump had drawn away from the remainder. At the last (265) Jay Trump (No. 5) is leading Freddie by a length, and there was a tense duel to the post, but Freddie was giving 5 lb. to Jay Trump and this weight advantage turned the scales in favour of the American challenger by three-quarters of a length.

This was the first victory in the National for a horse ridden by an American. Tommy Smith, the winning jockey — Crompton Smith III — a leading amateur in the United States, claimed Jay Trump out of a seller for his owner Mrs. Mary Stephenson from Ohio, and won two Maryland Hunt Cups and nine other races in America before they decided to try to win the National and to send him to Fred Winter to train. It is rarely such ventures have so happy an ending.

1966 — Anglo's year

For the second year running the gallant Freddie, owned, bred and trained in Scotland by Reg Tweedie at his farm in Berwickshire, was beaten by weight in the National. Starting a hot favourite he found the task of conceding 21 lb. to the 50–1 outsider Anglo well beyond him.

Coming to the Chair 42 of the field of 47 were standing — surely a record for the race. Several fell at the Chair and on the second circuit the field steadily dwindled.

At Becher's second time round (266) Forest Prince (No. 6) who had made all the running, was leading Greek Scholar (No. 13) and Kapeno (No. 10, D. Mould), who are both on the ground, though Kapeno's No. 10 number-cloth is visible. The tiring Valouis (No. 31, E. Prendergast) in the first picture in the sequence looks as if he will be all right but he is in fact brought down (267) as Greek Scholar struggles to his feet. As Valouis subsides, Freddie (No. 2) finds a leg, and continues in pursuit of Forest Prince. Highland Wedding (No. 41, O. McNally) is on the outside about to clear the fence in the third picture in the sequence (268). The head of Anglo (curious white

264

265

266

267

268

blaze) is also just visible on the right of this picture. It was the third time in succession that Kapeno had fallen at Becher's. Mrs. Dennis Thompson's hooded Forest Prince, wearing the colours of her grandfather Mr. Frank Bibby, who won with Kirkland and Glenside, was headed by Anglo two out.

269 Forest Prince was still in touch with Anglo (T. Norman) at the last (269), but lost second place in the run-in to Freddie, who could make no impression on Anglo.

As a two-year-old Anglo had unsuccessfully carried the colours of Major-General Sir Randle Feilden, for some time senior steward of the Jockey Club. General Feilden saw no possibilities in Anglo as a chaser and sold him out of a seller to a Huntingdon farmer for only 110 guineas — even pundits on racing are sometimes made to look foolish! Anglo was gaining his 13th victory in winning the National. Anglo, like Jay Trump, was trained by Fred Winter — a wonderful start to a training career in his first two seasons as a trainer.

1967 — Foinavon's year

270 This year there was the most ghastly pile-up (270 and 271) at the fence after
271 Becher's second time round (the 23rd) recalling to the elderly the pile-up at the Canal Turn thirty-nine years before when Easter Hero straddled the fence. A loose horse running down the fence caused the trouble at the 23rd. With one exception all horses still in the race were brought to a halt at this fence, and the one exception was the moderate Foinavon, who jumped the fence comparatively unimpeded, was left out on his own, and eventually won by an official 15 lengths from Honey End, who cleared the fence at the second attempt.

There was no hint of this disaster in the first two-thirds of this race. At
273 Becher's second time round (273) Foinavon (No. 38, J. Buckingham) is at the tail end of his field and nearly down (his light-coloured hood can be seen nearly touching the ground). Buckingham was almost tailed off as he
270 approached the disaster at the next fence (270 and 271). The picture of
271 P. Buckley trying to get his mount Limeking (No. 9) to his feet gives a
272 good idea of the shambles (272) as does Peter Biegel's painting of the scene (Colour Plate XIII), in which he depicts from left to right Game Purston, Different Class, Red Alligator, Kapeno, Honey End, and the winner. Foinavon alone got over the 23rd at the first attempt and jumped the last seven fences
274 on his own in cold blood to win from Honey End (274), who had been badly baulked early on the second circuit and had little chance as he approached

the 23rd. Seventeen horses took the fatal 23rd at the second or third attempt and finished the course. The winner, a cast-off of Anne, Duchess of Westminster, was the most moderate winner of the National of the century. His tote starting price of 444–1 reflected his chance. Neither his owner Mr. Cyril Watkins nor his trainer J. Kempton was at Aintree. Watkins watched the race on television, Kempton was at Worcester where he rode the winner of a novice's hurdle, trained by himself at Compton in Berkshire. Foinavon was saddled by the trainer's father.

1968 — Red Alligator's year

The American grandfather Tim Durant at the age of 68, riding in his third Grand National, fell at Becher's second time round, 'calling a cab', after making the mistake of going for a gap in the fence (275). He then gallantly remounted and completed the course on Highlandie to win a £500 bet, which he gave to a fund for injured jockeys. This retired New York stockbroker deserved the cheer which greeted him.

275

The race went to Red Alligator, a half brother of the 1966 winner Anglo (276), who is seen finishing clear of the rest. They were both bred by William Kennedy, a farmer near Downpatrick in Northern Ireland out of a mare called Miss Alligator, bought for only 70 guineas at the Dublin Sales of 1952 although she finished sixth in the Oaks of 1949 to Musidora.

276

Kennedy got only kudos, no financial gain for the two National winners Miss Alligator bred him, for he sold Anglo for £140 as a foal and Red Alligator for 360 guineas as a yearling. The only other mare to produce two winners of the National is Miss Batty, dam of Lord Coventry's 1863 and 1864 winners Emblem and Emblematic, who were full sisters.

Red Alligator won as easily as his half brother Anglo. The worst moment for his 19-year-old jockey Brian Fletcher was when Red Alligator (No. 22) had to jump (277) the prostrate Polaris Missile (N. Thorne) at Becher's first time round. At the time, he was following the hooded Great Lark (No. 15, T. Carberry) and the French-bred Quitte ou Double (No. 10, J. Ciechanowski). Red Alligator carried the colours of Mr. John Manners, a butcher from County Durham and a neighbour of the horse's trainer Denys Smith from Bishop's Auckland. The runner-up Moidore's Token was trained by Oliver in Scotland.

277

Owned in partnership by an American steeplechasing enthusiast Mr. T. H. McKoy, junior, and a Canadian Mr. C. F. W. Burns Highland Wedding won the National at the third attempt. Trained by Toby Balding in Hampshire, Highland Wedding ran in the Burns colours of white with a green maple leaf in 1966 and 1968, ridden by the stable jockey O. McNally. Owing to injury, McNally could not ride in 1969 and E. P. Harty, who represented Ireland in the Olympic Games of 1960, took McNally's place and won in the McKoy colours.

278
Two other Americans were not so fortunate. George Sloan, riding his own horse the grey Peccard is seen (278) ending up at Becher's first time round in an unpleasant position beneath the legs of his horse! His brother Paul rode Terossian, who refused soon afterwards at the fence after Valentines.

At Becher's first time round Michael Lyne captures the scene brilliantly (Colour Plate XIV) as Rondetto (No. 12, light and dark blue quarters) clears the fence. The leader is Castle Falls (grey, red sleeves), followed by Flosuebarb (brown and white hooped sleeves), The Fossa on inside (red jacket), Kellsboro' Wood (No. 6, yellow jacket) and Furore II (claret jacket).

279
At Becher's second time round another grey Tam Kiss (No. 25) and his owner-rider Jeremy Hindley part company in spectacular fashion, as the picture (279) shows.

280
At this fence (280) there was little to choose between Kilburn (No. 7, T. Carberry, nearest camera), Steel Bridge (No. 33, R. Pitman), Highland Wedding (No. 14, Harty on outside) and The Fossa (No. 20, Captain **281** A. Parker-Bowles, just behind Steel Bridge). Seconds later (281) Carberry and Kilburn have grounded, and Steel Bridge (No. 33) goes on from Highland Wedding (No. 14).

282
At the last (282) Harty on Highland Wedding is looking over his shoulder for possible danger as Steel Bridge in the centre (star on jacket) and old Rondetto follow him. Highland Wedding went on to win comfortably. Toby Balding's uncle Barnie Balding was fourth in the 1927 National on Drinmond, his father Gerald, a noted polo player, rode at Liverpool and his younger brother Ian saddled Mill Reef to win the 1971 Derby.

1970 — Gay Trip's year

This went to the top weight Gay Trip, ridden by Pat Taaffe in his final National, and trained by Fred Rimell at Kinnersley in Worcestershire where

Emblem and Emblematic, Forbra, E. S. B. and Nicolaus Silver were also trained.

Michael Lyne in his picture of the field jumping the third fence with the embankment behind (Colour Plate XV) vividly conveys the strong gallop which the leaders are setting — No Justice (No. 24) leading, Vulture (No. 32) the eventual runner-up, lying second and partly hiding Gay Trip the winner, (red and white hooped sleeves). French Excuse (No. 11) and The Otter (yellow cap) follow Gay Trip, and Assad (No. 16) leads the grey All Glory and Miss Hunter (green and white check).

At the Chair (283) the leaders included Assad (J. Gifford), The Otter (No. 13, T. Jones), No Justice (J. Guest) and almost level behind, taking the fence together are Vulture (S. Barker), Specify (J. Cook, spotted cap, half hidden by No Justice), and the winner Gay Trip (No. 2). **283**

At the water (284) Gifford, riding in his last National, led from No Justice, The Otter, Specify (about to land), Dozo (E. P. Harty), who was fourth, Ginger Nut (No. 22), who was fifth, and the winner Gay Trip, who is on the inside. **284**

At Becher's (285) Assad blundered, Gifford recovered, but T. Jones on The Otter was not so lucky, and as he fell seconds later (286) he brought down Specify (No. 5), who was going well at the time. Cook was to have better luck a year later. Taaffe rode a waiting race on the top weight Gay Trip, who jumped Becher's beautifully (287) and is out clear as he jumps the last (288). **285** **286** **287** **288**

1971 — Specify's year

This was one of the most exciting Nationals on record with five horses with winning chances in the run-in from the last fence. There were rumours before the race that Mrs. Topham was about to retire and the National was still in jeopardy. Such a magnificent race brought heart to those who feel it is high priority that its future should be secure.

Spectators at Becher's (289) had a fine view as Gay Buccaneer (No. 29) led a dozen horses almost in line including the hooded Lord Jim (No. 10, S. Mellor), Black Secret (No. 4, J. Dreaper), and the hooded Kellsboro' Wood (No. 33, A. Turnell). **289**

At the water (290) Flosuebarb (No. 28, J. Guest) is leading from the hooded Beau Bob (No. 18, R. Dennard), Sandy Sprite (No. 19, R. Barry), and Astbury (No. 22, J. Bourke, light-checked cap, nearest stands), with a **290** closely bunched group behind including Smooth Dealer (No. 20, A. Moore) and Black Secret immediately behind (black, white spots).

Beau Bob, leading at Becher's second time round and going well, unfortunately unseated his rider, and coming to the last, there were six still in it, Sandy Sprite leading from Black Secret, Bowgeeno, Astbury, Specify and Two Springs.

Sandy Sprite, who had broken down, weakened in the run-in and at the elbow the race lay between Black Secret, Bowgeeno, Astbury and Specify, who was coming from behind to challenge.

Specify (J. Cook) rather luckily found a gap on the inside and, finishing on the rails, won a thrilling race (291) by a neck from Black Secret. Astbury, the third, finished in the middle of the course and is not in the picture. Bowgeeno (white armlets) was fourth and Sandy Sprite (hooped cap) fifth.

291

1972 — Well To Do's year.

Just over half the field of 42 were still in the race as Fair Vulgan led at the Water on a rain-swept afternoon. The topweight and favourite L'Escargot had been brought down at the third, but the two previous winners in the field, Gay Trip and Specify, were both going well, as were Black Secret and Astbury, both close behind Specify in 1971.

Fair Vulgan was hampered by a loose horse as he jumped the water, and as they went away from the stands for the second time the field dwindled steadily. Just A Gamble, in the Tyrwhitt-Drake colours, fell at the first fence on the second circuit, interfering with The Otter and Vichysoise, and The Otter, after meeting with more interference at the next fence, made only a half-hearted attempt to jump the first open ditch, shooting his rider 'Buck' Jones over his head on to the top of the fence and bringing down Nephin Beg. In Plate 292, The Otter has extricated himself from the ditch and gone back towards the stands, and Nephin Beg is being led from the scene by his rider, P. Morris, to the disappointment of his trainer Lord Mostyn, whose great-great-grandfather owned Seventy Four, second to Lottery in the 1839 Grand National and again second three years later.

292

As they came to Becher's second time round (293) Black Secret (No. 3) led from Well To Do (No. 20) on the inside and right of the picture, the Irish trained General Symons (No. 25), Specify (spots on white cap), and Gay Trip (No. 2), with the white-faced Astbury (No. 27) just behind Gay Trip. These six had drawn clear, and the race lay between them.

293

During the first circuit of the course Terry Biddlecombe on Gay Trip had stuck fairly close to the rails, but on the second circuit he deliberately took a middle course, seeking faster ground, whilst Graham Thorner on Well To Do kept to the inside. As they crossed the Meling Road with two to jump, there was little to chose between the Irish-trained pair, Black Secret and General Symons, Gay Trip and Well To Do with Astbury now fifth. Gay Trip at this moment looked to be under pressure and beaten. There was little between the four at the second last but at the last (294) Well To Do on the right of the picture and General Symons jumped the fence together, with Black Secret (half hidden by Well To Do) and Gay Trip (half hidden by General Symons) just behind.

In the long run-in it was soon seen that Well To Do had the measure of the Irish pair but not yet of the ex-champion jockey Terry Biddlecombe and Gay Trip. At the elbow there was little to choose between the two racing wide of each other, but in spite of the drive and strength of Biddlecombe the weight told near the end and Well To Do, strongly ridden, too, by the reigning champion jockey Graham Thorner forged ahead again to win by two lengths. Gay Trip on sodden ground was attempting to give Well To Do twenty-two pounds. The honours of the race, if not the victory, surely went to this gallant little horse.

Clive Graham tells how Well To Do came to be bred—a mixture of French, English and Irish blood. It remains only to add that Well To Do's sire Phebus was bought in France by Mr. Tony Samuel, chairman of Barrie & Jenkins, the publishers of this book. Phebus showed himself a stayer of merit for Mr. Samuel and then went to stud in Cheshire.

CLIVE GRAHAM WRITES:

This victory by Well To Do did not lack the bitter-sweet note which has to be written into so many Grand National stories. Until her regrettably early death from cancer in June '71, Heather Sumner shared with her husband, John, member of a famous Oxfordshire sporting family, a close association with hunting and racing. On the advice of her trainer, Tim Forster, she bought this unbroken three-year-old gelding for £750 in 1966. Slow to reach maturity, Well To Do began to strike winning form in the 1970-71 seasons, gaining four successes in a row, but due to his owner's illness, the horse's racing engagements were cancelled after March and Mrs. Sumner bequeathed him to Tim in her will...

The idea of entering this gift-horse for the Grand National caused all sorts of heart-searching in the mind of the legatee. It was only on the insistence of Mr. John Sumner that the message was sent to Weatherby's half-an-hour before the closing of nominations. Later that day, Well To Do revealed his potential in the four-mile Fred Withington 'Chase at Cheltenham, with Black Secret and Astbury behind him.

Recurring doubts about the wisdom or rightness of running the horse for the Grand National were certainly not shared by the horse's breeder, Mrs. Hugh Lloyd-Thomas, widow of the pre-war amateur-rider and equerry to the Prince of Wales, whose horse, Royal Mail won the '37 National and who met his death in a riding fall the following year.

'This horse is bred for the job', she insisted. 'Is he not related to three of the greatest Grand National winners of all time—Gregalach, Reynoldstown and Royal Mail—and one of the unluckiest losers, Easter Hero?'

The mating with the French-bred Phebus, was purely fortuitous. The previous year, Lord Harlech was appointed H. M. Ambassador in Washington, and before leaving to take up the post, together with his wife, second daughter of Mrs. Lloyd-Thomas, the problem arose of the care of their five children, and the upkeep of their home near Oswestry in Shropshire. The children's grandmother gladly consented to make the move, on condition that she should be accompanied by her livestock. These included the pony-sized half-bred mare Puzzlement Princess (a daughter of the thoroughbred sire, Gregalach's Nephew), whose dam traces to a close relative of Royal Mail. Mrs. Lloyd-Thomas had set her ambition on breeding a Grand National winner, and seeing two horses sired by Phebus win at a local Shropshire point-to-point, and admiring their size and substance, she promptly booked a nomination for her little unbroken mare.

By the time he was weaned, Well To Do was nearly as big as his mother, and continued to thrive when sent back to Berkshire. He then spent another formative year roaming the paddock at the Sumner place, which had formerly been occupied by Reynoldstown's owner-trainer, Major Noel Furlong.

As the crowds, only a fraction of the vast throngs of twenty and more years ago, wended their way homewards, perhaps one question still stabbed their minds:

'Was this indeed the last-ever Grand National?'

At this time of writing, despite the promise of continued support by BP, the outcome seems almost as hard to predict as that of the annual race itself.

Grand National Personalities

(295)   Gilbert Cotton

This picture of Gilbert Cotton, Inspector of the Grand National Course for fifty years from 1920-1970, was taken in the garden of his home in Cheshire two months before he died of heart failure in 1971 at the age of 91.

295

(296)   Jim Bidwell-Topham, Gilbert Cotton, and Brigadier Tony Teacher

Jim Bidwell-Topham (on left), the present clerk of the Course at Aintree and nephew of Mrs. Mirabel Topham, is inspecting Becher's in 1963 before the National meeting with Gilbert Cotton (centre), and Brigadier Tony Teacher, who later became Senior National Hunt Inspector of Courses. Jim Bidwell-Topham became Clerk of the Course in 1956.

296

(297)   Sir Kenneth Gibson with the Queen Mother

Sir Kenneth Gibson, who followed Sir John Crocker Bulteel as clerk of the Course at Aintree, after an interval of one year, is seen with Queen Elizabeth the Queen Mother. Sir Kenneth rode Major H. R. Cayzer's Liffey Bank in the 1923 National. He was also a brilliant cricketer in his youth.

297

(298)   Sir John Crocker Bulteel

Sir John Crocker Bulteel, clerk of the Course at Aintree from 1936 to 1946, was son of Mr. J. G. Bulteel, the owner of the great Manifesto.

298

(299)   Mrs. Mirabel Topham and Mr. G. Malenkov

Mrs. Mirabel Topham is the remarkable managing director of Tophams, who have managed the Course for over a century. When this picture was

299

taken in 1956, Mrs. Topham was entertaining Mr. G. Malenkov, then Soviet Minister for Power Stations, in the year in which Devon Loch fell fifty yards from the post.

300 (300) Mr. Alec Marsh (left) and Captain Peter Herbert
Mr. Alec Marsh, Grand National starter for nearly twenty years from 1953 onwards, and a leading amateur rider before the Second World War, is seen returning to the paddock on the back of another horse after his mount Deslys had fallen at Becher's Brook in the 1939 National. He is with another leading amateur Captain Peter Herbert (right).

National Hunt trainers of note at Aintree

301 (301) Tom Coulthwaite (left) with Irish breeder T. K. Laidlaw
Tom Coulthwaite, who trained his third and last Grand National winner Grakle in 1931, is standing with Mr. T. K. Laidlaw, the early owner of Grakle, outside the corrugated iron hut on top of Cannock Chase between Hednesford and Rugeley which was built to accommodate the Duke of Windsor, when as Prince of Wales, he used to ride out and school his point-to-pointers. The Prince of Wales had a bed in this hut in which he could sleep at night before early morning work. Towards the end of his career, Coulthwaite lived partly in this hut and was based here when Grakle won the National. Mr. C. R. Taylor, the owner of Grakle, found him answering letters of congratulations in this hut, and giving his address as 'The Castle, Flaxley Green, near Rugeley'! Coulthwaite, who never lost his sense of humour, whatever his difficulties, was a most successful jumping trainer.

302 (302) Vincent O'Brien
Irishman Vincent O'Brien, an outstanding trainer, brought off a hat-trick with Early Mist, Royal Tan and Quare Times in the Nationals of 1953, 1954 and 1955. He now concentrates on flat racing, at which he is equally successful, and has three Derby winners to his credit.

303 (303) Neville Crump
Neville Crump, who trains at Middleham in Yorkshire, has had a fancied runner in the National in most years since 1946 and has saddled the winners Sheila's Cottage (1948), Teal (1952), and Merryman II (1960).

304 (304) Bobby Renton with the Grand National runner-up Tudor Line
Yorkshireman Bobby Renton trained one of the outstanding post-war Grand
National winners in Freebooter, and was probably unlucky not to win it a
second time with Tudor Line, who was runner-up both in 1954 and 1955.
Renton in his time saddled the winners of all the principal steeplechases at
Aintree.

305 (305) Willie Stephenson
Willie Stephenson is one of the few to train the winners of a Derby and a
Grand National. His National winner was Oxo in 1959. He was formerly a
competent flat race jockey, and as a trainer won the 1951 Derby with Arctic
Prince.

306 (306) Fred Rimell
Fred Rimell has won three Nationals with E. S. B. (1956), Nicolaus Silver
(1961) and Gay Trip (1970). Although leading National Hunt rider three
times, he had no luck in the race in his riding days. He trains at Kinnersley in
Worcestershire.

307 (307) Grand National Personalities by The Tout (P. R. G. Buchanan)
— 'A Grand National Nightmare — over and in Becher's.'

Racing Record 1839 to 1972

1837 THE DUKE (Mr. H. Potts) 1
THE DISO WNED
(Mr. A. McDonough) 2
4 ran. Time not taken.
N.B. *Only 2 horses finished.*

1838 SIR WILIAM
(Mr. A. McDonough) 1
SCAMP (Mr. Clarendon) 2
THE DUKE
(Captain M. Becher) 3
10 ran. Time not taken.

1839 LOTTERY (Jem Mason) 1
SEVENTY FOUR (T. Olliver) 2
PAULINA (Mr. Martin) 3
TRUE BLUE (Mr. Barker) 4
17 ran. Time: 14 min. 53 sec.

1840 JERRY (Mr. B. Bretherton) 1
ARTHUR
(Mr. A. McDonough) 2
VALENTINE (Mr. Power) 3
THE SEA
(Marquis of Waterford) 4
12 ran. Time: 12 min. 30 sec.

1841 CHARITY (Mr. A. Powell) 1
CIGAR (Mr. A. McDonough) 2
PETER SIMPLE (Walker) 3
REVEALER (Mr. Barker) 4
11 ran. Time: 13 min. 25 sec.

1842 GAYLAD (T. Olliver) 1
SEVENTY FOUR (Powell)
(Mr. A. Powell) 2
PETER SIMPLE (Mr. Hunter) 3
THE RETURNED
(Mr. W. Hope-Johnstone) 4
15 ran. Time: 13 min. 30 sec.

1843 VANGUARD (T. Olliver) 1
NIMROD (Scott) 2
DRAGSMAN (Crickmere) 3
CLAUDE DUVAL (Tomblin) 4
16 ran. Time: not taken.

1844 DISCOUNT (Crickmere) 1
THE RETURNED (Scott) 2
TOM TUG (Rackley) 3
CAESAR (Barker) 4
15 ran. Time: a little less than
14 min.

1845 CURE-ALL (Mr. W. J. Loft) 1
PETER SIMPLE (Frisby) 2
THE EXQUISITE (Byrne) 3
TOM TUG (Crickmere) 4
15 ran. Time: 10 min. 47 sec.

1846 PIONEER (Taylor) 1
CULVERTHORPE (Rackley) 2
SWITCHER (Wynne) 3
FIREFLY (L. Byrne) 4
22 ran. Time: 10 min. 46 sec.

1847 MATTHEW (D. Wynne) 1
ST. LEGER (T. Olliver) 2
JERRY (Bradley) 3
PIONEER
(Capt. W. Peel) 4
26 ran.   Time: 10 min. 39 sec.

1848 CHANDLER
(Capt. J. L. Little) 1
THE CURATE (T. Olliver) 2
BRITISH YEOMAN
(Mr. Bevill) 3
STANDARD GUARD (Taylor) 4
29 ran.   Time: 11 min. 21 sec.

1849 PETER SIMPLE
(Mr. T. Cunningham) 1
THE KNIGHT OF GWYNNE
(Capt. d'Arcy) 2
PRINCE GEORGE
(T. Olliver) 3
ALFRED (Wynne) 4
24 ran.   Time: 10 min. 56 sec.

1850 ABD EL KADER
(C. Green) 1
THE KNIGHT OF GWYNNE
(Wynne) 2
SIR JOHN (J. Ryan) 3
TIPPERARY BOY
(S. Darling) 4
32 ran.   Time: 9 min. 57½ sec.

1851 ABD EL KADER
(T. Abbot) 1
MARIA DAY (J. Frisby) 2
SIR JOHN (J. Ryan) 3
HALF-AND-HALF
(R. Sly, jr.) (late Small-Beer) 4
21 ran.   Time: 9 min. 59 sec.

1852 MISS MOWBRAY
(Mr. A. Goodman) 1
MAURICE DALEY
(C. Boyce) (late Flycatcher) 2
SIR PETER LAURIE
(W. Holman) 3
CHIEFTAIN
(Harrison)
24 ran.   Time: 9 min. 58½ sec.

1853 PETER SIMPLE (T. Olliver) 1
MISS MOWBRAY
(Mr. Gordon) 2
OSCAR (Mr. A. Goodman) 3
SIR PETER LAURIE
(W. Holman) 4
21 ran.   Time: 10 min. 37½ sec.

1854 BOURTON (Tasker) 1
SPRING (W. Archer) 2
CRABBS (D. Wynne) 3
MALEY (J. Thrift) 4
20 ran.   Time: 9 min. 59 sec.

1855 WANDERER (J. Hanlon) 1
FREETRADER (D. Meaney) 2
MAURICE DALEY
(R. James) 3
JANUS (H. Lamplugh) 4
20 ran.   Time: 10 min. 25 sec.

1856 FREETRADER (G. Stevens) 1
MINERVA (R. Sly, Jr.) 2
MINOS (R. James) 3
HOPELESS STAR
(W. White) 4
21 ran.   Time: 10 min. 9½ sec.

1857 EMIGRANT (C. Boyce) 1
WEATHERCOCK (C. Green) 2
TREACHERY (Poole) 3
WESTMINSTER (Palmer) 4
28 ran.   Time: 10 min. 6 sec.

1858 LITTLE CHARLEY
(W. Archer) 1
WEATHERCOCK
(Mr. G. Ede) 2
XANTHUS (F. Balchin) 3
MORGAN RATTLER
(T. Burrowes) 4
16 ran.   Time: 11 min. 5 sec.

1859 HALF CASTE (C. Green) 1
JEAN DU QUESNE
(H. Lamplugh) 2
THE HUNTSMAN
(B. Land, Jr.) 3
MIDGE (D. Meaney) 4
20 ran.   Time: 10 min. 2 sec.

1860 ANATIS
     (Mr. T. F. Pickernell)   1
     THE HUNTSMAN
     (Capt. Townley)   2
     XANTHUS (F. Balchin)   3
     MARIA AGNES (G. Stevens)   4
     19 ran.   Time: not taken.

1861 JEALOUSY (J. Kendall)   1
     THE DANE (W. White)   2
     OLD BEN ROE
     (G. Waddington)   3
     BRIDEGROOM
     (Mr. FitzAdam)   4
     24 ran.   Time: 10 min. 14 sec.

1862 THE HUNTSMAN
     (H. Lamplugh)   1
     BRIDEGROOM (B. Land, Jr.)   2
     ROMEO (Mr. C. Bennett)   3
     XANTHUS (R. Sherrard)   4
     13 ran.   Time: 9 min. 30 sec.

1863 EMBLEM (G. Stevens)   1
     ARBURY (Mr. A. Goodman)   2
     YALLER GAL (Mr. Dixon)   3
     FOSCO (Mr. G. Holman)   4
     16 ran.   Time: 11 min. 20 sec.

1864 EMBLEMATIC (G. Stevens)   1
     ARBURY (B. Land)   2
     CHESTER (W. White)   3
     THOMASTOWN
     (J. Murphy)   4
     25 ran.   Time: 11 min. 50 sec.

1865 ALCIBIADE
     (Capt. H. Coventry)   1
     HALL COURT
     (Capt. A. C. Tempest)   2
     EMBLEMATIC (G. Stevens)   3
     MISTAKE (Jarvis)   4
     23 ran.   Time: 11 min. 16 sec.

1866 SALAMANDER
     (Mr. A. Goodman)   1
     CORTOLVIN (J. Page)   2
     CREOLE (G. Waddington)   3
     LIGHTHEART (E. Jones)   4
     30 ran.   Time: 11 min. 5 sec.

1867 CORTOLVIN (J. Page)   1
     FAN (Thorpe)   2
     SHANGARRY
     (Mr. T. F. Pickernell)   3
     GLOBULE (G. Holman)   4
     23 ran.   Time: 10 min. 42 sec.

1868 THE LAMB (Mr. G. Ede)   1
     PEARL DIVER (Tomlinson)   2
     ALCIBIADE (Col. G. W. Knox)   3
     CAPTAIN CROSSTREE
     (W. Reeves)   4
     21 ran.   Time not taken

1869 THE COLONEL (G. Stevens)   1
     HALL COURT
     (Capt. A. C. Tempest)   2
     GARDENER (Ryan)   3
     ALCIBIADE (Col. G. W. Knox)   4
     22 ran.   Time: 11 min.

1870 THE COLONEL (G. Stevens)   1
     THE DOCTOR (G. Holman)   2
     PRIMROSE
     (Mr. W. R. Brockton)   3
     SURVEY (R. I'Anson)   4
     23 ran.   Time: 10 min. 10 sec.

1871 THE LAMB
     (Mr. T. F. Pickernell)   1
     DESPATCH (G. Waddington)   2
     SCARRINGTON (Cranshaw)   3
     THE COLONEL (G. Stevens)   4
     25 ran.   Time: 9 min. 35¾ sec.

1872 CASSE TETE (J. Page)   1
     SCARRINGTON (R. I'Anson)   2
     DESPATCH (G. Waddington)   3
     THE LAMB
     (Mr. T. F. Pickernell)   4
     25 ran.   Time: 10 min. 14½ sec.

1873 DISTURBANCE
     (Mr. J. M. Richardson)   1
     RHYSHWORTH (Boxall)   2
     COLUMBINE (Harding)   3
     MASTER MOWBRAY
     (G. Holman)   4
     28 ran.   Time: Watch stopped
     by accident.

1874 REUGNY
(Mr. J. M. Richardson) 1
CHIMNEY SWEEP (J. Jones) 2
MERLIN (J. Adams) 3
DEFENCE (Earl of Minto) 4
22 ran.   Time: 10 min. 4 sec.

1875 PATHFINDER
(Mr. T. F. Pickernell) 1
DAINTY (Mr. Hathaway) 2
LA VEINE (J. Page) 3
JACKAL (R. Marsh) 4
19 ran.   Time: 10 min. 22 sec.

1876 REGAL (J. Cannon) 1
CONGRESS
(Mr. E. P. Wilson) 2
SHIFNAL (R. I'Anson) 3
CHIMNEY SWEEP (J. Jones) 4
19 ran.   Time: 11 min. 14 sec.

1877 AUSTERLITZ
(Mr. F. G. Hobson) 1
CONGRESS (J. Cannon) 2
THE LIBERATOR
(Mr. T. F. Pickernell) 3
CHIMNEY SWEEP (J. Jones) 4
16 ran.   Time: 10 min. 10 sec.

1878 SHIFNAL (J. Jones) 1
MARTHA (Mr. T. Beasley) 2
PRIDE OF KILDARE
(Mr. J. Moore) 3
JACKAL (J. Jewitt) 4
12 ran.   Time: 10 min. 23 sec.

1879 THE LIBERATOR
(Mr. G. Moore) 1
JACKAL (J. Jones) 2
MARTHA (Mr. T. Beasley) 3
WILD MONARCH (Andrews)
18 ran.   Time: 10 min. 12 sec.

1880 EMPRESS (Mr. T. Beasley) 1
THE LIBERATOR
(Mr. G. Moore) 2
DOWNPATRICK (Gavin) 3
JUPITER TONANS
(Mr. J. F. Lee-Barber) 4
14 ran.   Time: 10 min. 20 sec.

1881 WOODBROOK
(Mr. T. Beasley) 1
REGAL (J. Jewitt) 2
THORNFIELD (R. Marsh) 3
NEW GLASGOW
(Capt. Smith) 4
13 ran.   Time: 11 min. 50 sec.

1882 SEAMAN (Lord Manners) 1
CYRUS (Mr. T. Beasley) 2
ZOEDONE (Capt. Smith) 3
THE LIBERATOR (J. Adams) 4
12 ran.   Time: 10 min. 42 sec.

1883 ZOEDONE
(Count C. Kinsky) 1
BLACK PRINCE (Canavan) 2
DOWNPATRICK
(Mr. T. Widger) 3
ZITELLA (Mr. T. Beasley) 4
10 ran.   Time: 11 min. 39 sec.

1884 VOLUPTUARY
(Mr. E. P. Wilson) 1
FRIGATE (Mr. H. Beasley) 2
ROQUEFORT
(Capt. Fisher-Childe) 3
ZOEDONE
(Count C. Kinsky) 4
15 ran.   Time: 10 min. 5 sec.

1885 ROQUEFORT
(Mr. E. P. Wilson) 1
FRIGATE (Mr. H. Beasley) 2
BLACK PRINCE (T. Skelton) 3
REDPATH (Mr. A. Coventry) 4
19 ran.   Time: 10 min. 10 sec.

1886 OLD JOE (T. Skelton) 1
TOO GOOD (Mr. H. Beasley) 2
GAMECOCK (W. E. Stephens) 3
MAGPIE (Mr. W. Woodland) 4
23 ran.   Time: 10 min. 14$\frac{3}{5}$ sec.

1887 GAMECOCK (W. Daniells) 1
SAVOYARD (T. Skelton) 2
JOHNNY LONGTAIL
(J. Childs) 3
CHANCELLOR
(Mr. W. Moore) 4
16 ran.   Time: 10 min. 10$\frac{1}{5}$ sec.

1888 PLAYFAIR (G. Mawson) 1
FRIGATE (Mr. W. Beasley) 2
BALLOT BOX
  (W. Nightingall) 3
RINGLET (T. Skelton) 4
20 ran.   Time: 10 min. 12 sec.

1889 FRIGATE (Mr. T. Beasley) 1
WHY NOT
  (Mr. C. J. Cunningham) 2
M. P. (A. Nightingall) 3
BELLONA
  (Mr. C. W. Waller) 3
20 ran.   Time: 10 min. $1\frac{1}{5}$ sec.

1890 ILEX (A. Nightingall) 1
PAU (Halsey) 2
M. P. (Mr. W. H. Moore) 3
BRUNSWICK (G. Mawson) 4
16 ran.   Time: 10 min. $41\frac{4}{5}$ sec.

1891 COME AWAY
  (Mr. H. Beasley) 1
CLOISTER (Capt. E. R. Owen) 2
ILEX (A. Nightingall) 3
ROQUEFORT (Guy) 4
21 ran.   Time: 9 min. 58 sec.

1892 FATHER O'FLYNN
  (Capt. E. R. Owen) 1
CLOISTER (Mr. J. C. Dormer) 2
ILEX (A. Nightingall) 3
ARDCARN (T. Kavanagh) 4
25 ran.   Time: 9 min. $48\frac{1}{5}$ sec.

1893 CLOISTER (W. Dollery) 1
AESOP (H. Barker) 2
WHY NOT (A. Nightingall) 3
TIT FOR TAT
  (G. Williamson) 4
15 ran.   Time: 9 min. $32\frac{2}{5}$ sec.
  (Record)

1894 WHY NOT (A. Nightingall) 1
LADY ELLEN II
  (T. Kavanagh) 2
WILD MAN FROM
  BORNEO (Mr. Jos. Widger) 3
TROUVILLE
  (Mr. J. C. Cheney) 4
14 ran.   Time: 9 min. $45\frac{2}{5}$ sec.

1895 WILD MAN FROM
  BORNEO (Mr. Jos. Widger) 1
CATHAL (H. Escott) 2
VAN DER BERG
  (W. Dollery) 3
MANIFESTO (T. Kavanagh) 4
19 ran.   Time: 10 min. 32 sec.

1896 THE SOARER
  (Mr. D. G. M. Campbell) 1
FATHER O'FLYNN
  (Mr. C. Grenfell) 2
BISCUIT (E. Matthews) 3
BARCAL WHEY (C. Hogan) 4
28 ran.   Time: 10 min. $11\frac{1}{5}$ sec.

1897 MANIFESTO (T. Kavanagh) 1
FILBERT (Mr. C. Beatty) 2
FORD OF FYNE
  (Mr. F. Withington) 3
PRINCE ALBERT
  (Mr. G. S. Davies) 4
28 ran.   Time: 9 min. 49 sec.

1898 DROGHEDA (J. Gourley) 1
CATHAL (Mr. R. Ward) 2
GAUNTLET (W. Taylor) 3
FILBERT (Mr. C. Beatty) 4
24 ran.   Time: 9 min. $43\frac{3}{5}$ sec.

1899 MANIFESTO (G. Williamson) 1
FORD OF FYNE
  (E. Matthews) 2
ELLIMAN (E. Piggott) 3
DEAD LEVEL (F. Mason) 4
19 ran.   Time: 9 min. $49\frac{4}{5}$ sec.

1900 AMBUSH II (A. Anthony) 1
BARSAC (W. Halsey) 2
MANIFESTO (G. Williamson) 3
BREEMONT'S PRIDE
  (Mr. G. S. Davies) 4
16 ran.   Time: 10 min. $1\frac{2}{5}$ sec.

1901 GRUDON (A. Nightingall) 1
DRUMCREE
  (Mr. H. Nugent) 2
BUFFALO BILL (H. Taylor) 3
LEVANTER (F. Mason) 4
24 ran.   Time: 9 min. $47\frac{4}{5}$ sec.

1902 SHANNON LASS
    (D. Read) 1
    MATTHEW (W. Morgan) 2
    MANIFESTO (E. Piggott) 3
    DETAIL (A. Nightingall) 4
    21 ran. Time: 10 min. $3\frac{3}{5}$ sec.

1903 DRUMCREE (P. Woodland) 1
    DETAIL (A. Nightingall) 2
    MANIFESTO (G. Williamson) 3
    KIRKLAND (F. Mason) 4
    23 ran. Time: 10 min. $9\frac{2}{5}$ sec.

1904 MOIFAA (A. Birch) 1
    KIRKLAND (F. Mason) 2
    THE GUNNER
      (Mr. J. W. Widger) 3
    SHAWN ABOO
      (A. Waddington) 4
    26 ran. Time: 9 min. 59 sec.

1905 KIRKLAND (F. Mason) 1
    NAPPER TANDY
      (P. Woodland) 2
    BUCKAWAY II (A. Newey) 3
    RANUNCULUS
      (C. Hollebone) 4
    27 ran. Time: 9 min. $48\frac{4}{5}$ sec.

1906 ASCETIC'S SILVER
      (Mr. A. Hastings) 1
    RED LAD (C. Kelly) 2
    AUNT MAY (Mr. H. Persse) 3
    CRAUTACAUN
      (I. Anthony) 4
    23 ran. Time: 9 min. $34\frac{2}{5}$ sec.

1907 EREMON (A. Newey) 1
    TOM WEST (H. Murphy) 2
    PATLANDER (J. Lynn) 3
    RAVENSCLIFFE (F. Lyall) 4
    23 ran. Time: 9 min. $47\frac{1}{2}$ sec.

1908 RUBIO (H. Bletsoe) 1
    MATTIE MACGREGOR
      (W. Bissill) 2
    THE LAWYER III
      (Mr. P. Whitaker) 3
    FLAXMAN (A. Anthony) 4
    24 ran. Time: 10 min. $33\frac{1}{5}$ sec.

1909 LUTTEUR III (G. Parfrement) 1
    JUDAS (R. Chadwick) 2
    CAUBEEN (F. Mason) 3
    TOM WEST (H. Murphy) 4
    32 ran. Time: 9 min. $53\frac{1}{5}$ sec.

1910 JENKINSTOWN
      (R. Chadwick) 1
    JERRY M (E. Driscoll) 2
    ODOR (Mr. R. Hall) 3
    CARSEY (G. R. Morgan) 4
    25 ran. Time: 10 min. $44\frac{1}{5}$ sec.

1911 GLENSIDE
      (Mr. J. R. Anthony) 1
    RATHNALLY (R. Chadwick) 2
    SHADY GIRL (G. Clancy) 3
    FOOLHARDY
      (Mr. MacNeill) 4
    26 ran. Time: 10 min. 35 sec.

1912 JERRY M (E. Piggott) 1
    BLOODSTONE (F. Lyall) 2
    AXLE PIN (I. Anthony) 3
    CARSEY
      (Mr. H. Tyrrwhitt-Drake) 4
    24 ran. Time: 10 min. $13\frac{2}{5}$ sec.

1913 COVERTCOAT
      (P. Woodland) 1
    IRISH MAIL
      (Mr. O. Anthony) 2
    CARSEY
      (Mr. H. Tyrrwhitt-Drake) 3
    N.B. Only 3 finished
    23 ran. Time: 10 min. 19 sec.

1914 SUNLOCH (W. J. Smith) 1
    TRIANON III (C. Hawkins) 2
    LUTTEUR III (A. Carter) 3
    RORY O'MOORE
      (Mr. P. Whitaker) 4
    20 ran. Time: 9 min. $58\frac{4}{5}$ sec.

1915 ALLY SLOPER
      (Mr. J. R. Anthony) 1
    JACOBUS (A. Newey) 2
    FATHER CONFESSOR
      (A. Aylin) 3
    ALFRED NOBLE (T. Hulme) 4
    20 ran. Time: 9 min. $47\frac{4}{5}$ sec.

1916 VERMOUTH (J. Reardon) 1
IRISH MAIL (C. Hawkins) 2
SCHOOLMONEY
  (A. Saxby) 3
JACOBUS (A. Newey) 4
21 ran. Time: 10 min. 22 sec.
N.B. The race was run at Gatwick

1917 BALLYMACAD (E. Driscoll) 1
CHANG (W. Smith) 2
ALLY SLOPER
  (I. Anthony) 3
VERMOUTH (J. Reardon) 4
19 ran. Time: 10 min. $12\frac{2}{5}$ sec.
N.B. The race was run at Gatwick

1918 POETHLYN (E. Piggott) 1
CAPTAIN DREYFUS
  (J. Reardon) 2
BALLYMACAD (I. Anthony) 3
BERNERAY (S. Avila) 4
17 ran. Time: 9 min. $50\frac{2}{5}$ sec.
N.B. The race was run at Gatwick

1919 POETHLYN (E. Piggott) 1
BALLYBOGGAN (W. Head) 2
POLLEN (A. Escott) 3
LOCH ALLEN (J. J. Kelly) 4
22 ran. Time: 10 min. $8\frac{2}{5}$ sec.
N.B. The race returned to Aintree

1920 TROYTOWN
  (Mr. J. R. Anthony) 1
THE TURK II (R. Burford) 2
THE BORE
  (Mr. H. A. Brown) 3
SERGEANT MURPHY
  (W. Smith) 4
24 ran. Time: 10 min. $20\frac{2}{5}$ sec.

1921 SHAUN SPADAH
  (F. B. Rees) 1
THE BORE
  (Mr. H. A. Brown) 2
ALL WHITE (R. Chadwick) 3
TURKEY BUZZARD
  (Capt. G. H. Bennet) 4
35 ran. Time: 10 min. 26 sec.
N.B. Only 4 finished, and the
winner was the only horse which
did not fall

1922 MUSIC HALL
  (L. B. Rees) 1
DRIFTER (W. Watkinson) 2
TAFFYTUS (T. Leader) 3
SERGEANT MURPHY
  (C. Hawkins) 4
32 ran. Time: 9 min. $55\frac{4}{5}$ sec.

1923 SERGEANT MURPHY
  (Capt. G. H. Bennet) 1
SHAUN SPADAH
  (F. B. Rees) 2
CONJUROR II
  (Mr. C. Dewhurst) 3
PUNT GUN (M. Tighe) 4
28 ran. Time: 9 min. 36 sec.

1924 MASTER ROBERT
  (R. Trudgill) 1
FLY MASK (J. Moylan) 2
SILVO (G. Goswell) 3
DRIFTER (G. Calder) 4
30 ran. Time: 9 min. 40 sec.

1925 DOUBLE CHANCE
  (Maj. J. P. Wilson) 1
OLD TAY BRIDGE
  (J. R. Anthony) 2
FLY MASK
  (E. C. Doyle) 3
SPRIG (T. Leader) 3
33 ran. Time: 9 min. $42\frac{3}{5}$ sec.

1926 JACK HORNER
  (W. Watkinson) 1
OLD TAY BRIDGE
  (J. R. Anthony) 3
BRIGHT'S BOY
  (E. Doyle) 3
SPRIG (T. Leader) 4
30 ran. Time: 9 min. 36 sec.

1927 SPRIG (T. Leader) 1
BOVRIL III
  (Mr. G. W. Pennington) 2
BRIGHT'S BOY
  (J. R. Anthony) 3
DRINMOND
  (Mr. J. B. Balding) 4
37 ran. Time: 10 min. $20\frac{1}{5}$ sec.

1928 TIPPERARY TIM
(Mr. W. Dutton) 1
BILLY BARTON
(T. Cullinan) 2
42 ran. Time: 10 min. 27 sec.
N.B. Only 2 horses finished

1929 GREGALACH (R. Everett) 1
EASTER HERO
(J. Moloney) 2
RICHMOND II (W. Stott) 3
MELLERAY'S BELLE
(J. Mason) 4
66 ran. Time: 9 min. 47 sec.
*N.B. This is the biggest field in the
history of the race. Only 10 finished*

1930 SHAUN GOILIN
(T. Cullinan) 1
MELLERAY'S BELLE
(J. Mason) 2
SIR LINDSAY
(D. Williams) 3
GLANGESIA
(J. Browne) 4
41 ran. Time: 9 min. $42\frac{2}{5}$ sec.

1931 GRAKLE (R. Lyall) 1
GREGALACH (J. Moloney) 2
ANNANDALE (T. Morgan) 3
RHYTICERE (L. Niaudot) 4
43 ran. Time: 9 min. $32\frac{4}{5}$ sec.

1932 FORBRA (J. Hamey) 1
EGREMONT
(Mr. E. C. Paget) 2
SHAUN GOILIN
(D. Williams) 3
NEAR EAST
(T. McCarthy) 4
36 ran. Time: 9 min. $44\frac{3}{5}$ sec.

1933 KELLSBORO' JACK
(D. Williams) 1
REALLY TRUE
(Mr. F. Furlong) 2
SLATER (Mr. M. Barry) 3
DELANEIGE (J. Moloney) 4
34 ran. Time: 9 min. 28 sec.
(Record)

1934 GOLDEN MILLER
(G. Wilson) 1
DELANEIGE (J. Moloney) 2
THOMOND II (W. Speck) 3
FORBRA (G. Hardy) 4
30 ran. Time: 9 min. $20\frac{2}{5}$ sec.
(Record)

1935 REYNOLDSTOWN
(Mr. F. Furlong) 1
BLUE PRINCE (W. Parvin) 2
THOMOND II (W. Speck) 3
LAZY BOOTS (G. Owen) 4
27 ran. Time: 9 min. $20\frac{1}{5}$ sec.
(Record)

1936 REYNOLDSTOWN
(Mr. F. Walwyn) 1
EGO (Mr. H. Llewellyn) 2
BACHELOR PRINCE
(J. Fawcus) 3
CROWN PRINCE
(Mr. R. Strutt) 4
35 ran. Time: 9 min. 37 sec.

1937 ROYAL MAIL (E. Williams) 1
COOLEEN (J. Fawcus) 2
PUCKA BELLE
(Mr. E. Bailey) 3
EGO (Mr. H. Llewellyn) 4
33 ran. Time: 9 min. $59\frac{3}{5}$ sec.

1938 BATTLESHIP (B. Hobbs) 1
ROYAL DANIELI
(D. Moore) 2
WORKMAN (J. Brogan) 3
COOLEEN (J. Fawcus) 4
36 ran. Time: 9 min. $29\frac{4}{5}$ sec.

1939 WORKMAN (T. Hyde) 1
MAC MOFFAT (I. Alder) 2
KILSTAR (G. Archibald) 3
COOLEEN (J. Fawcus) 4
37 ran. Time: 9 min. $42\frac{1}{5}$ sec.

1940 BOGSKAR (M. Jones) 1
MAC MOFFAT (I. Alder) 2
GOLD ARROW (P. Lay) 3
SYMAETHIS (M. Feakes) 4
30 ran. Time: 9 min. $20\frac{3}{5}$ sec.

1941-45 No race, owing to World War II

1946 LOVELY COTTAGE
    (Capt. R. Petre)   I
    JACK FINLAY (W. Kidney)   2
    PRINCE REGENT (T. Hyde)   3
    HOUSEWARMER
    (A. Brabazon)   4
    34 ran. Time: 9 min. $38\frac{1}{5}$ sec.

1947 CAUGHOO (E. Dempsey)   I
    LOUGH CONN
    (D. McCann)   2
    KAMI (Mr. J. Hislop)   3
    PRINCE REGENT (T. Hyde)   4
    57 ran. Time: 10 min. $3\frac{1}{5}$ sec.

1948 SHEILA'S COTTAGE
    (A. P. Thompson)   I
    FIRST OF THE DANDIES
    (J. Brogan)   2
    CROMWELL
    (Lord Mildmay)   3
    HAPPY HOME (G. Kelly)   4
    43 ran. Time: 9 min. $25\frac{2}{5}$ sec.

1949 RUSSIAN HERO
    (L. McMorrow)   I
    ROIMOND (R. Francis)   2
    ROYAL MOUNT (P. Doyle)   3
    CROMWELL
    (Lord Mildmay)   4
    43 ran. Time: 9 min. $23\frac{4}{5}$ sec.

1950 FREEBOOTER (J. Power)   I
    WOT NO SUN
    (A. P. Thompson)   2
    ACTHON MAJOR
    (R. J. O'Ryan)   3
    ROWLAND ROY (R. Black)   4
    49 ran. Time: 9 min. $24\frac{1}{5}$ sec.

1951 NICKEL COIN (J. Bullock)   I
    ROYAL TAN
    (Mr. A. O'Brien)   2
    DERRINSTOWN
    (A. Power)   3
    BROOMFIELD (R. Emery)   4
    36 ran. Time: 9 min. $48\frac{4}{5}$ sec.

1952 TEAL (A. P. Thompson)   I
    LEGAL JOY (M. Scudamore)   2
    WOT NO SUN (D. V. Dick)   3
    UNCLE BARNEY (J. Boddy)   4
    47 ran. Time: 9 min. $20\frac{3}{5}$ sec.

1953 EARLY MIST (B. Marshall)   I
    MONT TREMBLANT
    (D. V. Dick)   2
    IRISH LIZARD (R. Turnell)   3
    OVERSHADOW (P. Taaffe)   4
    31 ran. Time: 9 min. $21\frac{3}{5}$ sec.

1954 ROYAL TAN (B. Marshall)   I
    TUDOR LINE (G. Slack)   2
    IRISH LIZARD
    (M. Scudamore)   3
    CHURCHTOWN
    (T. Taaffe)   4
    29 ran. Time: 9 min. $32\frac{4}{5}$ sec.

1955 QUARE TIMES (P. Taaffe)   I
    TUDOR LINE (G. Slack)   2
    CAREY'S COTTAGE
    (T. Taaffe)   3
    GIGOLO (R. Curran)   4
    30 ran. Time: 10 min. $20\frac{3}{5}$ sec.

1956 E. S. B. (D. V. Dick)   I
    GENTLE MOYA
    (G. Milburn)   2
    ROYAL TAN (T. Taaffe)   3
    EAGLE LODGE
    (A. Oughton)   4
    29 ran. Time: 9 min. 21 sec.

1957 SUNDEW (F. Winter)   I
    WYNDBURGH
    (M. Batchelor)   2
    TIBERETTA (A. Oughton)   3
    GLORIOUS TWELFTH
    (B. Wilkinson)   4
    35 ran. Time: 9 min. $42\frac{2}{5}$ sec.

1958 MR. WHAT (A. Freeman)   I
    TIBERETTA (G. Slack)   2
    GREEN DRILL (G. Milburn)   3
    WYNDBURGH
    (M. Batchelor)   4
    31 ran. Time: 10 min. $1\frac{1}{5}$ sec.

1959 OXO (M. Scudamore)   1
WYNDBURGH
  (T. Brookshaw)   2
MR. WHAT (T. Taaffe)   3
TIBERETTA (A. Oughton)   4
34 ran.   Time: 9 min. $37\frac{1}{5}$ sec.

1960 MERRYMAN II (G. Scott)   1
BADANLOCH (S. Mellor)   2
CLEAR PROFIT
  (B. Wilkinson)   3
TEA FIEND (P. Madden)   4
26 ran.   Time: 9 min. $26\frac{1}{5}$ sec.

1961 NICOLAUS SILVER
  (H. Beasley)   1
MERRYMAN II (D. Ancil)   2
O'MALLEY POINT (P. Farrell)   3
SCOTTISH FLIGHT (W. Rees)   4
35 ran.   Time: 9 min. $22\frac{3}{5}$ sec.

1962 KILMORE (F. Winter)   1
WYNDBURGH (T. Barnes)   2
MR. WHAT (J. Lehane)   3
GAY NAVARREE
  (Mr. A. Cameron)   4
32 ran.   Time: 9 min. 50 sec.

1963 AYALA (P. Buckley)   1
CARRICKBEG
  (Mr. J. Lawrence)   2
HAWA'S SONG
  (P. Broderick)   3
TEAM SPIRIT
  (G. W. Robinson)   4
47 ran.   Time: 9 min. $35\frac{4}{5}$ sec.

1964 TEAM SPIRIT
  (G. W. Robinson)   1
PURPLE SILK (J. Kenneally)   2
PEACETOWN (R. Edwards)   3
ETERNAL (S. Davenport)   4
33 ran.   Time: 9 min. 47 sec.

1965 JAY TRUMP
  (Mr. T. Crompton Smith)   1
FREDDIE (P. McCarron)   2
MR. JONES (Mr. C. Collins)   3
RAINBOW BATTLE
  (G. Milburn)   4
47 ran.   Time: 9 min. $30\frac{3}{5}$ sec.

1966 ANGLO (T. Norman)   1
FREDDIE (P. McCarron)   2
FOREST PRINCE (G. Scott)   3
THE FOSSA
  (T. Biddlecombe)   4
47 ran.   Time: 9 min. $52\frac{4}{5}$ sec.

1967 FOINAVON (J. Buckingham)   1
HONEY END (J. Gifford)   2
RED ALLIGATOR
  (B. Fletcher)   3
GREEK SCHOLAR
  (T. Biddlecombe)   4
44 ran.   Time: 9 min. $49\frac{3}{5}$ sec.

1968 RED ALLIGATOR
  (B. Fletcher)   1
MOIDORE'S TOKEN
  (B. Brogan)   2
DIFFERENT CLASS
  (D. Mould)   3
RUTHERFORDS (P. Buckley)   4
45 ran.   Time: 9 min. $28\frac{4}{5}$ sec.

1969 HIGHLAND WEDDING
  (E. Harty)   1
STEEL BRIDGE (R. Pitman)   2
RONDETTO (J. King)   3
THE BEECHES (W. Rees)   4
30 ran.   Time: 9 min. $30\frac{4}{5}$ sec.

1970 GAY TRIP (P. Taaffe)   1
VULTURE (S. Barker)   2
MISS HUNTER (F. Shortt)   3
DOZO (E. Harty)   4
28 ran.   Time: 9 min. 38 sec.

1971 SPECIFY (J. Cook)   1
BLACK SECRET
  (Mr. J. Dreaper)   2
ASTBURY (J. Bourke)   3
BOWGEENO (G. Thorner)   4
38 ran.   Time: 9 min. $33\frac{4}{5}$ sec.

1972 WELL TO DO (G. Thorner)   1
GAY TRIP (T. Biddlecombe)   2
BLACK SECRET (S. Barker)   3 ⎤
GENERAL SYMONS   ⎬
  (P. Kiely)   3 ⎦
42 ran.   Time: 10 min. $8\frac{4}{5}$ sec.

168

Index of Names

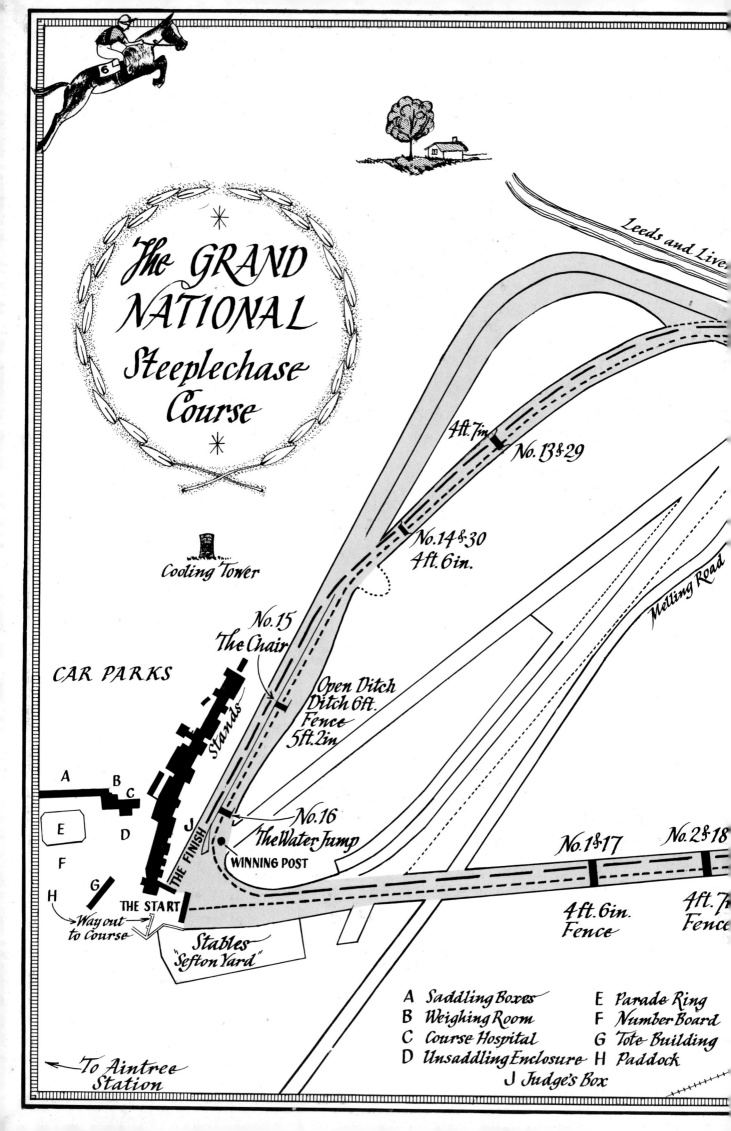

The GRAND NATIONAL Steeplechase Course

Leeds and Liver...

4ft. 7in.
No. 13 & 29

No. 14 & 30
4ft. 6in.

Melling Road

Cooling Tower

No. 15
The Chair

CAR PARKS

Stands

Open Ditch
Ditch 6ft.
Fence
5ft. 2in.

A   B
C
E
D
F
G
H

J

THE FINISH

No. 16
The Water Jump
WINNING POST

No. 1 & 17

No. 2 & 18

4ft. 6in.
Fence

4ft. 7...
Fence

THE START

Way out
to Course

Stables
"Sefton Yard"

To Aintree
Station

A   Saddling Boxes
B   Weighing Room
C   Course Hospital
D   Unsaddling Enclosure
E   Parade Ring
F   Number Board
G   Tote Building
H   Paddock
J   Judge's Box